THE MIND OF
THE CATHOLIC LAYMAN

THE MIND

of the

CATHOLIC LAYMAN

Daniel Callahan

✠✠✠

CHARLES SCRIBNER'S SONS

New York

For my parents

Vincent F. and Anita Hawkins Callahan

CONTENTS

PREFACE

Every book, like every person, has a history. This one is a child of the times. It was conceived at a moment when the problem of the layman was just beginning to strike the American Catholic Church with full force. The pioneering work of a number of European theologians, especially Father Yves Congar, had begun to capture the attention of many laymen and priests. The various lay movements in America, after a hesitant and slow start, were beginning to attract wide support and could boast exploding membership rolls. Here and there, however delicately, a number of laymen were coming to voice complaints about their seemingly negligible role in the Church. And a Catholic, for the first time, was about to enter the White House.

Since that time, the Church has been in the midst of an intense period of ferment; and the end is nowhere in sight. What the lay renaissance could not accomplish single-handed, the Second Vatican Council could. Throughout the Church, in America as well as the rest of the world, renewal and reform have become the challenge offered and the challenge accepted. Thus this book is born at a moment when the Church stands on the threshold of a new era. It is an era, however, in which much will depend upon the layman. Without his active participation, the renewal will be in vain. If the lay renaissance which we are now witnessing does not come into full bloom, then it is difficult to see how anything else in the Church can either. The question of the layman is not simply one more problem facing the Church; it stands in the very forefront.

Yet it is one thing to recognize the importance of the layman and still another to understand him as he lives out his life in the world. That many attempts are being made to fashion a theology of the laity is evident; that many laymen are intensely concerned about how best to mediate the Church to the world is no less apparent; that the clergy are coming to see the significance of the layman in the Church cannot be doubted. Who can fail to see that these rapid developments have thrust upon the Church the urgent task of bringing to fruition the seeds of discussion, debate and activity which have been amply sown in recent years?

But who is the layman? Who is this person whose presence is now felt by all? What is he and where did he come from—and where is he going? These are the very broad and very difficult questions which this book attempts to answer.

How, in the first place, should one go about such a task? One way is clear and traditional: by exploring the theological problem of the layman. That is not the way I have chosen in this book, however vital and important such work is. Instead, my purpose is to explore the history and the present state of the American Catholic layman. It has been written with the conviction that very little is known about him. In itself, there is little reason to be disturbed by this fact. No matter how intensive the efforts of sociologists, historians and intelligent observers, it is doubtful that anything so elusive as the mind of the layman could be analyzed with satisfactory accuracy. What is surprising, however, is that so few have tried. If the theological literature is as yet scant, it far surpasses in quantity what has been written on the layman from other vantage points. There exists no history of the American Catholic layman's role in the Church; there exists no full-fledged social history of the layman; there are few sociological studies of the laymen available; and there have been few things written on the layman which cannot be called either hortatory or theological.

It is the aim of this book to fill some of these gaps. But it is not only the existence of these gaps which makes such an aim pertinent. More fundamentally, it seems to me impossible to understand the layman if he is approached exclusively from a theological point of view; and we understand him even less if we hear only about what the layman ought to be rather than what he is. For the layman does not live in a vacuum. In reality, what the layman has been, what he is, and what he will become, represent the interaction of many forces: historical, sociological, political, cultural and theological. Thus if we are to understand the present outburst of interest in the layman, it is not sufficient merely to point to recent papal statements and assume that there lies the explanation. On the contrary, the experience of a democratic society, the increase in the number of educated laymen, the changing image of the priest all come into play as well. What the layman comes to be in our society and in the Church will not be only the result of theological investigations and refinements. They will determine part of the equation; but the other part will be determined by how the layman responds to all those other influences in his life, many of which come from outside of the Church.

Any attempt, however, to analyze the layman is beset with difficulties. The absence of historical studies has meant that I have had to pick my way through territory where few others have been; in this respect, I still barely scratch the surface. It has been aptly observed that, until very recently, Church history has been conceived of as hierarchical and institutional history. The truth of this observation will be borne home very quickly to anyone who surveys the work of American Catholic historians on the layman. To judge from the attention paid him, he might just as well not have existed. This is not to assert that individual laymen have not been studied; nor that such matters as the layman's poverty, piety and patriotism have not been written about. But as a rule the intent of most such writing seems to have been to praise him, to affirm his good citizenship, to chronicle the saga of his humble roots and rapid rise. What he thought about, how (in fact rather than fiction) he got along with the clergy, how his understanding of Catholicism shaped his reaction to non-Catholics, how he interpreted his duties toward Church and society—these things are rarely mentioned.

But if an historical analysis of the layman is difficult to fashion, the present situation of the layman poses no fewer obstacles. As fast as the Church changes, America changes. As fast as the layman confronts one challenge, another is there to take its place. And no two laymen are alike. What troubles one may be of no consequence to another; what concerns the layman in Boston or Peoria may be different from what concerns him in New Orleans or Los Angeles. What irritates those with a college education may mean a great deal to the less educated. Hence anyone who attempts to write very broadly about the layman does so at his own risk. He can only catch glimpses of the real life which goes on below the surface of statistics. He can hardly ever know who, among the many models he may have in mind, represents the "typical" layman; whatever is said will, in the eyes of some, miss the mark.

Despite these difficulties, the task cannot be evaded. The American layman has his historical roots which must be uncovered to see the way he has emerged. At the same time, the life he lives today is a complex one. He stands astride two realities: that of the Church to which he belongs and that of the society in which he lives. Each will present him with demands on his time, his loyalty and his conscience. Somehow, he must reconcile these demands; somehow, he must find a coherent and meaningful way of relating them to one another, sacrificing neither his integrity nor his contact with reality. The Church has called upon the layman to redeem the world by restoring all things in Christ. But the world also makes calls upon the layman, some good and some bad. Ideally, there is no conflict between the role of the Catholic as a faithful member of the Church and his role as a good citizen in our constitutional democracy. In practice, however, agonizing conflicts and obscure dilemmas assail the layman at every turn. It is these realities which concern me here; and it is the way these realities shape the layman of today that I have tried to reveal.

It must be confessed at this point that I once thought a study of this kind could be done in an "objective" way. I now believe this to be impossible. As soon as one faces the question of choosing material, of deciding what should be emphasized and what can be ignored, it becomes obvious that there are no platonic heavens from which one can gaze in a detached fashion. The most that can be done in such a situation is to strive for balance in the selection of material; but in a domain as controversial as that of the layman, one man's idea of balance is likely to be another's idea of distortion. So be it; there is no escape.

However, balance is not the only demand made upon one who would write about the layman. There are also the duties of candor and fairness. As for candor, there is simply no use at all in writing about the layman if one plans systematically to ignore the discrepancies between ideals and reality. This is particularly pertinent for a book of this kind—one which is meant as an investigation rather than a call to the colors. Fairness is just as essential, but far harder to achieve than candor. Almost every issue discussed in these pages is the subject of vigorous debate within American Catholicism; thus it is inevitable, despite all efforts, that some perceptions and some viewpoints will appear to have been slighted. Above all, there is always the danger that a book of this type, which concentrates on the problems of the Church and the layman, will seem to neglect those vast constructive and regenerative forces at work in American Catholicism. They exist and they cannot be denied. If I appear to give them inadequate recognition, the reason has more to do with the particular aims of this book than anything else.

I have not hesitated to be candid and I have tried to be fair. Whether I have succeeded, especially in the latter respect, will have to be judged by others.

This book would not have been possible without the help of many people. To the Right Reverend John Tracy Ellis, of Catholic University, I am especially indebted for the trouble he took to provide me with a valuable list of books and articles. Without that list I would have been lost. To Father Thomas T. McAvoy, C.S.C., of Notre Dame, my debt throughout this book is obvious; more than anyone else he has opened the door to American Catholic social history. His personal encouragement was equally helpful. A special word of thanks must go to Father Joseph H. Fichter, S.J., whose work I have drawn upon heavily and who, through a few timely letters, helped to make me aware of the pitfalls in venturing any generalizations about the layman. I also want to thank Michael Novak for many a lively discussion about the layman and for his support and encouragement. I am likewise indebted to Christopher Dawson for teaching me just how wrong Henry Ford was in his famous remark that "history is bunk." Finally, I want to express my great appreciation to James O'Gara for his careful reading of my manuscript and for his many helpful suggestions; and to my wife, Sidney, for many valuable insights and unfailing support. I am, of course, solely responsible for the opinions I express.

DANIEL CALLAHAN

Part One

Part One

CHAPTER 1

A New Land, a New Layman

THROUGHOUT its two-thousand-year history, the Catholic Church has had constantly to respond to new challenges, new cultures, new dangers, new intellectual and theological frontiers. As a missionary Church, it has on innumerable occasions embarked on the arduous task of evangelizing strange countries, converting men whose values and mores were at striking variance with the message and the Word of the Savior. In almost every instance, great ingenuity was required. New languages had to be learned, the Gospel translated into unfamiliar idioms, the practices of the Church adapted to the ways of the milieu in which it found itself. Where it has done so successfully, the Church has flourished. Where it failed to bridge the gap, the Church remained weak and ineffectual. Where the Church approached a new culture with an open mind ready to show that Catholicism was compatible with anything good that men had created, it was readily able to incarnate itself. When is has been fearful, when it believed it could not retain its purity apart from the culture familiar to the missionaries, it has found itself rebuffed and unwelcome.

Yet apart from specifically missionary work, the Church has on occasion followed its people. That is, the Church has seen its people moving to new lands, seeking new freedoms or opportunities, and has then sent its priests and its bishops after them to care for their spiritual welfare. That, pre-eminently, was the situation in the America of the colonial days. True, the Church had, especially in its French and Spanish missionaries, seen the New World as mission territory. But it was the Indian whom the missionaries sought, and not the European immigrant. Yet by the end of the seventeenth century, it had become clear that the main work of the Church universal in the New World would be that of caring for Catholic immigrants: Catholics who, for one reason or

3

another had sought in America a chance to make a fresh beginning, to tap the resources of a vast land whose limits were still unknown.

At the same time, however, for all the European ways which the early settlers brought with them, America was a new country. If the anti-Catholicism which the English Protestant settlers brought with them was familiar enough, the country to which they brought it was not. For the main fact was that there were an increasing number of Catholics coming to this new land and living under conditions far more unique than familiar. If, in one sense, the Catholic people came before the Church, it nevertheless remained true that the Church could not care for these people unless it had the same kind of open outlook which characterized the most imaginative type of missionary work. Nor could the Catholic retain his faith unless he himself was prepared to face the fact that his situation was a new one. Both Church and Catholics were from the first put on their mettle.

Now it can be said immediately that the contemporary discussion of the Catholic laity merely raises in a new garb questions which have persisted in the American Church since its earliest days. To be sure, American civilization in the twentieth century has presented the institutional Church and the laity with some strikingly new dilemmas and challenges. Yet underlying most of them are some that are very old: the relationship of Church and society, of clergy and laity, bishop and layman, the threats and possibilities of a pluralistic society, and the layman's role in the work of the Church. One problem in particular has been persistent. How ought the Catholic layman adapt himself, both as citizen and believer, to the society in which he lives? Put another way, what ought the Catholic give to the society in which he lives and what ought he to take from it?

In an important way, the Church itself has been compelled to raise an analogous set of questions. As one historian has strikingly noted: "The Church as an institution-in-law in Europe had to become in the new nation merely another private corporation, a society that had to conform with first colonial and then state laws simply to exist. In a sense, the whole history of the Church in the United States has been the gracious accepting of that change, a constant adaptation to that life in a new and secular environment."[1] For his part, the layman had also

---

[1] Henry J. Browne, "Catholicism in the United States," *The Shaping of American Religion*, Vol. I, *Religion in American Life*, edited by James Ward Smith and A. Leland Jamison (4 vols.; Princeton, 1961), p. 75.

to adapt himself. He could neither depend on the law to favor or sustain his beliefs nor could he depend on a consensus of opinion among his neighbors to provide a milieu in which his faith could weather the ordinary stresses of a genuinely Catholic life. Like his Church, the layman was also a "private corporation," forced to make his own way and to choose, day in and day out, what kind of a life he wanted. Like his Church, the possibilities of adaptation were numerous. He could choose to identify himself totally with the culture he found about him or he could choose to ignore or oppose that culture, drawing about himself a heavy coat of defensive armor. Yet the layman had one further choice which, properly speaking, the Church itself never had. He could, as one free of legal or social coercion, reject the Church entirely—and many did precisely that. If the situation of the Church in America was unique, the situation of the layman was no less so.

Before considering the situation of the layman in more detail, it will be well to recollect the place of the Church in the colonial and early national days. The year 1790 provides a convenient point of focus, for it was in that year that John Carroll was installed, in Baltimore, as the first American bishop. In other parts of the world in 1790 the fortunes of Catholicism were at a low point, with worse to come. The French Revolution, barely a year old, was preparing the end of the *ancien régime* and the favored place of the Church in France. In Germany, the cumulative effect of the system of ecclesiastical territories, separating Catholics from the main stream of German life, had reduced the Church to a seriously weakened state, ripe for the revolutionary upheavals about to strike it in the next few decades. The Church in England had still to wait thirty-nine years for the Emancipation Bill. In Latin America, the destructive consequences of the *patronato real* were being felt to the full in a frequently corrupt and venal Church life. Almost everywhere the old world was giving way to the new—and the privileged Church was about to become a persecuted, struggling Church.

Quite the contrary was the case in America in 1790. Behind the Church lay the worst of its troubles: the repressive penal laws common in the American colonies from about the mid-seventeenth to the final decades of the eighteeenth century. While antagonism to Catholics was hardly dead, Catholic loyalty during the Revolutionary War had done much to reduce it. By 1790, the Catholic could at least feel some optimism. Within a year Georgetown Academy would be founded, soon to become the first American Catholic college. Within a year as well a group of French Sulpicians would open St. Mary's Seminary in Baltimore, thus providing the start of clerical education in America. In each of the major cities along the Eastern seaboard one could find a few prominent and respected Catholics. Moreover, there were signs of a growing cooperation between Catholics and Protestants.[2] In short, while the Church in Europe and Latin America had only trouble and decline to look forward to in 1790, the American Church was on the verge of a great expansion and an era of promise.

To be sure, Catholics were still a distinct minority, barely thirty-five thousand in all, concentrated in Maryland, Pennsylvania and New York. Yet with the appointment of Bishop Carroll, it became possible for the first time to see the American Church as a living and significant reality. Nothing could be more important in the years to come when the immigrant waves began to crash with greater and greater frequency on the American shore, bringing not only many undisciplined and ill-trained priests but poor, uneducated and often lax laymen. Immediately following the year 1790, however, the Church was to have a few decades in which to get ready for those crises which lay ahead—and to consolidate and develop the gains which it had taken many years to bring about.

Yet if we are to understand fully the situation of the laity and of the Church by 1790, one must note more forcefully the one overriding circumstance which was so decisive for both: anti-Catholicism. The justly traditional theme of all Catholic histories of the colonial period is that of a small Catholic minority beleaguered and oppressed by a Protestant majority. "It was not," as one historian has put it, "that there was any ferocious persecution. This was not necessary: the hard smooth surface of social disapproval was itself sufficient to discourage Catholicism . . ."[3] The roots of this anti-Catholicism were many, stemming, eventually, back to the Elizabethan period in England. But during the seventeenth century there were still more concrete causes: the English trade wars with France and Spain kept anti-Catholicism alive in England and its colonies. In America this meant a special fear of the French in Canada and of the Spanish in Florida. The fact that Catholics were an insignificant minority was of little help. On the general principle that to be

[2] Cf. Thomas O'Brien Hanley, S.J., "The Emergence of Pluralism in the United States," *Theological Studies*, XXIII (June, 1962), pp. 207-232.

[3] Theodore Maynard, *The Story of American Catholicism* (New York, 1941), p. 98.

forewarned is to be forearmed, the various colonial charters of the seventeenth century provided for proscriptions against Catholics and the establishment of penal laws to hamper any that might slip through. Only in Maryland did Catholics have some measure of freedom.

Ironically, however, the 1649 Act of Toleration in Maryland marked the high point of Catholic freedom in the seventeenth-century colonies. In 1691, during the reign of William and Mary, Maryland became a royal colony and the penal laws in force in England were fully instituted in Maryland. Nor were Catholics in the leading counties of New York to fare any better. After some seven years of toleration under Thomas Dongan, a Catholic governor appointed in 1682, the Church of England was legally established, supported by the usual repressive laws against non-conformists. Only in William Penn's Pennsylvania Colony, founded in 1681, did Catholics consistently find an open atmosphere and genuine toleration. With the exception of Pennsylvania, the first half of the eighteeenth century brought no respite. Up and down the coast, Catholics were disenfranchised, excluded from public life, forbidden to establish schools and hampered in conducting religious services. This early tradition of repression was to leave a strong imprint on the Church and its members—an imprint which left Catholics at a social disadvantage for decades to come, which made them timid, conformist and retiring, and which made their religion a personal as well as a social burden. Even when the atmosphere began to change by the 1770s, and even more so after the Revolution, it was to be a long while before Catholics would begin to reshape their ingrained defensive habits.

Response of the Clergy

How did Catholics, in practice, respond to their situation? How did the clergy and bishops view their situation in the years just before and just after the Revolution? Let us look first at the clergy, as well as at some of the problems which faced Bishop Carroll. The very response to the question of the appointment of a bishop, which arose during the 1780s, says very much about the clergy and the way they approached the problems of the Church. Despite considerable confusion among both clergy and laity about the sources of authority in the American Church, many Catholics were by no means eager to see a bishop appointed. As late as 1783, Catholics had legal equality in only five states and were still highly sensitive to their general unpopularity. Moreover, they were acutely aware of the particular Protestant distaste for bishops; this was something the Anglicans had already learned in a painful way. Few Catholics had any desire to bring new troubles on their heads after years of trying to get rid of the old. The clergy shared this attitude every bit as strongly as did the laity. In addition, the clergy were afraid of a change in American Church government which might work to their disadvantage. Even John Carroll himself, in the years just before his own appointment, was no hearty advocate of an American episcopacy. Above all, he was doubtful that Rome had a clear understanding of the American Catholic situation and was uncertain whether Rome would give an adequate hearing to the opinions of the American clergy.

In time, nonetheless, many of the common doubts diminished. Disorder among clergy and laity in Philadelphia and New York, contending priests and fractious laymen, made it evident that order was needed and that the governance of the Bishop of London would no longer suffice.[4] By 1788 the American clergy were prepared to accept a bishop and petitioned Pope Pius VI that they be allowed to elect one. Despite the irregularity of the request that the clergy make their own choice, the petition was granted and Carroll was elected by an overwhelming majority.

Yet as the earlier reluctance of the clergy to have a bishop suggests, the clergy who came under Carroll's jurisdiction were by no means entirely a vigorous or zealous lot. Some, to be sure, were industrious, hard-working men, forced to ride by the hour to care for scattered groups of Catholics. Others, unfortunately, were in poor health, aged or too much cowed by Protestant ill-favor to be very effective.[5] A few, invited by local Catholic immigrant groups from Ireland, had dubious credentials for the hard work required of them. One of Carroll's first tasks would be to strengthen the clergy and to bring order among them. More than that, it was essential that there be more clergy and especially native American clergy.

As for the laity, there could be little to boast about. Many, it is true,

---

[4] John Tracy Ellis, *Catholics in Colonial America.* Reprinted from the *American Ecclesiastical Review*, CXXXVI, Jan.-May, 1957 (Washington, D.C., n.d.), pp. 66ff.

[5] Cf. John Carroll's report to Propaganda, March 1, 1785, in *Documents of American Catholic History*, edited by John Tracy Ellis (2nd ed., Milwaukee, 1962), pp. 149-150.

persevered in their faith despite a lack of Catholic education, the sparsity of priests and a rare reception of the sacraments, not to mention the inevitable inroads of Protestantism which dominated the scene. But many more fell away from the Church. In 1785, about all that (then) Father John Carroll could find to say about the Catholics of America was that, "In Maryland a few of the leading more wealthy families still profess the Catholic faith introduced at the very foundation of the province by their ancestors. . . . As for piety, they are for the most part sufficiently assiduous in the exercises of religion and in frequenting the sacraments, but they lack that fervor, which frequent appeals to the sentiment of piety usually produce, as many congregations hear the word of God only once a month, and sometimes only once in two months."[6] If these words hardly suggest a happy state of affairs, worse still could be said about the newer immigrants, most of whom ignored even the most minimal Church requirements. The numerous Irish Protestants in the South today bear witness to the extent of the early defections. What was difficult for the few wealthy Catholics in Maryland was all but impossible for the common man.

For his part, Carroll was also inclined to see the problem as the inevitable effect of "unavoidable intercourses with non-Catholics" which led in one direction toward a looseness of morals and, with equal danger, toward intermarriage.[7] It was this latter problem which he found especially vexing. As he wrote to a friend in England in 1798, "Here our Catholics are so mixed with Protestants in all the intercourse of civil society and business public and private, that abuse of intermarriage is almost universal and it surpasses my ability to devise an effectual bar against it. No general prohibition can be exacted without reducing many of the faithful to live in a state of celibacy."[8] How much this problem worried Carroll is further emphasized by the comment of another of Carroll's biographers who notes that, after 1785, there was "scarcely a letter to Rome which does not ask for a stipulated number of dispensations for mixed marriages, and every report to Rome contains the note of fear on this score."[9] That Carroll had good grounds for his

[6] *Ibid.*, pp. 148-149.
[7] *Ibid.*, p. 149.
[8] Letter from John Carroll to Charles Plowden, Oct. 10, 1798, quoted in Annabelle M. Melville, *John Carroll of Baltimore* (New York, 1955), p. 241.
[9] Peter Guilday, *The Life and Times of John Carroll, Archbishop of Baltimore, 1735-1815* (2 vols.; New York, 1922), II, p. 774.

fears can be seen in the family of Dominick Lynch (1754-1825), a prominent New York merchant and a pillar of the Church in that city. Despite the fact that Lynch fathered thirteen children, within a couple of generations almost all of the descendants of his family were lost to the Church, primarily through mixed marriages.[10]

Still another problem for Carroll and the suffragan bishops soon appointed was the nationalistic factions and disputes in the Church. In the late eighteenth and early nineteenth centuries, the main source of discord lay in the fact that most of the clergy were French *émigrés;* and, as it turned out, they became the pastors of an increasingly large number of Irish immigrants who were not at all pleased by the arrangement. Not only did this encourage some of the excesses of lay trusteeism, but it also led to the establishment, in Philadelphia in 1787, of the first schismatic American parish. In that instance, however, it was the dissatisfaction of German-born Catholics with English priests which led to the break.

Finally, one cannot overlook the question of Catholic education. If the American bishops have been consistent in any one thing, it has been in their concern for education. From the outset of his episcopacy until the end, this was a theme constantly reiterated by Bishop Carroll. "To devise means for the religious education of Catholic youth—that precious portion of pastoral solicitude," was the way he described his task in his installation sermon in Baltimore on December 12, 1790.[11] And when he wrote his first Pastoral Letter in 1792, the letter opened with an exhortation to his flock to support the newly-opened Georgetown Academy. Again, in "The Pastoral Letter to the Laity" issued by the First Provincial Council of Baltimore in 1829, the urgency of Catholic education occupied a prominent part—and one of the values of a Christian education which that letter stressed was that children would more naturally be influenced by their parents, "in that most important of all temporal concerns, the selection of a wife or husband."[12]

However strong the desire for Catholic educational facilities came to be, Carroll was himself, at one point, not eager for a separate system of education. Nor was there any conception during the early part of the

[10] Thomas F. Meehan, "Some Pioneer Catholic Laymen in New York—Dominick Lynch and Cornelius Heeney," *Historical Records and Studies,* IV (1906), pp. 285-301.

[11] John Tracy Ellis, *Documents, op. cit.,* p. 173.

[12] *The National Pastorals of the American Hierarchy, 1792-1919,* edited by Peter Guilday (Westminster, Md., 1954), p. 26.

nineteenth century of mass education. Indeed, it was from the start understood that Georgetown would prove too expensive for many. In itself there was nothing unusual in that: the tradition of a Christian education for the upper classes was a strong one and it was to this class that the first efforts were directed. Hopefully, their influence would make up for their smallness in number.

The net result, however, of these early efforts at creating educational facilities was not very striking. For one thing, there was not quite the sense of urgency that was felt when the immigrants began to arrive in droves in the thirties and forties of the nineteenth century. For another, there simply was not enough money available to do anything on a large scale. One almost inevitable outcome of the slow development of Catholic higher education was to retard the development of a substantial American tradition of Catholic intellectualism, both among the clergy and the laity. In 1818, Archbishop Ambrose Maréchal, the second successor to Archbishop Carroll in Baltimore, commented on the native American clergy that "They are acquainted with only the necessary ecclesiastical sciences. The reason for this is the fact that before their ordination they can spend only a few years in studying the humanities, letters and theology, and afterwards they are impeded from further study because of the ever pressing need of their ministry. So they find it difficult to talk on more erudite topics."[13] Nor, despite its early beginnings, did Georgetown in its lay graduates ever come near to exerting the kind of influence on American thought and letters that might have been hoped for. The coming of the immigrants merely further retarded an intellectual and cultural development in the Church which did not, in the first place, get off to a very rapid or auspicious start.

Archbishop Carroll, then, and his immediate successors as well as the occupants of the other early sees faced a number of formidable problems. From the viewpoint of the hierarchy, the prospects were both hopeful and demanding: the clergy had to be organized and brought under discipline; the laity had to be educated and the great leakage from the Church stemmed; churches had to be built and native clergy found, educated and supported to staff them; and the rising number of immigrants had to be cared for. The freedom which the Revolution slowly brought Catholics did, indeed, open a new era for the Church. It also introduced new complications.

[13] Report of Archbishop Ambrose Maréchal to Propaganda, Oct. 16, 1818, in Ellis, *Documents, op. cit.,* p. 210.

Response of the Laity

Yet if it was clear from the viewpoint of Archbishop Carroll that the Church had paid heavily for its years of repression, how had the laity adapted to their situation? For many, of course, there was little problem of adaptation. If they had been weak Catholics in the first place, there was little to induce them to become stronger Catholics: their Church was socially unacceptable, their clergy were few and the milieu was Protestant if at all religious. But if they were intent on remaining Catholic and had the good fortune to live in an area where a church and a priest were available, and at least a few other Catholics to sustain them, the problem of adaptation was mitigated—but hardly annulled. They still had to cope with the society in which they lived.

For the upper classes, particularly in Maryland and Pennsylvania, the problem was less acute than for the lower and middle classes. For one thing, they were able to retain and support private chapels and chaplains. For another, they had a strong tradition of giving their children a Catholic education. Prior to the establishment of Georgetown and Georgetown Visitation Convent, they sent their children abroad for their education, normally to France. Again, they had a close relationship with the clergy, strengthened by a common tradition of English persecution. The result was a sizable group of cultured and trained Catholics, strong in their own faith and of great assistance to the clergy.[14] Their Catholicism was at least comparatively solid and their resistance to the climate of opinion firmer. The lower classes, particularly the scattered Irish indentured servants, had no such advantages. For the struggling farmers, shopkeepers and port laborers, who formed the greater body of Catholics, there was little to fall back on. That in many instances they were desperately eager to preserve their faith can hardly be doubted; that the odds against them were overwhelming is open to even less doubt.

Yet it is especially worth considering the wealthier class of Catholics, English for the most part, and plantation owners by occupation. Not only did they have the material means to preserve their faith, but they also had other advantages in coping with the world in which they lived. Their greatest advantage lay in the fact that they were English; they shared, at least, a common cultural background with their non-Catholic neighbors. Unlike the Irish immigrants, it was impossible for them to be

[14] Cf. John LaFarge, "The Survival of the Catholic Faith in Southern Maryland," *Catholic Historical Review*, XXV (1935-36), pp. 1-20.

considered foreigners and cultural interlopers. Their only real problem
was their religion. In other matters they were at one with those about
them. They were acceptably conservative, had the right sort of social
pedigrees, spoke the language of their neighbor in the idiom of their
neighbor, were not troublesome about their rights as Catholics and
were, in almost all things, accepted men of their times with an influence
proportionate to their numbers.

The instance of Charles Carroll of Carrollton (1737-1832) is particularly instructive. While the Carroll family had been for some decades
a prominent family in Maryland, it had, like all other Catholic families,
no national importance. But by virtue of Charles Carroll's productive
pen, he became a well-known personage recognized for his able attacks,
in the *Maryland Gazette* in February 1773, against the actions of the
royal governor, Robert Eden. He soon became the only Catholic signer
of the Declaration of Independence. However distinguished Carroll was
for his patriotism, there was little that was outstanding about his Catholicism. Unlike his somewhat aggressive father, Charles Carroll of Annapolis, the son was passive and had little of the apostolic drive in him. In
his relations with the clergy, he was loyal but at the same time critical of
the Jesuits. While there is little to confirm the opinion of Carroll held
by one Anglican rector, it is at least suggestive: "I am satisfy'd there
are some *Roman* Catholic Gentlemen of Fortune and Family, both here
and in England, who do not swallow implicitly all the Impositions of
that Church, though they hold external Communion with it."[15]

What it may suggest, of course—and many present-day American
Catholics have met the same type of judgment for no apparent reason—
is that Carroll simply did not live up to a certain stereotype of what a
Catholic ought to be like. But it also suggests that Carroll was not one to
make an issue of his Catholicism. Like other Catholics of his time,
Carroll was not prone to mix his religion and his politics nor did the
clergy attempt to influence the laity in their politics. "The lack of numbers," Father Thomas T. McAvoy laconically notes, "gave the Catholics
of that day little inclination to bring their religion into politics and the
social position of Catholics was determined chiefly by the circumstances
of their birth and property."[16]

A few other Catholics were no less successful, if less prominent than

15 Ellen Hart Smith, *Charles Carroll of Carrollton* (Cambridge, 1942), p. 37.
16 Thomas T. McAvoy, C.S.C., "The Catholic Minority in the United States,
1789-1821," *Historical Records and Studies*, XXXIX-XL (1952), p. 40.

Carroll. Matthew Carey (1760-1838), a vigorous opponent of the penal code in Ireland and a refugee to the United States, was an important publisher and probably the first genuine American Catholic liberal. An advocate of regulated trade, prison reform and public education, Carey stood at the other end of the ideological spectrum from his fellow Catholic Philadelphian Robert Walsh (1784-1859). Walsh was a Federalist and a conservative, the founder of a quarterly, the *American Review of History and Politics*, an enthusiastic supporter of a *laissez-faire* trade policy, and an opponent of the early labor movement and of mass public education.

More famous, however, than Walsh and Carey were such men as Roger Brooke Taney (1777-1864) and William Gaston (1778-1844). Taney, who served under Jackson as Secretary of the Treasury and became, finally, Chief Justice of the Supreme Court, was passionately interested in protecting Negro rights, whether slave or free. Yet he was basically a Southerner in his attitudes and his role in the Dred Scott decision was conservative. As a Catholic he followed the usual pattern: he was devout but by no means aggressive—he refused, in fact, to let Catholic friends attempt to convert his Protestant wife and daughter. Gaston, known as a humanitarian, rarely sought public office (though he did serve in Congress as a representative from North Carolina from 1813-1817) but despite that was famous as a public speaker. In New York, Francis Cooper (1764-1850) and Cornelius Heeney (1754-1853) achieved considerable prominence, Heeney for his wealth and charitable works and Cooper as the first Catholic elected to the New York state legislature. Others, like Dominick Lynch in New York and Thomas FitzSimons, the Brents and the Digges families in Maryland, all made attempts to further their social and political position. All, with the exception of Cooper and Heeney, were quiet and circumspect about their Catholicism. And it is worth recalling that, in the early nineteenth century in New York, Catholics made some small mark for themselves in the literary world, though more as publishers and booksellers than as writers.[17]

If there was any one overriding characteristic about the upper-class Catholics—and those below them for that matter—it was their conformity to the values of the day. The plantation system, which was the

[17] Thomas F. Meehan, "Catholic Literary New York, 1800-1840," *Catholic Historical Review*, IV (1919), pp. 399-414.

source of the wealth of the Maryland Catholics, had the effect of making Catholics participate in the value system of the landed aristocracy. Land tenure, the dependence upon slaves, and the practice of indentured servitude were easily accepted by Catholics. It was not so much a question of Catholics imitating their non-Catholic neighbors as it was a generally unquestioning attitude toward the commonly-held values of the period. "Belonging to the landed classes, attached to the royal party both by choice and by circumstance, and sharing the usual economic motives for colonial enterprise, they were not inclined to examine critically the social and economic systems of their time."[18] In politics they were, for the most part, Federalists—they had little enthusiasm for Jefferson's egalitarianism. Yet whatever their political opinions, Catholics of all classes were acceptably patriotic. They took a part in the Revolution compatible with their numbers and, in Charles Carroll and Daniel Carroll, Thomas FitzSimons, Stephen Moylan and John Barry, American Catholicism was able to boast some outstanding revolutionary spirits.

If there was any one difficulty in the assimilation of the Anglo-American Catholics, it was precisely the fact that they so easily adapted themselves to the mores of the day. Even granting their small numbers and their good reasons always to attest, perhaps excessively, to their patriotism, it meant in the long run that Catholics took no leadership in their society. Anyone who would have looked, say, to Catholics to raise their voice against slavery would have been sadly disappointed. Nor was there any inclination on their part to confront the great intellectual movements of the eighteenth and early nineteenth centuries; they had no part in the radical ferment created by the French Revolution, and their values were not such as to produce fiery and influential intellectual leaders. In all things they were passive and docile. Not until the Irish immigrants began arriving in large numbers was there any counter-force to this early conservatism; not until the Irish immigrants came was there any serious Catholic thinking done on the implications of American democracy. As one who shared the values of the wealthy and the settled, the early Catholic was as suspicious of the masses as the next man—and as resistant to his rise. The Catholic, when he was not aristocratic in his inclinations, was bourgeois; no other choice attracted him.

Yet there was one distinct advantage in the combination of passivity

[18] C. Joseph Neusse, *The Social Thought of American Catholics, 1634-1829* (Washington, D.C., 1945), p. 282.

and acceptance of the dominant culture. It did gain upper-class Catholics a place among their neighbors and, with that in hand, they could be of use to the immigrant Catholics. It was not surprising, then, that the established English-Catholic group became the cultural leaders in the Church. For one thing, they were almost alone in having some measure of education. For another, they provided the immigrant with a pattern for assimilation and acceptance into the established social order. Most importantly, they formed "the chief connecting link between the history of the Catholic immigrant and that of the native Protestant."[19] While this subject will be of greater concern in subsequent chapters, it is worth noting at this point that the cultural leadership provided by the Anglo-American Catholic was soon to come into sharp conflict with the more aggressive stance of the immigrants. If the Anglo-Americans were not more aggressive in asserting their rights, one reason was that they were not "ghetto" Catholics: they did not live in physical isolation from their non-Catholic neighbors nor in cultural isolation. After some early struggles, they had the acceptance of those about them. Inevitably, they were to find the aggressiveness of the more sorely pressed immigrant distasteful. Like all men, they too were embarrassed by their poor relatives. They knew how to get along; the latecomers didn't. But it was the latecomer who was finally to dominate American Catholic culture; sheer numbers more than made up for the disadvantage of unpromising beginnings.

Yet even when the immigrant came finally to dominate, one problem was to continue down to our own day. Ought the Catholic, when faced with a hostile society, attempt to coerce the opposition by political and legal pressure, or as the Anglo-Catholics were prone to believe, use the gentler means of persuasion and a quiet appeal to the mind and conscience? The Anglo-American Catholics worked out one pattern of response, the immigrants another. In a wider sense, however, two views of the role the Catholic ought to play in American pluralism were at stake: that of unobtrusive and gradual assimilation versus that of active, pressing assimilation. It suffices here to mention this conflict; it will loom much larger in subsequent history.

So far I have attempted to describe, first, the hierarchy's view of the situation of the Church in the colonial and early national period and,

[19] Thomas T. McAvoy, C.S.C., "The Formation of the Catholic Minority in the United States, 1820-1860," *Review of Politics*, X (Jan., 1948), pp. 16-17.

secondly, the place of the layman in this society. Now it is time to turn to the third and perhaps most momentous question. What was the role of the layman in the early American Church? No sooner does one ask this question than a single phrase comes to mind—lay trusteeism. For if there is any one facet about the Church which bears most heavily on the problem of the layman, it is the fact that almost until the 1860s, the control of local church finances was in the hands of groups of lay trustees.

Trusteeism: Power and Abuse

This control was both a great opportunity and a great temptation to the layman. Lay trusteeism meant, on the one hand, that the layman was intimately involved in the running of the churches and, on the other, capable of creating havoc and disunity when he abused his power. He could, and sometimes did, refuse to accept a priest assigned by the bishop, discharge a priest whom he did not like, shout down in church an unpopular preacher and, with musket loaded, keep out a contending group of trustees. Had abuses not been apparent from the beginning, the history of the American Catholic layman could have been considerably different. As it turned out, the Church was forced to act against the whole system: the layman had his wings clipped, the clergy became more rigidly disciplined and the hierarchy expanded its power and control. Yet, "regarded a priori," Archbishop John Hughes was to say in 1853, "no system could appear to be less objectionable, or more likely, both to secure advantages to those congregations, and at the same time to recommend the Catholic religion to the liberal consideration of the Protestant sentiment of the country."[20]

What was the trustee system and why, at first, did the Church find it unobjectionable? In its remote origins, trusteeism was an integral part of the organization of individual churches. While the Church always held that it had the right to administer ecclesiastical property, it allowed this right to be delegated to either clergy or laity. Those to whom this right was delegated were known as *fabrique de l'église*, or trustees. These trustees in turn had the responsibility, amounting to a right, to

[20] *Brooksiana; or The Controversy Between Senator Brooks and Archbishop Hughes Growing Out of the Recently Enacted Church Property Bill* (New York, 1855), p. 5.

distribute and control that part of church revenues contributed for the maintenance of a church. This system was almost universal until the sixteenth century and was recognized by the Council of Trent.[21]

In America, trusteeism became the established custom for a number of reasons. In the early colonial period, the Church was allowed to own no property; hence it became necessary for the Jesuit missionaries to keep what little ecclesiastical property they had in the names of individual priests, willing it on their death to other individuals. This was a tolerable system because of a certain unity among the Jesuits. With the coming of secular priests, it was less than satisfactory. Eventually, after disestablishment and in conformity with most state laws which recognized only designated members of any given congregation as legal owners of church property, it fell to the lot of the laity to select a few of their number to hold the property in their own names. The state laws, not unexpectedly, envisaged the normal Protestant congregational arrangement for the holding of property—yet it was an arrangement compatible with Catholic church government as well.

In theory, then, lay trusteeism had some weight of Catholic tradition behind it and was, as well, required by most of the states. At first Bishop Carroll tolerated trusteeism, believing it would be conducive to the raising of funds and the building of parishes. Yet he soon came to regret the whole business. In his own diocese he was to witness, at one of his Baltimore churches, the spectacle of one faction of the congregation assembling to repel another faction by force of arms; to see an excommunicated priest installed by rebellious trustees in a Philadelphia church; and to be taken to court on one occasion for daring to assert his episcopal authority.

The reasons for the abuse of trusteeism were many. Without suggesting any order of priority, the following causes were most apparent: undisciplined and refractory priests, mainly Irish; rebellious and ignorant laymen; nationalistic clashes; the example and inspiration of the Protestant churches; and the general spirit of democracy. The pattern of the trustee disputes was almost invariably the same: an itinerant immigrant priest, assigned by Bishop Carroll or one of his successors to some unserviced church, would gather about him a group of laymen and set himself against the bishop. For this act he would be suspended, whereupon he and his faction would go into schism.

---

[21] Cf. Guilday, *The Life and Times of John Carroll, op. cit.,* I, pp. 782ff., for a good account of the legal origins of trusteeism.

But such a schematic account does little justice to the complexities involved. Each instance often saw a different weighting of the common elements. In 1787 in Philadelphia, for instance, the German-born parishioners of St. Mary's Church, dissatisfied with their English-speaking priests, legally incorporated themselves and hired a wandering German priest as their pastor. In other instances, Irish congregations resented French priests—almost the only priests that Bishop Carroll had for many years; thus, nationalism was a factor of importance in many of the disputes. Or it might be a congregation wanting to have a better preacher; regardless of the rights of the bishop, it would simply expel the appointed priest and install its own man. In other instances, it was the desire of an unruly priest to be free of the influence of his bishop —and all he needed was the support of the trustees. Finally, as in the Norfolk-Charleston schism of 1804, the desire of the trustees to manage entirely their own affairs, spiritual and temporal, was the cause of the trouble. In most instances, however, it took two or three elements working together to bring about a real crisis: a pliant or machiavellian priest and an ignorant or rebellious group of trustees.

Today we find it difficult to imagine how such things could have happened. Even more significantly, the question arises whether these abuses were not inevitable. For an answer, one must look more closely at the situation of both the clergy and the laity. The first thing to be kept in mind is that Carroll and the other early bishops had little choice about the quality of the clergy. A great many of the priests under their jurisdiction were uninvited. They were priests who, for one reason or another, had left their native land and sought refuge in America. In too many instances, they were priests who had been in trouble with their bishops at home and expected less trouble in America—this was notably true of the Irish clergy. Carroll, while often reluctant to accept them, was desperate for priests. Moreover, until the establishment of the hierarchy in 1790, there was practically no organized control of the clergy. Informality and freedom from discipline were a deeply engrained tradition. One of Carroll's first tasks was to bring about some order where, for over a hundred years, there had been no order at all.

Secondly, in the absence of adequate educational facilities, the laity for the most part had only the dimmest understanding of canon law and especially that part pertaining to the rights of a bishop. There was an easy leap in logic from control of the finances to control of the priest and the spiritual functions of a church. Since it was their money which had built and maintained their church, many trustee groups felt that they had the right to name their own pastor or to depose the pastor appointed by the bishop. It was also common to claim *jus patronatus*: the privilege of a church benefactor to present to the hierarchy the name of a person acceptable to him to fill a church vacancy. Important, too, was the fact that the state laws were usually on the side of the trustees. It was the legally elected board of trustees which had the right, under law, to manage church affairs as they saw fit. Disputes between trustees and bishops were matters which fell outside the jurisdiction of the courts. A more subtle but ever present source of trouble was the example of the Protestant churches: it was tempting to imitate their freedom from hierarchal control and to want the same right to "call" and discharge clergy as their Protestant neighbors had.

Nor can one fail to observe the potent influence of American democracy. Catholics, like all Americans, were caught up in the spirit of freedom. For if America meant anything, it meant the right to religious and civil freedom. As the board of trustees of the church in Norfolk and Portsmouth in 1819 put it in a letter to Archbishop Carroll, who had summoned one of their priests, his request was "a most glaring violation of their civil right and religious liberties and in direct opposition to the state laws of Virginia."[22] And this kind of language was not uncommon, just as it was not uncommon for the trustees to take their complaints to court. While it would be a mistake to overstress this point, it is evident that these American Catholics found some obvious points of conflict between the laws of their Church and the mores and laws of their society.[23] Here, for the first time in America, the layman was forced to reconcile the values of the political system under which he lived with the radically different hierarchical structure of his Church. As we shall see, it would not be the last time.

But more decisively, it is important to recognize that the ignorance and conflicting values of the laity also encouraged the rebellious priests. Lacking any solid education themselves, it was a fairly easy matter for

[22] Ellis, *Documents, op. cit.,* p. 221.
[23] Cf. R. F. McNamara, "Trusteeism in the Atlantic States, 1785-1863," *Catholic Historical Review,* XXX (July, 1944), pp. 135-154. McNamara, however, puts entirely too much stress on this cause of trusteeism in my opinion. Bishop John England of Charleston was considerably more charitable about the trustees. Cf. *Works of John England,* edited by Sebastian G. Messmer (7 vols.; Cleveland, 1903), IV, p. 291.

a group of trustees to be even more misled when they had a priest to goad them on and suggest to them rights which the Church itself did not in fact grant. As Bishop John England of Charleston was to complain of some of the Irish priests: "Scarcely do they set foot on American soil when, intoxicated with the spirit of liberty, they seem to lose their heads."[24] And what logic could not do, eloquence, in an age when eloquence counted for much, often could. While in most instances it is impossible to exonerate the lay trustees, it is not altogether fair to treat them as malicious usurpers either. Ecclesiastical discipline was often as new to them as to many of their priests; many of the laymen simply could not believe they did not have all the rights they claimed. Moreover, since the clergy had been allowed to elect their own bishops in the instance of the first three American bishops—Carroll, Graessl and Neale—it seemed only reasonable to some that they should be able to elect their own pastors.

But if Rome had been willing to make a concession in the case of the bishops it was hardly inclined to do so with the laymen; nor were the elected bishops themselves willing to make such a concession. Yet the fact that some bishops were slow to act, worked against them in the long run. Episcopal tolerance encouraged the trustees to expect ecclesiastical action to be taken only as a last resort. In the instance of Carroll and the other early bishops there was normally a bending over backwards to give the laity as much freedom as possible; to adapt, in the end, the American Church as much as possible to the American scene and the temperament of American Catholics. In this respect, Carroll was not just being practical. He was himself firmly committed to the American freedoms which he and his flock enjoyed with all other Americans.

If concessions to either the desires of the laity or the biases of Protestants were necessary, Carroll was willing to make them so far as it was within his authority to do so. As he wrote in 1785: "We desire that the faith in its integrity, due obedience towards the Apostolic See and perfect union should flourish; and at the same time that whatever can with safety to religion be granted, shall be conceded to American Catholics in ecclesiastical affairs. In this way we hope that distrust of Protestants now full of suspicion will be diminished and that our affairs can be solidly established."[25] In 1820, a Father Harold, writing to the *Congre-*

[24] Quoted by Neusse, *op. cit.*, p. 177.
[25] Carroll to Cardinal Antonelli, Feb. 27, 1785; quoted by Melville, *op. cit.*

gation de Propogation Fide, could express a similar attitude: "The Sacred Congregation in legislating for the Church, should never forget, that the Sovereign Power in these States, is the will of the people. . . . In such a state of things, it will, I trust, appear evident to your Eme. that the wishes of the people, when they do not pass the bounds of duty, nor encroach the sacred limits of Church discipline, should be treated with great mildness and intelligence."[26]

Nevertheless, when pressed too far, the bishops could and did stand firm. As Archbishop Jean Dubois expressed it to a group of trustees who threatened to cut off his income, "Gentlemen, I have seen the horrors of the French Revolution, and I could meet them again. I am an old man. I can live in a cellar or a garret; but, gentlemen, whether I come up from my cellar or down from my garret, you must remember that I am still your bishop."[27] But until trusteeism became a clear threat to the spiritual authority of the bishops, they showed little inclination to make an issue of their rights and prerogatives. They were not only physically close to their people but they also enthusiastically shared the general American love of freedom from authoritarian restraint. Nor was their attitude in this respect devoid of a desire to see the American Church find its own patterns and be free of a slavish obedience to Rome.

Although Rome did for the most part stay out of the trustee disputes, it made its voice heard on one important occasion. As an aftermath of the notorious Hogan schism in Philadelphia, led by Father William Hogan who was excommunicated for his refusal to accept episcopal authority, Pope Pius VII in August, 1822, addressed a brief, *Non sine magno,* to Archbishop Maréchal and to all American Catholics. In his brief, the Pope stated that trusteeism was, in principle, acceptable to the Church provided that "the trustees . . . administer the temporalities of the Church in union of mind and heart with the Bishop." "But," he added, "that trustees and laymen should arrogate to themselves the right . . . of establishing for pastors, priests destitute of legal faculties, and even not infrequently bound by censures . . . and also of removing them at their pleasure, and of bestowing the revenues among whom they please, is a practice *new* and *unheard of* in the Church. And if these

---

[26] Peter Guilday, "Trusteeism," *Historical Records and Studies* (1928), p. 11.
[27] Gerald C. Treacy, "Evils of Trusteeism," *Historical Records and Studies,* VIII (1915), p. 153.

things have been performed in the manner, in which it has been announced to us, how could so great a subversion of laws, not only ecclesiastical but divine, be borne with? For in that case the Church would be governed, not by *Bishops*, but by *laymen*, the *Shepherd* would be made subject to his flock, and laymen would usurp the power, which was given by Almighty God to Bishops."[28]

Draconian Measures

Trusteeism was slow in dying. Not only was it to take many decades for state laws to be changed to allow local bishops to hold church property as a corporation sole, but the advent of nativism and know-nothingism in the thirties and forties of the nineteenth century was to make it all the more difficult for the hierarchy to have the laws changed. As late as 1855, the New York legislature, at the instigation of a group of trustees of St. Louis Church in Buffalo, passed the Putnam Act giving the trustees the right to overrule the bishop—in that case, Archbishop John Hughes of New York. And it was not until 1935 that a law enacted in 1855 forbidding episcopal control of church property was finally repealed in Pennsylvania.

After the 1840s, however, serious disputes became less and less frequent. One reason for this was that the First Provincial Council, which met in Baltimore in 1829, had urged the bishops not to consecrate any church unless the deed had been made in trust to them. Then, too, the bishops had discovered that it was possible to appeal, in many instances, directly to the rebellious trustees; when confronted with a reasonable request to desist in their claims they were often willing to give way to the bishop. As Father Harold shrewdly noted: "These people yield a willing obedience to authority when exercised coolly and with mildness, but if their feelings and opinions are treated with violent and contemptuous disregard, they become obstinate and incorrigible."[29]

To pass judgment on the trustee system is, in one way, simple. It obviously led to abuses, discord and schism. To have been successful, it would have required a far more mature and theologically sophisticated type of layman than the early Church could boast; just as it would have

[28] Peter Guilday, *The Life and Times of John England, 1786-1842* (2 vols.; New York, 1927), I, p. 357.
[29] Guilday, "Trusteeism," *op. cit.,* p. 9.

required far more stable priests than were then available. Because of the obvious troubles and dangers, it is not hard to see why the hierarchy turned against it and took steps to bring it to an end. Yet from another point of view, there is good reason to regret that it was, finally, so sharply rejected. It was a system which, in theory at least, offered the layman a very active part in parish life. Under a trustee system it would hardly be possible to say that the Church was a purely clerical matter—unhappily, the early trouble was just the reverse.

Even more concretely, the trustee problem convinced the hierarchy that rigid discipline of both clergy and laity was absolutely essential. The reaction, when it finally set in, was sharp: the layman was a person to be wary of, one who, given his head too much, was prone to be carried away by his sense of power into thinking he had rights within the Church which neither priests, bishop nor pope could annul. Once allowed to meddle in Church business, however temporal and worldly the business might be, there was no telling what he would do—especially when he lived in a society which made much of human freedom, democratic values and Protestant mores. The only safe course was to exclude the layman entirely from any part in the management of Church affairs or property. For the layman, this meant that he was denied a voice in the use of the funds he contributed. He might complain and mutter but there was little he could do to make his criticism effective.

For the individual priest, the effect of the reaction was no less constricting. If, earlier, he had been too much at the mercy of his congregation, he was soon to be very much at the mercy of his bishop. The power over pastors that the trustees had wielded was not transferred entirely back to the pastors; rather, it was given to the bishop, who henceforth would have the decisive control over Church matters, both spiritual and temporal. Inevitably, genuine cooperation and a sense of fellowship between priests and laymen suffered. From being bound tightly—too tightly—to their parishioners, pastors and curates would now be bound far more tightly to the bishops. If the bishop did not provide leads for new initiatives within the churches, then there would be little a pastor could do to make progress at his own pace or to show a sensitive readiness to respond to the needs of his flock. Whatever the needs or desires of his people, a priest had first to think of his bishop. What would he say? Would he approve? What would other priests say?

The strengthening of the power of the hierarchy and the introduction of clear patterns of discipline and responsibility were, then, a loss as well as a gain. It is hardly a coincidence that the Archdioceses of Philadelphia and New York, the scenes of some of the worst trustee disputes, have ever since been notably sluggish in encouraging or allowing lay activities or initiatives—or that the clergy in those archdioceses have always had heavy hands laid upon them whenever they incurred the displeasure of the Ordinary. In New York, in particular, the stern tradition of Archbishop John Hughes, who set out forcefully and effectively to end trusteeism in that city in the 1850s, lingers on up to the present day. The moral which the hierarchy drew from trusteeism was that firm authority and discipline were imperative, far more imperative than even perfectly legitimate lay freedom and autonomy. In the light of the trustee wrangles, with their clear threat to the spiritual authority of the bishops, it seemed the only moral possible.

Yet the Church was to pay a high price for the establishment of firm episcopal authority. As one contemporary American bishop has written: "Trusteeism had to be crushed, no doubt about that. . . . But as in the case with almost every draconian measure, the rooting out of trusteeism meant also the damaging of the original American Catholic spirit which has been identified here with Archbishop Carroll. Essential as was the victory for the divinely established authority of the bishops to rule their dioceses as successors of the Apostles, and not as chairmen of governing boards, it nevertheless resulted in a situation where the part of the laity in this cooperative effort which is the work of the Church was reduced to a minimum."[30]

Amidst these "draconian" measures, it is worth recalling one imaginative attempt made to resolve a trustee crisis. This was Bishop John England's adoption of a diocesan "constitution" for Charleston, the aim of which was to provide an alternative means to trusteeism by which laymen could have a significant role in Church affairs, as well as to provide a workable basis for Church government.[31] Bishop England had very clearly seen the dangers of trusteeism in the North and was determined that his own diocese of Charleston would not experience a repetition of

[30] Bishop Robert J. Dwyer (Bishop of Reno), "The American Laity," *The Commonweal*, LX (Aug. 27, 1954), p. 506.
[31] The only full account of Bishop England's Constitution is to be found in Peter Guilday's *The Life and Times of John England, 1786-1842, op. cit.*, I, pp. 343-377.

those evils. At the same time he believed that the laity, as well as the lower clergy, should be cooperatively bound to the bishop while still having a significant voice of their own. To this end, he drew up an elaborate diocesan constitution, specifying the authority and rights of the bishop and the rights and duties of the laity. To gain the support of clergy and laity, he called for the "First Convention of the Roman Catholic Church of South Carolina," with lay and clerical delegates, which met on November 24, 1823, in Charleston. That convention unanimously approved the constitution, although it was not until 1839 that it was printed in its final amended form.

There were a number of details about the constitution which need not concern us here. Most relevant, however, was the provision which called for a yearly convention. The convention consisted of three parts: the Bishop, a House of the Clergy, and a House of Lay Delegates. All of the clergy of the diocese were expected to attend the convention with each parish or district, according to population, sending an allotted number of lay representatives. It was the duty of the Lay House of Delegates to elect its own president and appoint its own officials. To all intents and purposes, the House of the Clergy and the House of the Delegates were on a basis of equality. The aim of the convention, as Bishop England envisioned it, was not participation in the ecclesiastical government of the diocese; that was the bishop's responsibility alone. Instead, the two Houses were, in his words, "to be considered rather as a body of sage, prudent and religious counsellors to aid the proper ecclesiastical governor in the discharge of his duty."[32] Specifically excluded from the authority of the convention were such matters as Church doctrine and discipline, appointments, ordinations, administration of the sacraments, and superintendence of the clergy. What the conventions did take up regularly were Catholic education, seminary training, social welfare work, the Catholic press, works of charity and means of defending and extending the faith.

In almost every respect, Bishop England's hopes for the constitution and for the conventions were achieved. Altogether, fifteen conventions were held at Charleston for the District of South Carolina (1823-1838), eight at Augusta for the Georgia District (1826-1835) and two at Fayetteville for North Carolina (1829-1831).[33] And in the words of the

---

[32] *Ibid.*, p. 375.
[33] Full reports on these conventions were carried in the pages of England's diocesan paper, *The United States Catholic Miscellany*.

Bishop, "Under the Charleston Constitution, I can truly say that the clergy, and especially the bishops, are entirely free; and on the other hand the laity are empowered to cooperate but not to dominate." Unfortunately, the other American bishops were, from the start, suspicious. Bishop Cornwell of Philadelphia, alarmed by the insistence of many laymen in New York and Philadelphia that the constitution be adopted in those dioceses, was particularly opposed, seeing in it a danger of democratizing the Church. Despite efforts of some of the bishops to have the constitution condemned by Rome, Bishop England himself weathered all opposition. But the constitution did not survive his death in 1842: neither his successor nor any of the other bishops ever adopted it. Only today, when some diocesan synods have formally made place for lay participants, do we hear echoes of this ingenious arrangement.

CHAPTER 2

The Layman as Immigrant:
1830-1880

EVERY nation has a personality, those subtle traits and characteristics which enable us to distinguish the American from the Englishman, the Dane from the Italian, the Arab from the Japanese. Though sometimes less immediately discernible, it is just as possible to distinguish, within a nation, various sub-cultures: those cultures which, while possessing much that is common to all, have their own life and their own set of values, mores and goals. But is it equally possible to note and character-ize—for the naked eye and not just for a sociological monograph—a change in tone, color and direction of a particular religious group as it adjusts to a new situation? Can one pick out, with any assurance, just how, why and where a group changes?

If one observes the American Catholic community as it passed from the relatively stable, if struggling, years just after the Revolution to the years when the immigrants began quite literally to swamp the Church, the answer is decisive. Not only is the change evident in charts and statistics, but it was even more visible in the daily life of the Church and its members. One might be tempted at first to say the change was only from chaos to chaos. For did not Bishop Carroll and the other early bishops have to surmount a troublesome clergy, a frequently turbulent and obstructionist laity, heavy losses from the Church, wholly inade-quate finances and facilities? That is perfectly true. But it was also true that the first bishops soon had a fairly clear idea of what they needed to do; and one could find in almost every important community Catholic laymen accepted and respected, men who could not only help the Church financially and socially but who could also be of assistance to the at first comparatively small number of immigrants. There were, in

28

short, the rudiments of a viable structure and the outlines of a consistent, workable approach to the problems which confronted the Church. Even if, as misfortune would have it in the instance of trusteeism, part of the hierarchy's approach meant the quelling of the laity and the establishment of stricter ecclesiastical order, there still remained flexibility and the possibility of slow and informal experimentation. The main road had been charted and the rest of the way could be worked out in time.

There never was time, however. In the 1820s somewhere in the vicinity of 54,000 Catholics came to America. They were, to be sure, a problem. But compared with the 1840s, when approximately 700,000 arrived, the earlier situation was almost idyllic. By 1900 close to 5,000,000 immigrants had swept into the Church's orbit. And how did they arrive? They came for the most part penniless, desperate, by turns fearful and hopeful, uneducated and bewildered. They came, not back to the land which as peasants most of them had left, but to crowded, impersonal and disorderly cities. They lacked in most cases the skills and talents which an urban, increasingly industrialized society demanded of them. They fled the famine-ridden villages of Ireland and the oppression of the English only to find that one could come close to starving in America and be as oppressed by one's fellow Americans as by any masters they had left behind. They fled the revolutions of Germany only to find that a wretched tenement house could breed as much confusion and violence as any contending ideologists. And when, after the Irish and the Germans had come and staked out their own place during the middle of the nineteenth century, the Italians and the Slavs came later in the century, they found that one could be as resented by other immigrants as by the most imperious, well-bred Yankees.

Equally important was their discovery that their religious world had been shattered. No longer could they count on society to provide a matrix for their belief. No longer could they see their religion intimately intertwined with their work and their leisure. No longer could they count on the sustaining cycle of publicly recognized feast-days, the blessing of their work and their tools, the intimate connection between soil and deity. They came into a world with jagged economic edges; and they came as well into a world with jagged religious edges, a world which offered them far more in the way of temptations and spiritual threats than it did in hope and spiritual meaning. If, economically, they had nowhere to go but up, theologically it was possible to go down and out. What poverty, inadequate priestly care and a new and strange religious milieu could not accomplish, a violent anti-Catholicism might. For the hierarchy, their task could hardly have been more demanding. They had, on the one hand, to cope with the overwhelming numbers of the immigrants: churches had to be built, schools opened, hospitals and orphanages constructed, and competent priests found. On the other, they had to devise ways to relate the immigrant's Catholicism to the new American setting. They not only had to keep him as a member of the Church, but they also had to find ways to enable him to deal with the temptations and obstacles which could all but destroy his faith by robbing it of vigor and vitality. It was hardly surprising, then, that it should be the hierarchy and the clergy who were the most concerned about the fate of the immigrant. The immigrant himself could, initially, do little to improve his state; he had to depend almost exclusively on the abilities of those who were already here to help him make his way. And it was the hierarchy and clergy who were the best organized to help him, the one native group most sympathetic to him and the one group with whom he shared an immediate and natural bond.

My purpose here, however, is not to recount the story of the Catholic immigrant. Rather, it is necessary to understand how the experience of immigration shaped his consciousness—how, finally, it shaped the layman and provided him with a set of attitudes, beliefs and expectations about his place in the Church and in American life.

Two conclusions can immediately be anticipated. First, the immigrant started out at the bottom of the social ladder; he began his life as an American in a very unfavorable position. There was little to commend him to the established elements of society—other than the cheapness of his labor. There was little he could do to shape the life around him in its broader aspects. The most he could do was to make the little world he inhabited tolerable. And the only way he could do this was to stick closely to his fellows, to band together with them to ward off the threats and attacks directed at him. He became, in short, defensive, parochial, insular and sectarian. Second, since it was the clergy which most directly took charge of his fortunes, he became in very short order dependent upon them to direct his spiritual and cultural progress. Lay initiative was not only rare in fact, it was even in theory all but impossible; the immigrant had neither the education nor the self-confidence to direct himself. Perforce, he left the task to his betters.

Yet it would be a mistake to see the development of parochialism among the immigrants and the hegemony of the hierarchy and clergy as two distinct movements. In many ways, it was precisely the fact that the clergy held such sway that confirmed and strengthened the separatism of the immigrant. For in order to strengthen the immigrant's Catholicism and to build up the Church in America, the hierarchy and clergy had to induce a sense of group solidarity.[1] In order to develop and maintain loyalty to the faith, they had to develop loyalty to the Catholic community, loyalty to one's fellow Catholics. To be sure, the Church served the immigrant's material as well as spiritual needs. But one direct result of its ministrations was to keep the immigrant isolated from his non-Catholic neighbor. In part, this result was intentional, stemming from a desire to keep the immigrant close to the Church. But in greater part perhaps it was unintentional, for the hierarchy and clergy shared with the immigrant many of the same problems and fears. As natural as it was for the immigrants themselves to band together with those they knew, as natural was it for the hierarchy and clergy to do the same. Together, they had to withstand the forces of disintegration within the Catholic community and the hostile forces outside.

It was of particular importance that the task of answering attacks upon the Church fell heavily on the bishops. Beginning in the 1830s, nativism became a strong and virulent force working against the advancement of the immigrants. Nativism was not, of course, purely anti-Catholic. It was as much an expression of hostility against the economic threat of the immigrant and of repugnance at the fact that the immigrant was, in origin and lingering culture, a foreigner and an outsider. Anti-Catholicism was merely its most dramatic manifestation. It took such forms as the establishment, in 1830, of an explicitly anti-Catholic paper, *The Protestant*, the formation of the American Protestant Association in 1842, and of the Know-Nothing Party c. 1854. The task of meeting these anti-Catholic attacks, carried on by pamphlets, haranguing street preachers, and occasional acts of violence, fell naturally to the bishops. During the 1830s and 1840s it was not uncommon for priests and bishops to debate in public with Protestant ministers. Armed with the

---

[1] As Archbishop John Hughes of New York put it, "In short, [I had] to knead them up into one dough to be leavened by the spirit of Catholic faith and of Catholic union." From "The Archdiocese of New York a Century Ago: A Memoir of Archbishop Hughes, 1838-1858," *Historical Records and Studies*, XXXIX-XL (New York, 1952), p. 183.

power of words and a natural indignation, they had no hesitation about meeting the attacks head-on: they defended the Church from the pulpit, in the burgeoning Catholic press and from the debate platform. In this defense, they spoke not only for the Church universal but also for the American Catholic: the bishops became, by their own intent and by tacit popular acclaim, the champions of the people.

But if, as could have been expected, the internal problems and external attacks on the Church and on Catholics effectively erected a wall between Catholics and Protestants and resulted in a consequent turning of Catholics upon themselves, they did have the effect of strengthening Catholic solidarity. The unfortunate consequence of these attacks, however, was to solidify the trend, begun early in the nineteenth century, toward the formation of Catholic ghettos in the large cities of the Eastern seaboard. In cities like New York, Boston and Philadelphia, the newly-arrived Catholic immigrant could find wholly Catholic neighborhoods. In them he could find those who spoke his language, shared his religion, ate the same foods and were, like him, struggling to better their economic lot. While these ghettos did have the advantage of helping him make the transition from the old country to the new, they also kept him tied to his old culture for a far longer time than if he had been thrown immediately into the strange life of a growing America. To be sure, many of the immigrants had no desire to remain in the cities. Many, in particular, wanted to return to the land, to carry on in America the life they knew best, that of tilling the soil. But it was no easy task to find the funds to escape from the cities; and, once established within a sheltering ghetto, it was psychologically difficult to uproot themselves once more to start a new life again on the American frontier.

From the viewpoint of the hierarchy there was much to be said for the cities despite the great moral and social ills they bred. In the cities, with a high density of Catholics, it was far easier to raise the money needed to support charitable institutions, to build schools and churches, than it was on the frontier or in the established rural areas. Moreover, the solidarity that the ghettos fostered made it easier for the Church to retain the spiritual loyalty of the immigrants: they could be reached more easily, and the social atmosphere in the ghettoes provided a milieu in which Catholicism could flourish. There the whole panoply of ritual and popular piety could be sustained with little outside interference. Indeed, those Catholics who wanted to help the immigrants to escape from the city often found to their dismay that some Eastern bishops opposed any efforts toward that end.[2]

Given the fact of so many of the immigrants arriving in cities, of the opposition of some bishops to a westward movement, and of the psychological security of the urban ghetto, American Catholicism became, by the end of the nineteenth century, an urban religion, and the American Catholic an urban man. In the classic American social struggle between the rural and the urban populations, the Catholic was to be identified almost solely with the latter group. His religion, his class, his native roots and his life as a city-dweller all set him apart.

A Natural Conservatism

The experience of immigration and the subsequent forming of urban ghettos had still another important effect on the Catholic, both lay and clerical. It confirmed and strengthened his natural conservatism. "Village religion," Oscar Handlin has noted, "was, as a matter of course, conservative. Peasants and priests alike resisted change."[3] Then, too, in Ireland and in Germany religion had been a source of stability amidst the upheavals of the eighteenth and nineteenth centuries. Religion symbolized all that the old life meant, a life that was slowly destroyed by the fact of famine and the less obvious but just as real fact of the industrial revolution. These same attitudes were transferred to America where the one real hold the immigrant had on his old life was his Catholicism. It became a solid rock in a country where everything else was new and constantly changing.

In short, the immigrant was no lover of "progress." His experience in his native land had taught him to look with distrust at all those developments which were to usher in the modern age: tools, machines, modern agricultural economics—these had all been his enemies. Then again, from what he knew of repressive governments on the continent and in Ireland, the immigrant was hardly disposed to seek his salvation in the virtues and powers of the state. On the contrary, the state was some-

---

[2] *Documents of American Catholic History*, edited by John Tracy Ellis (2nd ed., Milwaukee, 1962), p. 320. Cf. also H. J. Browne, "Archbishop Hughes and Western Colonization," *Catholic Historical Review*, XXXVI (Oct., 1950), pp. 257-285.

[3] Oscar Handlin, *The Uprooted* (Boston, 1951), p. 119.

thing to be wary of; the less power it had the better. Altogether, there was little of the progressive or the utopian idealist in the immigrant's outlook. The world was hard, tough and oppressive and the grandiose schemes of the social visionary were regarded with suspicion.

The conservativism of the immigrant did, however, prove useful to the Church. For one thing, it made it easier for the hierarchy to gain the support of the masses for the numerous private and Church-sponsored welfare organizations. With little inclination to turn to the state for relief, the immigrant was ready to support those charities which, run by those he knew and trusted, promised immediate and direct assistance. For another, the very fact that it appeared natural for Catholics to look after themselves and to find their own methods of relief fostered a sense of unity and common purpose. It was the Church which provided both spiritual and physical support, thus avoiding the possibility of counter-allegiances tugging the immigrant away from the Church.

Yet this conservatism was not without its ironies. If there was ever a genuine Irish Catholic hero it was Daniel O'Connell. Revered both in America and in Ireland for his dynamic drive for Irish Emancipation, O'Connell was a genuine liberal. He stood not only for Irish freedom but also for freedom of religion, the separation of Church and State and the abolition of slavery. More than that, through O'Connell the drive for emancipation became primarily a lay-directed movement. He was, "a rare sort of Catholic for his day, a Catholic radical. Bentham did not lose completely to Bellarmine and Bossuet; they shared a sincere, if sometimes truculent devotee."[4]

But however attractive O'Connell's drive for Catholic rights was, few Irishmen were attracted to his liberalism. If, as has sometimes been contended, the Irish-Catholic immigrant brought to America a tradition of democratic agitation, he did not necessarily bring with him the ideological trappings which normally accompany such a tradition. He knew better how to agitate for his own rights than he did to construct the theoretical basis for a democracy which, working through the machinery of government, could assure attention to the rights of all. He might be counted upon to protest the harm done to his conscience by the reading of the King James Bible in the public schools; but for the rights of Negroes or women or for civil liberties in general he had little en-

[4] James A. Reynolds, *The Catholic Emancipation Crisis in Ireland, 1823-1829* (New Haven, 1954), p. 33.

thusiasm or interest. Nor could the earlier generation of immigrants and their children be counted upon to favor later generations of immigrants —Italians, Poles, Slavs and Jews.

Still another irony was the natural attraction of the immigrants to the Democratic party. During the early national period, as noted in the preceding chapter, the prosperous and settled English-American Catholics were largely Federalist in their political leanings; that party was the natural choice for men whose social position and wealth gave them a conservative bent. The immigrants, however, were more prone to become Jacksonian Democrats than Whigs when the Federalist Party finally collapsed. The Whig Party, founded in 1834, quickly became the party supported by the nativists and anti-Catholics; however attractive its conservatism might have been, it was still the party supported by the enemy. The Democrats, by contrast, were more positive in their support of religious freedom and, most importantly, were sympathetic and receptive to the immigrants. At the same time, ironically, the Democratic Party was the natural habitat of the agnostic or Protestant social reformer, with heavy support from the liberal academic and clerical community in New England. It stood for exactly those rights which the immigrant cared little about; but its one saving virtue was that it also stood for the immigrants' rights and that was sufficient to offset its other predilections.

In retrospect, it would now appear that the combination of Democratic Party affiliation and a natural, though rough-hewn conservatism was not particularly helpful to the immigrant or to the Church. The fact that the immigrant was aligned with the Democrats meant that his conservatism would not, until very recently, have any great impact on American conservative (normally Republican) politics. Of equal significance, the attachment of the immigrants to the Democratic Party was to make comparatively little difference in the shaping of a liberal ideology. Until the end of the nineteenth century, Catholics had almost no influence on party policy. Moreover, the ideological base of the party continued for some time to be shaped by those Yankees and intellectuals who, as a group, were the least congenial to the immigrants. That they fought for immigrants' rights was about the only thing in their favor; their other causes—women's rights, abolition, civil liberties—were a mark against them in the eyes of the immigrants.

If one were to seek the reason why Catholics, even Catholic liberals, have never been close to the central stream of American liberalism, one would have to confront the paradox of conservative Catholics giving their support to a liberal Democratic Party: the support of the party was strictly a matter of the practical help that the Democrats gave to the immigrants. This meant that the Catholic immigrant could receive help from the party but could not bring himself to share wholeheartedly in its general values. As with the Republican Party, the immigrant was from the outset excluded, almost by his own choice, from high policy-making decisions, and consequently from exerting any significant influence on the shaping of American liberal opinion.

But there was one crisis in particular which did more than anything else to alienate the immigrant from the American liberals. That was the question of abolition. Of all the rallying cries of the liberals, none was heard more loudly than that of "free the slaves." Yet almost without exception, Catholics, lay and clerical, were anti-abolitionists. The reasons are many. Most notably, the American Catholic theological attitude toward slavery was ambiguous and evasive. Although trade in slaves had been condemned by Pope Gregory XVI in December, 1839, the consensus of the theologians was that whenever slavery was not patently inhuman, it was not necessarily evil. In America, this view was upheld by the most important Catholic theologian, Bishop Francis P. Kenrick of Philadelphia. In his eyes, slavery was not demonstrably incompatible with the natural law. Moreover, the agitation over abolition was a threat to peace and order; the laws of the states allowed slavery and the laws should not be contravened in the name of some abstract good.[5] No doubt, too, the kind of people who supported abolition, men like William Lloyd Garrison and John Brown, furnished another argument. Added to the timidity of the bishops was fear on the part of the immigrants at the prospect of economic competition from Negroes. The lynching of freed slaves by Irish immigrants in New York in 1863 was simply a tragic expression of a general attitude.

In short, the Catholic was of little help in doing away with the injustice of slavery. For those who saw how important the issue was—and that included the main body of American intellectuals—the prevailing Catholic opinion was, at best, disturbing and, at worst, appalling. Even after the Civil War, and after the "development of doctrine" which the

[5] Francis P. Kenrick, *Theologia moralis* (Philadelphia, 1841), I, p. 257. Cf. John Tracy Ellis, *American Catholicism* (Chicago, 1956), pp. 87-90.

Union victory stimulated, it took the Catholic community many decades to speak out on Negro rights. The call of the Second Plenary Council in October, 1866, for religious instruction of the Negro, was almost universally ignored. In the South particularly, Catholics shared the general opinion of their white Protestant brethren. The religious orders were averse to educating Negroes; the laity were equally opposed. The age-old drug of the *status quo*, the unwillingness of Catholics to arouse antagonism and the conformity of Catholics to local values all worked against any kind of crusade in behalf of the Negro. The much-vaunted Catholic leadership on racial problems in the South is thus something of recent origin. Many Southern Catholics, faced with desegregation in schools and churches, could well complain that they had never heard that segregation and discrimination were immoral.

The issue of abolition and slavery constituted a notable occasion on which the American Church failed in its duty to promote vigorously human justice and freedom. Bishops, priests and laity equally shared the blame. In this context, it is necessary to note, however, that the bishops did not attempt to influence the political views of the laity in any major dispute around the middle of the nineteenth century. In practice as well as theory the bishops disclaimed any right to influence the political judgment of the laity or, for that matter, the clergy. This was made perfectly clear in the Pastoral Letter issued by the Fourth Provincial Council in May, 1840.[6] At the same time, it may be said that there was little reason for the bishops to entertain the idea of influencing a laity that had no part in the radical movements of the day. In their political opinions they were one with their bishops, at least in the sense that they were as quick to reject radical liberalism as were their shepherds. Equally, the immigrant had no desire to be an agitator—this took the kind of self-confidence that only the solidly rooted Yankee possessed. The Protestant or Yankee intellectual could afford to throw away his reputation on a social cause. But as one who aspired to the bourgeois life and who still had to make a place for himself, the immigrant was not attracted to radicalism, nor was there anything in his background which would have made him susceptible. The bishops had little to worry about in this respect.

This is not to suggest that Catholics were uniform in their political

[6] *The National Pastorals of the American Hierarchy, 1792-1919*, edited by Peter Guilday (Westminster, Md., 1954), p. 142.

opinions. They were not, nor were the bishops and priests. But differences remained within the spectrum of the respectable and acceptable. If the bishops had any warnings to offer, they were directed against extremism and political strife: "Do then, we entreat of you, avoid the contaminating influence of political strife, keep yourself aloof from the pestilential atmosphere in which honor, virtue, patriotism and religion perish."[7] This was certainly good advice. But it was the kind of advice which confirmed the layman's aloofness from vigorous participation in those social movements which were to shape the American social consciousness. The Catholic was from the start, by circumstance and by choice, cut off from all those social developments which were to triumph eventually—and which in the end he supported as much as the next man. But by then—only in the last few decades—it was hard for the American reformer to take the Church seriously as a potent force for social justice.

Confronting American Society

If slavery, the rights of workers and of women and the cause of civil liberties did not produce any genuine debate and leadership within the Church, there was one important issue which did. That was the question of the kind of stance the Catholic ought to take toward his non-Catholic fellow countryman. Reduced to its simplest terms (and they were anything but simple) the question was whether Catholics ought to make a positive effort to abandon defensiveness and engage in an outright attempt, first, to convert America to Catholicism and, second, to adapt the Church systematically to American life and mores.

The question might never have arisen, or not so sharply, had it not been for a number of eminent and dynamic converts to the Church between 1840 and 1860. From among the ranks of the Protestant clergy had come such men as Levi Silliman Ives, Thomas S. Preston and James Roosevelt Bayley. More notable still were the conversions of Isaac Hecker and Orestes Brownson—two men closely tied to the upper strata of American intellectual life and solidly secure in their social position. By temperament and class the converts were much closer to the older strain of the Anglo-American Catholics than they were to the incoming immigrants; and like this older Catholic group, they were often unhappy with the immigrants.

[7] *Ibid.*, p. 143.

But there was one significant difference between the views of converts like Brownson and Hecker toward the immigrant and those of the
Anglo-Catholic group. The latter objected to the immigrants because
they had the effect of lowering the social status of the Church and of
undoing the image of respectability so assiduously developed; there was,
to put it bluntly, a strong admixture of snobbery in their attitude. Hecker
and Brownson had a different set of aspirations and a different type of
objection.

The Anglo-Catholics were hardly apostolic; they wanted to be accepted and respected and had little inclination to convert those about
them. Brownson and Hecker, however, were vigorously apostolic. They
saw no reason why the Church ought not to aspire to convert Americans
in droves and make it a policy to attempt just that. Such an aspiration
entailed one essential preliminary task: both Catholics and non-Catholics
had to be convinced that Catholicism and the American way of life were
eminently compatible. Furthermore, unlike the Anglo-Catholics, Hecker
and Brownson specifically objected to the immigrants' defensiveness.
Their political conservatism was objectionable enough, but even more
distressing was their dogged attachment to the inappropriate customs and
attitudes of the "old country." When the immigrant was aggressive, and
he was normally timid and isolated, he was aggressive in the wrong
fashion: he liked to make a public display of just those elements of his
religion which had meant so much in the cultures from which he had
come. More than that, he was prone to be hostile to things American,
suspicious of the ruling and well-to-do classes, and only too ready to fight
back in a crude manner when attacked. The immigrant's aggressiveness
was that of a man on the defensive, determined to maintain for as long
as possible all those ways of life which had traditionally meant much
to him.[8]

In the eyes of Hecker and Brownson all this was hopelessly misguided.
What was needed was a vigorous attempt to do away with old-country
religion and to shape a Catholicism appropriate to the American scene.
However difficult, the immigrant had to cease looking upon the white,
Anglo-Saxon Protestant as his natural enemy; what the situation required was a systematic attempt to win over this group to the Church
or, at the very least, to build some strong and enduring bridges to this
dominant majority. The Church had no need to be defensive nor ought

[8] Cf. Thomas T. McAvoy, C.S.C., "The Formation of the Catholic Minority in
the United States, 1820-1860," *Review of Politics*, X (Jan., 1948), pp. 13-34.

it, really, take anti-Catholicism too seriously. Would the Church but adopt the stance of confidence, promote the intellectual and cultural life, replace old ways with new, then opposition to the Church would diminish and America would see it in its true, glorious and universal garb.

Not unexpectedly, these views did little to endear Hecker or Brownson to the bishops, nor did they attract much attention among the immigrant laity. Brownson, in particular, forcefully expressed opinions which rubbed just about every sensitive nerve the bishops had: he criticized the Irish, the native-born clergy, seminary education, Catholic higher education, Catholic insensitivity to the slavery question and did not view with the appropriate alarm the threat posed to the temporal power of the papacy by the movement for Italian reunification. More deeply still, many of the bishops found it all but impossible to share Brownson's optimism about the place of the Church in America, his judgment on the fundamental good sense and good will of Protestants, and his distaste for the immigrant. In the face of nativism and know-nothingism, the bishops' first desire was self-defense; the idea of ignoring these attacks and proceeding to build the needed bridges to the non-Catholic world had little appeal.

To make matters worse, Brownson was not one to play a fawning-layman role. He said what was on his mind and nothing was too sacred or too sensitive for his comments. The converts, Archbishop Hughes said (no doubt of Brownson in particular) "have been disposed to find fault with everything that has been done, at least to point out how much more might have been accomplished. But especially they take pleasure in suggesting to the Prelates and clergy what is to be done for the present and coming time. . . . Appropriating to themselves the words of encouragement which the Supreme Head of the Church addressed under peculiar circumstances to certain eminent lay editors of Europe, they have been disposed to look upon themselves as an unofficial but approved portion of the Catholic hierarchy. I have set my face against the exceptional parts of all this."[9]

The reason for the self-confidence felt by the converts, their buoyant optimism for the Church and their willingness to speak freely to bishops,

---

[9] "The Archdiocese of New York," *op. cit.*, p. 186. Cf. also Thomas T. McAvoy, C.S.C., "Orestes A. Brownson and Archbishop John Hughes in 1860," *Review of Politics*, XXIV (Jan., 1962), pp. 19-47, for a particularly good account of the relationship between Brownson and Hughes.

priests and laymen alike, is not hard to guess. They were themselves at one time members of that group which they most wanted to convert; the fact of their own conversion was a type of empirical evidence that the Church could have a strong appeal to the educated Protestant. As men who had been perfectly secure socially in their old habitat and accepted members of American society, they came into the Church with a sense of social security which the immigrant could not possibly feel. Their practice of free speech in the Church stems from the same root: they had been accustomed before to speaking out as they saw fit and acting independently at all times. Their very conversions required independence of a high degree; and it was unlikely that they would suddenly lose those characteristics which had enabled them to stand the rebuffs of their former Protestant friends.

Despite the comparative weakness of the influence of the converts, their lasting significance should not be underestimated. They gave the Church, first, some inkling of the kind of freedom and confidence that an American Catholic could have—a freedom to move easily in non-Catholic society, to speak out frankly to the clergy, and to face American life with equanimity. Secondly, they gave the American Church a foretaste of what a genuinely educated American Catholic would look like; the values that the converts stressed were, as we shall see, just those values which are now on the whole praised by all Catholics. Thirdly, the converts did, in fact, make many acceptable contributions to the Church of the immigration period. They did much to raise intellectual standards, they were often of great help in assisting charitable activities, and, to some Protestants at least, they presented a facet of Catholicism rarely seen among the immigrants.[10]

Finally, the converts made a major, though often unappreciated, contribution. Through public debate within the Church, they initiated and sustained a spirit of Catholic self-criticism. For if there was any one thing the immigrant Church lacked it was a genuine concept of self-criticism. There were, undeniably, many complaints about the troubles of the Church and its financial difficulties, its loss of members and its often beleaguered state. But there was very little tendency to criticize the quality of its successes. Whatever progress was made was accompanied by the rhetoric of self-congratulation. The converts, especially Brownson, were loath to engage in this kind of activity. Their criticism was directed

[10] Cf. John Gilmary Shea, "Converts—Their Influence and Work in This Country," *American Catholic Quarterly Review*, VIII (July, 1883), pp. 509-529.

at just those parts of Church life by which the immigrants set most store; they measured the Church and its forward movement not just by its earlier state but also by a comparison with the historical glories of the Church universal and, at times, with non-Catholic American institutions. The following doggerel, written as it happens by a priest who was not a convert but who had fallen under Brownson's spell, expresses very well the new self-critical spirit:

> Like little Jack Horner,
> We squat in a corner,
> And, jollily winking, agree
> That each Catholic college
> Is a fountain of knowledge
> And cry, 'What a great people are we.'[11]

While this type of attack was hardly likely to win many friends it was sorely needed. That it did little good is beside the point: it said what needed to be said.

In the preceding pages, I have laid heavy stress on two points: the situation of the immigrant, which served to reinforce his natural conservatism and stimulate in him an attitude of aggressive insularity, and the place of the convert, who was to present to the Church a different, more confident approach to American life. It is now possible to turn directly to the place of the layman within the Church. Yet the very first thing to be said about that "place" is that there is terribly little to say. In the decades between approximately 1830 and 1870, especially during the peak years of the Irish immigration, the layman had as little influence in the Church as he has ever had in American Church history. The very activity and vigor of Orestes A. Brownson merely shows in a sharp light how far the layman sank into obscurity during this period. The real question to be asked about the immigrant layman is not what he did in the Church but why he did practically nothing at all. The layman, as we have seen, did have a certain importance in colonial and early national days; and in the closing decades of the nineteenth century he was to experience a resurgence of power and influence. But what happened during the period between? Without suggesting an order of importance, let us first turn to the

[11] William J. Barry, *Brownson's Quarterly Review*, 3rd series, VIII (Dec., 1860).

bishops and clergy and the role they played in the overshadowing of the layman. The experience of the colonial and early national Church had taught the episcopacy two important lessons: the necessity of organization and discipline, and the necessity of keeping a tight rein upon the laity. Without a systematic approach to the problems faced by the Church there could hardly be any kind of orderly progress, either spiritual or material. If churches were to be built, schools founded, seminaries established, charitable institutions created, and competent clergy trained and governed, then there could be no escaping the creation of an efficient organization. But efficiency can only be maintained where there are rigid lines of command, clearly established duties and obligations, comparatively little emphasis on individual rights that can muddy the waters, and an overwhelming emphasis on the ends to be attained. It was precisely the disorderly and carefree ways of the colonial and early post-colonial days which had, together with the seductions of American values and mores, led to the scandals of trusteeism and the rebelliousness and ineffectuality of some of the clergy.

At all costs, then, the whole drift of internal Church life had to be changed. The weaknesses of the past had to be uprooted and the acute needs of the present and future provided for. In practice this meant a strengthening of the power of the episcopacy at the expense both of the freedom of the lower clergy and of the laity. In a sense, the bishops could only have power and control by taking it from others. Thus, neither the lower clergy nor the laity could be allowed to retain those rights which, practically though not juridically, they had exercised in the early days of the Church. Besides, the general hostility toward the Church was in itself almost enough to turn the bishops into generals in charge of an army under siege, and it confirmed them in their view that only by taking complete charge of both the defense and the defenders could the attack be met.

Yet it is important to stress here that this development does not bespeak a personal hunger for power on the part of the bishops. On the contrary, their motivation was the good name, the good order and the good defense of the Church. If they often seemed more like generals than bishops, they were not without reasons for their conduct. If they were wary of giving too much freedom to the clergy and especially to the layman, much of their attitude was determined by the clear and distinct harm done by the early spirit of chaotic freedom. The matter could hardly be put much better than it was by Father Boniface Wimmer,

O.S.B., founder of the American Benedictines, in a letter to Ludwig I of Bavaria on February 13, 1852: "The ecclesiastical condition of America is still in its infancy; the will of the bishop is the only law. The bishop can expect no support from the state against refractory priests, and much less from the Protestant, or better, atheistic state and the democratic inclinations of its citizens. Accordingly they are naturally distrustful of every attempt to deprive them more or less of their unrestricted power, or to insure oneself against their arbitrariness."[12]

The Roots of Lay Passivity

Nonetheless, however understandable the bishops' reaction, there can be little doubt that their power was gained at the expense of the vigor and self-responsibility of the lower clergy and the laity. In this instance as in so many others throughout history, what counts in the long run is what happened and not the motives of those who brought it about. What happened was the diminishing of the laity, the coming into being of a cautious and repressed clergy—and, it can equally be admitted, the rise of a vigorous and strong institutional establishment.

Amidst the successes of the bishops in the direction of financial solvency, the recruitment of clerical manpower and the sustaining of the immigrant there was, then, a price to be paid. In this respect, restrictions on the freedom of the lower clergy were just as significant as those on the laity. Not only does a tight disciplining of the clergy tend to separate the clergy from the laity by making the clergy first and foremost members of the clerical establishment—more loyal and deferential to their bishops and fellow priests than to their lay parishioners—but it also and sometimes fatally leads to a general confusion between the kind of obedience a priest owes his superior and the kind of obedience appropriate to a layman in the world.

It was during this period of American Church history that any real possibility of either lay or clerical initiative was effectively uprooted, not to be replanted for many generations. Just as it is common today to

---

[12] Colman J. Barry, O.S.B., *The Catholic Church and the German Americans* (Milwaukee, 1953), p. 17. See also the Pastoral Letter of 1866 which lays far heavier stress on the authority of the Church and the bishops than was ever characteristic of the earlier pastorals—and this at a time when there was practically no threat whatever against the bishops' authority. Guilday, *The National Pastorals, op. cit.*, pp. 198ff.

bemoan some of the unfortunate consequences of post-tridentine theology, it might also be appropriate, *mutatis mutandis*, to regret the post-trustee episcopal hegemony. In both cases time was to show that more creative solutions would have been far more healthy for those generations which had to live with the consequences.

Despite those considerations, it must be reiterated that the obscuring of the place of the laity in the Church was by no means entirely the doing of the bishops. Of equal importance was the temper of the immigrant layman himself. Had there been a significantly large class of educated and articulate laymen, the bishops might well have felt differently about their role. Had there been enough laymen or lay-minded clergy able to set before their eyes some alternatives to unrestricted episcopal sway, the situation could have been quite otherwise than it turned out. There were very few such laymen and priests. With the notable exception of Brownson and Hecker, there were simply no men who could place before the Church a different vision than the one entertained by the bishops. Thus if the bishops desired to consolidate and extend their power, they had, by default, the help of laymen and clergy who were timid and passive. No *via media* between the abuse of trusteeism and total control by the episcopacy was seen or sought.

The reason for lay passivity was twofold. First, the immigrants brought over with them, from Ireland in particular, a long tradition of clerical dominance combined with an unusually strong personal affection for the clergy. Secondly, the fact that the immigrant arrived in this country in a state of confusion and fearful uncertainty, eager for help and leadership, helped to keep alive the traditional old-country relationship of laity and clergy. "When nothing is left to a people but its religion, priests become its leaders."[13] In Ireland, as a consequence of the penal laws enacted between 1695 and 1746, the people were stripped of land, economic security and political power; nothing remained to them but their religion.[14] In America, the newly-arrived immigrant was, for different reasons, in somewhat the same state. Here the laws did not operate

[13] Stephen Gwynn, *Ireland* (London, 1924), p. 160.
[14] As de Tocqueville observed of Ireland: "There is an unbelievable unity among the Irish clergy and Catholic population. The reason for that is not only that the clergy are paid by the people, but also because all the upper classes are Protestants and enemies. The clergy, rebuffed by high society, has turned its attention to the lower classes . . . [a] state of affairs altogether peculiar to Ireland." *Journeys to England and Ireland*, ed. by J. P. Mayer (London, 1958), p. 132.

against him; but poverty, nativism and ignorance did. Once in America, the Irish-American layman had little desire to change the old tradition. The clergy performed here many of the same functions as they had performed before. As in Ireland, the laity cared very little about their rights or opportunities as members of the Church. What they did care about was food, housing, jobs and the right to free and accessible worship. They were happy enough to leave the management of the Church entirely in the hands of the clergy—that was not their concern or their problem. They were ready and willing to give their money and their support. If they were not also called upon to provide ideas, to cooperate as equals, then that also was fine with them. They had nothing to say about higher ecclesiastical policy, anyway.

An additional comment is necessary here. It has been customary among American churchmen for decades to hold the American Church up as the very model of a happy relationship between clergy and laity. On the whole, this was certainly true of the immigration period, which is normally chosen as the archetype. What has to be kept in mind, however, is that the relationship during that period was almost exclusively of a one-way kind: the clergy wanted to lead and the laity were happy to follow. Under those circumstances, there was no reason why friction should develop. Both the clergy and laity had what they wanted. This certainly does not deny the validity of the proud assertions of clerical-lay harmony. Yet it does cast this relationship in a significantly different light. When today's orator harkens back to the glorious immigration days and decries the threatened loss of that early harmony between clergy and laity, he almost always fails to note how different the character, temperament, background and education of the laity were at that time. With the rise of an educated, self-confident laity, this early stability could hardly last. A harmonious bond between clergy and laity is always a fine ideal. But it is surely doubtful that the immigrant pattern provides an appropriate model for the middle of the twentieth century.

Despite the general run of the laity, and despite their normally passive state during the early to mid-immigration period, a few lay voices were heard that rendered great service to the Church and the hierarchy. They were found mainly in the Catholic press, in Catholic fund-raising, and in charitable and philanthropic work. However, only one man, Orestes Brownson, wrote and spoke consciously of the laymen's role in the Church. For the most part, the other active laymen worked very closely with the Church, occasionally differing with the bishops; they defended the immigrant, retorted to charges against the Church, solicited funds and used their technical skills to further the Church. What they did not do was to reflect on the theoretical implications of their own work, much less agitate for a greater part in the making of policy or a more creative use of the laity.

A man such as James A. McMaster, editor of the New York *Freeman's Journal* and next to Brownson the most prominent American layman, had strong if not violent opinions on most questions.[15] Though he generally supported his Archbishop, John Hughes, he did not hesitate to differ with him when he saw fit. But his differences turned on practical and immediate questions and were entirely devoid of any abstract references to the rights of laymen. In almost all areas, the lay editors of the early and middle immigration period were, like their bishops, conservative, which meant that their voices carried more weight in relationship to the non-Catholic world, against whom they defended the laity, than within the institutional boundaries of the Church. The same can be said of the few Catholic book publishers; like their journalist brothers they depended for their livelihood and reputation on the good will of the hierarchy and clergy and were, in any event, little inclined to differ with them.

Of mixed significance also was the place of the layman in education, charitable works and fund-raising. With the great spurt in parochial schools beginning in the 1840s and the almost total reliance on them by mid-century, the layman from the first played an important part in education—but as teacher rather than as administrator. The bishops depended heavily upon lay teachers; but their ideal was always to have the schools staffed by religious. This meant that laymen were always liable to be displaced by nuns or brothers if they could be found. Yet laymen were in fact present in the schools in great numbers; there could hardly have been an extensive system of parochial schools without them. What they never succeeded in doing was making their influence on school policy commensurate with their numbers; they were, as the expression today has it, "second-class citizens," used only when the bishops had no other choice. Two Catholic colleges founded and staffed by laymen— Calvert College and Cecil College, started, respectively, in 1850 and

[15] McMaster, more than anyone else, helped establish the phrase "Godless public schools" in the American Catholic vocabulary.

1860—had a very short life, foundering on the apathy of both clergy and laity.[16]

In the field of charitable works and Church fund-raising the layman had a similar status. Clearly, the hierarchy had to depend upon the laity, especially the more prosperous, to contribute the money necessary to build churches and schools and support the clergy. And the laity were noble and self-sacrificing in doing what was needed. But the frightening memory of trusteeism prevented the laity from having practically anything to do with how these funds were to be used. The laymen gave and the bishops disposed. For the more wealthy among the immigrants, access to the bishop was then (as today) something of a mark of Catholic social success. It was enough for these men that the bishop favored them with his good will and esteem in return for their generosity; they had no desire to attach strings to their donations, much less to exert influence to see their money put to what they might have thought useful purposes. Only in a few benevolent societies did the laity have some importance. The German Central Catholic Verein organized in 1855, the Irish Catholic Benevolent Union established in 1867, and the St. Vincent de Paul Society, first organized in America in 1845, after Frederic Ozanam's successes in France—all of these organizations were, in the main, lay oriented and lay directed.

The laity were seen but rarely heard in the Church. Ancestral history, deeply ingrained traditions, the consolidation and extension of hierarchical power, lay passivity, and the defensiveness induced by a hostile nativist element in American life, all conspired to reduce and minimize the laity's place. What the bishops gained the laity lost. If this meant, on the one hand, an institutional American Church which was the wonder of the Western world in its financial and organizational progress it meant, on the other, that a firm pattern of lay subordination was established. The interruption of this tradition for a short time toward the end of the nineteenth century does not invalidate the generalization. (It is precisely the challenging of this tradition which explains the present crisis of the layman's role in the Church of mid-twentieth-century America.)

Brownson's Prophetic Voice

The only person who, with brilliant penetration, saw the significance of the developing pattern of lay-clerical relations during the middle of the

[16] Cf. Edward J. Power, *A History of Catholic Higher Education in the United States* (Milwaukee, 1958), pp. 32-33.

nineteenth century was Orestes Brownson. Brownson alone gave the matter the attention it deserved and Brownson alone had the prophetic power to project a more daring vision. What Brownson most deplored was the transplantation of the Irish tradition of lay-clerical relations to the United States. Noting that in Ireland "the clergyman was for the poor but faithful people, not only the parish priest, but the chieftain of the clan," he added that, "It was natural, inevitable and salutary at the time, but cannot survive, and it is not desirable it should survive, the growth of the intelligence and civil importance of the Irish laity."[17] Nor could it survive in America. "The modern world," he wrote on another occasion, "is to a great extent laic, and if the laity are not frankly recognized, and freely permitted to do whatever laymen can do, we shall find that they will undertake . . . to do more than they have any right to do. . . . There is not now the distinction in education and intelligence between the clergy and laity which formerly existed. . . . The whole theory of ecclesiastical training, aside from what pertains to faith and universal discipline, has to be modified so as to permit every layman to be treated, in principle, very much as temporal princes professing the Catholic religion have heretofore been treated."[18]

In general, Brownson envisioned two broad tasks for the laity. He held, first of all, that the laity have a special obligation to temporal society and a special role to perform in it: "In a highly civilized state of society, where intelligence is generally diffused among the people, the laity necessarily and rightfully rise in importance, and do themselves many things which in a less advanced civilization . . . are necessarily done by the clergy. Catholicity embraces both religion and civilization, and civilization is, where they are capable, the province of the laity. Here is the sphere of the laity and in this sphere they owe to the clergy only that general subordination in which the temporal is always placed to the spiritual."[19]

Secondly, Brownson held it to be the right of the laity to speak out in the Church on disputed questions, a right shared partly with the clergy. "There is a mission of genius, of intelligence in the Church, which is not necessarily restricted to the clergy, and may be committed to laymen. We see nothing uncatholic in this non-hierarchical mission, any more

[17] *The Works of Orestes A. Brownson* (20 vols.; Detroit, 1882-1907), Vol. XX, pp. 229-230.
[18] *Ibid.*, Vol. XII, pp. 383-384.
[19] *Ibid.*, Vol. XX, p. 234.

than there was under the Old Law in the mission of the prophets. . . .
In discussion the layman, under responsibility, we hold, may take the
initiative, and not await it from authority. He may open such questions
as he deems important, and the business of authority is not to close his
mouth, but to set him right, when and where he goes wrong."[20] In
Brownson's own case, he did not hesitate to write on the most delicate
questions of the day: the relationship between Church and State, current
theological disputes, papal authority and religious education. Though
often under attack by the bishops, some of whom wanted Rome to
condemn him, he nevertheless showed that, for the layman who knew
what he was about and the ground on which he stood, it was possible to
gain a hearing and avoid suppression.

What undoubtedly enabled Brownson to say things which other laymen did not say (assuming they thought of them at all) was his sensi-
tivity to hierarchical worries and his frequent protestations of loyalty to
the Church. He took special pains, on the one hand, to make clear that
he recognized the possible dangers which American values posed to the
authority of the bishops and priests: "In a country like ours there is
always danger of disrespect and disobedience to authority. . . . Catholics
who mingle much with Protestants, and in general American society,
catch something of the Protestant tone, and there is always as much
danger with us of the laity tyrannizing over the clergy, as there is of the
clergy tyrannizing over the laity."[21] On the other hand, he was well
aware of the episcopal fear that those who urged a freer hand for the
laity were secretly intent on changing the authoritarian, hierarchical
structure of the Church's teaching authority: "He who ventures to assert
that the clergy are functionaries in the Church and for the Church, that
the laity are an integral part of the Church and not mere 'hewers of
wood and drawers of water' to the hierarchy, with neither voice nor souls
of their own, is at once suspected of wishing to democratize the Church,
of having Congregational predilections or reminiscences, if not of being
animated by an unavowed hostility to the hierarchical constitution of the
Church herself."[22]

At the same time Brownson held that a rigidity of authority and
obedience was not the way to meet the possible danger. "The Catholic

[20] *Ibid.*, pp. 270-271.
[21] *Ibid.*, Vol. XIV, p. 568.
[22] *Ibid.*, Vol. XX, p. 272.

lay society is not a monastery, and cannot be governed on the monastic principle of obedience. . . . To forget this, to regard every spiritual person as the superior of a convent . . . would only lead to a practical spiritual despotism as repugnant to spiritual welfare as to secular freedom."[23] The ideal that Brownson held up to the American Church was one which, on the contrary, both took account of the American love of liberty and reflected a highly spiritual conception of Christian freedom. "Under the American system, she [the Church] can deal with people as free men, and trust them as free men, because free men they are. . . . Blind obedience even to the authority of the Church cannot be expected of the people reared under the American system, not because they are filled with a spirit of disobedience, but because they insist that obedience shall be *rationabile obsequium*, an act of the understanding, not of the will or the affections alone."[24] The kind of obedience that the Church ought to seek from the layman, "an intelligent, free, willing obedience, yielded from personal conviction, after seeing its reasonableness, its justice, its logic in the Divine Order—the obedience of a free man, not of a slave— is far more consonant to the spirit of the Church, and far more acceptable to God, than simple blind obedience."[25]

Here, then, was a lofty and realistic vision of the layman. But Brownson's words fell on deaf ears; he could hardly have been more out of step with the spirit of the times. Wittingly and unwittingly, the American Church had charted a different course. The prophet was talking to himself. Yet a seed had been planted. Toward the end of the nineteenth century the layman would stage a brief comeback. A change was in the offing.

[23] *Ibid.*, Vol. XII, pp. 385-386.
[24] *Ibid.*, Vol. XX, p. 420.
[25] *Ibid.*, p. 421.

CHAPTER 3

Lay Renaissance, Lay Decline:
1880-1917

WERE it possible to chart graphically the progress of the Catholic Church in the United States, we would see a series of rises and declines. The lowest point on the chart would come during the penal-law years of the seventeenth and eighteenth centuries. With the American Revolution the curve would rise, continuing upward until about 1830. From 1830-1860, however, it would again descend; the impact of the Irish immigration, the strain on Church resources, the upswing of anti-Catholicism, would all show their effects. From 1860-1900 a new rise would become apparent; but then the curve would level off and decline slightly until World War I.

I want to turn now to that broad period of Church history which extends from the post-Civil War days to the advent of the Great War. As in the preceding period, immigration continued on a massive scale. To the numbers of the Irish were added successive waves of Germans, Eastern and Southern Europeans.

In one sense the Church's problems and difficulties were to continue unabated. Yet the particular significance of this period was that the Church and the Catholic people slowly came face to face with the problem of what to do with their new situation once the initial hurdle of simple survival had been surmounted. What was the Church to do once it had established solid roots in America? What was the Catholic layman to do once he found a place for himself in American society? What was to be the relationship between the integrated layman and his Church, the integrated layman and his country? As Archbishop John Ireland of St. Paul wrote to James Cardinal Gibbons of Baltimore toward the end of the nineteenth century: "In Archbishop Carroll's time the Church was truly American. Later the flood of Catholic foreign immigration overpowered us, and made the Church foreign in heart and in act. Thank God we are recovering from this misfortune."[1]

But as Ireland himself discovered by the turn of the century, the way the Church recovered was to bring many new problems. The most notable was the violent dispute instigated by the attempt of Archbishop Ireland and others to find a positive way in which the Church could meet the needs of the American scene—an attempt which, in the end, was to suffer the fate of an apparent papal condemnation. No less important was a significant re-awakening of the laity. It is impossible here to recount all of the rich events of this period. It is possible, however, to trace that sequence of events and its attendant climate of opinion which saw the laity come to a new awareness of their importance toward the end of the century. For the prophetic vision of Brownson was, if only for a relatively short period, in part realized by the generation which came after him.

Before confronting this lay renaissance directly, it is necessary first to delineate the new social situation of the laymen. As in every other period of American Church history, the fortunes of the layman in the Church were very closely related to his fortunes within American society, and to the fortunes of his Church. And one striking thing about the American Catholic in the decades after the Civil War was his more favorable position among his non-Catholic neighbors. To be sure, if he was a first- or second-generation German immigrant, an escapee from the political turmoil of the German unification movement in the 1870s and the *Kulturkampf* in the 1880s, he would have to suffer many of the pains that the Irish had suffered before him (and, indeed, continued to suffer). Again, if he was a Polish immigrant he would find himself exploited and scorned for a time in the great cities of the Midwest. If he was Italian he would come to know what it was like to be thrown into a strange and unfriendly Eastern seaboard city.[2] Yet despite the fact that the later immigrants had to make most of the same painful adjustments as did

[1] John Tracy Ellis, *The Life of James Cardinal Gibbons, Archbishop of Baltimore, 1834-1921* (2 vols.; Milwaukee, 1952), I, p. 413.

[2] Sometimes, too, the Italian immigrant would find the Irish Catholicism which he encountered every bit as strange as American secular society. As one perceptive Irish priest was quick to note in the late 1880s, "The fact is that the Catholic Church in America is to the mass of the Italians almost a new religion." In Bernard J. Lynch, "The Italians in New York," *Catholic World*, XLVII (1888), p. 72.

their predecessors, they had at least before their eyes some signs of Catholic success.

For one thing, it was not long before the Irish politician came to dominate New York and Boston. If the sheer numbers of Irish in those two cities were a source of social ostracism and Protestant fears, they also provided a fine base from which to capture political control. The very clannishness of the Irish, their gift for political organization (not to mention intrigue), and their unerring eye for the tight interpersonal relationships necessary to maintain a political machine, were too much for the less organized Yankee. And if at first the Italians or the Poles found themselves excluded by these same Irish, it would not be long before they too learned how to master the political techniques—though it did take them longer than the Irish who had the advantage of speaking English.

Less dramatically, but in many ways far more importantly, more and more Catholics were finding ways to escape from the urban ghettos. Among the Irish, some found ways of returning to the land as farmers or settlers on the opening frontiers of the Western plain states. Still more found work in the labor gangs of the great railways which were spreading westward. For many, unhappily, a job with the railroads was little better than a form of indentured servitude; what money the terms of their contract did not eat up, the families they had to leave behind did. Yet, for a considerable number, it was far more attractive to stay where they were in the Middle or Far West than it was to return to the cities from which they had come. Though as manual laborers the Irish would start at the bottom of the ladder, the social climate they found beyond the Alleghenies was a far healthier one than in the East. Especially in the Middle West, there was not a great mass of struggling immigrants and the Irish newcomer in such cities as Cincinnati, Cleveland, St. Louis or Omaha was not forced to compete so much with his own kind nor was he so readily identifiable as a member of the lowest social stratum. Then, too, the society of the Middle Western cities did not have the fixed and rigid character of the Eastern cities: hard work and enterprise afforded the newcomer an access to the larger community.

For the German, except for one important distinction, assimilation in the Midwestern cities and even more in the rural areas was also comparatively easy. He met little initial hostility, his number was not great enough or concentrated enough to incite much fear, and his industrious work habits and ways of life commanded admiration. The German's real problem came more from his ambivalent attitude toward American society than from its attitude toward him. Even more fervently than the Irish, the German believed that it was essential for the preservation of his faith to maintain the traditions of his native land, especially the German language. Any conservatism the German immigrant did not supply of his own accord, his clergy were likely to supply for him. What saved the German in the end from complete cultural isolation was the simple fact that most of them were scattered over wide areas. They could form cultural pockets of resistance to Americanization but these were for the most part too small to resist the erosion of time and circumstance.[3]

Middle-Class Aspirations

In general, it was the period between the end of the Civil War and the turn of the century which saw American Catholicism establish its predominantly middle-class character; or perhaps it would be more accurate to say its middle-class aspirations. For in fact one can hardly speak of a Catholic middle class until the opening decades of the twentieth century. For the most part, the Catholic social world could be neatly divided into an upper-class Anglo-American group and a lower-class immigrant working group. In between, however, occupying a grayish, indistinct area, was the makings of a Catholic middle class. Whenever possible, those Catholics who sought a higher education were apt to aim either for business or for the professions of law, medicine or dentistry. To that group can be added numerous men who, by one means or another, managed to establish their own businesses or to rise to a position of respectability in non-Catholic firms. A very few were outstandingly successful. Thomas Fortune Ryan (1851-1928), for instance, orphaned at an early age, managed by wit and energy to rise from the position of a Wall Street messenger to the small ranks of the genuine American tycoon. Another man, Edward Douglas White (1845-1921), a graduate of Georgetown, was (after Taney) the second Catholic Democrat to achieve the position of Chief Justice of the Supreme Court. By the 1880s, in New York, it has been estimated that half of the

[3] Cf. Colman J. Barry, O.S.B., *The Catholic Church and German Americans* (Milwaukee, 1953), esp. Chaps. I and VI.

journalists were Catholics. Yet as one observer noted, "This influential body of writers in all departments, of theater attachés, of doctors, of journalists, of political officials, was quite unknown to and therefore never used by the ecclesiastical authorities. Its service to religion was purely personal, accidental, and negative; yet even thus the service was valuable and worthy of record."[4]

Still another man, Charles Joseph Bonaparte, prominent during the first decade of the twentieth century as Secretary of the Navy and later as Attorney General, was the first Catholic to be elected a trustee of Harvard. Not surprisingly, however, Bonaparte's background was that of a solid member of the upper classes. His career would seem to prove that a Catholic could gain acceptance as a full-fledged member of the upper reaches of the Anglo-Saxon Protestant world—provided he did not start out as an immigrant. In this respect, the only Catholics who managed to move easily in Protestant society were the descendants of the Anglo-American Catholics and those converts from Protestantism who already had behind them an established social position. Although the former group was soon swallowed up by the massive preponderance of the immigrants, they still existed in large enough numbers to maintain the kind of connections their predecessors had enjoyed ever since colonial days.

On the whole, however, with the exception of cities like New York and Boston, the Catholic exercised little influence either in politics or civic affairs—only in the business world was he of some importance. As a group Catholics had to be taken into account, if only because manpower was needed and they were so numerous. But as individuals capable of influencing events and shaping cultural or political trends, their presence was hardly felt. Doubtless, the humble and unfavorable circumstances of the great immigration waves account for much in the position of the Catholic in the American social spectrum. Nevertheless, as Daniel P. Moynihan has observed, "A good part of the surplus that might have gone into family property has gone to building the Church. This has almost certainly inhibited the development of the solid middle-class dynasties that produce so many of the important people in America."[5]

[4] J. T. Smith, The Catholic Church in New York (2 vols.; New York, 1905), II, p. 451.
[5] "The Irish," a paper prepared for the Joint Center for Urban Studies of Harvard University and M.I.T., p. 22.

Amidst the efforts of the Catholic layman to stake out a place for himself, the role of the bishops in assisting him cannot be overlooked. However, their role was ambiguous and subject to fluctuations. In the 1870s and 1880s there seems little doubt that the bishops were far more concerned to perfect the hierarchical structure of the American Church and to strengthen its sacramental character than they were to clarify the role of the Church or of individual Catholics in American life. Their main interests were the preservation of faith, the building of schools and churches and the education of the young; they showed little interest in the social, economic or political problems of their flock in its relationship to the outside world. "It can be said," Father McAvoy has written, "with some validity that hardly any official Church decrees took notice of the American social and economic problems until the period of World War I."[6]

Perhaps in no area was the episcopal concern for faith and morals so apparent as in the parochial school. By the time of the Third Plenary Council in 1884, almost all traces of any dependence upon public education had disappeared. At that council, not only were all pastors directed to construct, within a period of two years, parochial schools attached to their churches, but parents were commanded to send their children to these schools. Voted down only by the narrowest margin was a decree which would have excluded from the sacraments parents who sent their children to public schools. In this respect it is worth noting that, beginning with a fairly mild urging of parochial education and parochial school construction by the First Provincial Council in Baltimore in 1829, the decrees of Provincial and Plenary Councils over the years became increasingly stringent on the need for Catholic education.[7] Behind this stringency lay an intense fear of the secularizing influence of the public schools; the failure of almost all attempts to find a *modus vivendi* with the public schools brought about a complete despair of their serving the religious needs of Catholic children. However understandable, this attitude unfortunately did much to contribute to the continuing failure on the part of Catholics to take the kind of interest in the

[6] Thomas T. McAvoy, C.S.C., *The Great Crisis in American Catholic History, 1895-1900* (Chicago, 1957), p. 44.

[7] Cf. J. A. Burns, *The Growth and Development of the Catholic School System in the United States* (New York, 1912), esp. Chap. VII, "School Legislation," pp. 181-196; also, Francis P. Cassidy, "Catholic Education and the Third Plenary Council of Baltimore," *Catholic Historical Review*, XXXIV (Oct., 1948), pp. 257-305.

public schools which is needed to sustain them as important institutions in American life.

As if to underscore Catholic aloofness from the American economic and social scene, there was almost no interest in the great reform surge engendered by the Progressive Movement after the turn of the century. For all practical purposes Catholics continued to rely, with an ideological fervor, upon private charitable institutions.[8] Indeed, the overriding fear of most members of the hierarchy was Communism and socialism; this fear merely strengthened existing predispositions. To make matters worse, the antipathy between Catholics and Progressives was mutual. The Progressive saw urban reform as one of the great needs of the time. But urban reform meant, in great part, the ousting of the corrupt political machines run by Irish Catholics.

There was one important social problem which rose shortly after the Civil War and was, over the years, to be a continuing problem to the hierarchy. That was trade unionism. Partly as a result of the great labor unrest of the 1870s, especially the murderous activities of the Molly Maguires in the Pennsylvania coal fields, and partly because so many Catholics were laborers, the question of unionism was one which could not be ignored. From the viewpoint of the hierarchy, the fact that so many of the early trade unions were secret societies, complete with rituals and oaths, posed a major problem. Their anxiety was heightened by a fear of Communistic radicalism. As Archbishop James Roosevelt Bayley put it in 1875, "The idea (of labor organizations) is communistic, and no Catholic with any idea of the spirit of his religion will encourage them."[9] At the same time, it soon became clear that a great number of Catholics were joining these unions.

Fortunately, cooler heads among the hierarchy were to prevail. Too many Catholics were involved in the unions to make an outright condemnation reasonable or practicable; moreover, by the late 1880s a gradual awareness of the worker's stake in unionism began to lessen some of the earlier animosity. The turning point was to come with the successful

[8] Aaron Abell, *American Catholicism and Social Action: A Search for Social Justice, 1865-1950* (New York, 1960), Chap. II, "The Urban Welfare Crusade: Charity Phase, 1865-85," pp. 27-53.

[9] *Ibid.*, p. 46. Even the moderately liberal Bishop John Lancaster Spalding of Peoria believed that trade unions would "wean them [Catholics] from the Church." *The Religious Mission of the Irish Race and Catholic Colonization* (New York, 1880), p. 205.

efforts of Archbishop Gibbons of Baltimore in 1887 to keep Rome from condemning the most important labor organization of all, The Knights of Labor.[10] From that time on a different climate of opinion was apparent, though it spread only gradually. "The outcome," as Father Henry J. Browne perceptively notes, "was that some Catholic members of organized labor were saved when they did not have to make a choice between earthly and heavenly bread."[11] More than that, the Church succeeded, however fearfully at first, in being thought of as a friend of labor; and after the turn of the century the bond between the Church and labor became still firmer.

Nonetheless, it seems difficult to find sufficient evidence to overthrow Father Browne's judgment that "Catholic concern with the American social scene even up to the 1930s" was marked by "a deeply negative character."[12] What Daniel P. Moynihan says of the Irish in New York can, I believe, be said of Catholics in general: "The Irish were immensely successful in politics. They ran the city. But the very parochialism and bureaucracy that enabled them to succeed in local politics prevented them from doing much else. . . . They never thought of politics as an instrument of social change—their kind of politics (patterned on that of Ireland) involved the processes of a society that was not changing."[13]

The Americanist Crisis

One must here add an important qualification to the sketch just presented of the hierarchy's role in the assimiliation of the immigrant. On the surface, there was little manifestation of interest in the social and economic welfare of the immigrant. The hierarchy's central concern was the organizational structure of the Church, the preservation and nurturing of the immigrant's faith. Yet, and not apparent to the public eye, an important ideological debate broke out in the mid-eighties among members of the hierarchy. This debate, generally referred to as the Ameri-

[10] Cf. Henry J. Browne, *The Catholic Church and the Knights of Labor* (Washington, D.C., 1949).

[11] Henry J. Browne, "Catholicism in the United States," *The Shaping of American Religion*, Vol. I, *Religion in American Life*, edited by James Ward Smith and A. Leland Jamison (4 vols.; Princeton, 1961), p. 98.

[12] *Ibid.*, p. 101.

[13] "When the Irish Ran New York," *The Reporter*, June 8, 1961, p. 34.

canist crisis, turned on the question of the extent to which the Church ought to enter the mainstream of American political, social and economic life.[14] The Church could do either of two things (and urge the faithful to do likewise): it could attempt a wholehearted embrace of American life and institutions or it could adopt a policy of aloofness, protectionism and cultural separation.

By the time of the Third Plenary Council in 1884 it had become apparent that Rome was favoring the latter choice; and the decrees of that Council, which originated in Rome, clearly showed this inclination. Yet for a number of outstanding and articulate American bishops, only the former choice seemed to offer any hope for the viability of the Church in America. The most important figure to take this position was Archbishop John Ireland. "The Church in America," Ireland said, "must be, of course, as Catholic as in Jerusalem or Rome; but so far as her garments may be colored to suit environment, she must be American."[15] There was no good reason, Ireland held, why Catholics could not cooperate with non-Catholics, why they could not to give up the lingering vestiges of their foreign origins, and why they could not hope, as equal partners, to exert an important influence in American life. In short, Catholics ought to seek a rapid assimilation, adopt a progressive and optimistic outlook, and work in all things to unite Catholicism and American culture. Sharing Ireland's viewpoint, in varying degrees, were James Cardinal Gibbons of Baltimore, the leader of the American hierarchy, Bishop John J. Keane, the first rector of Catholic University, Monsignor Denis O'Connell at the American College in Rome, and the Paulist Fathers, strongly imbued with the spirit of Isaac Hecker. Together, they formed a powerful force.

But this group was opposed by a coalition almost as strong. In particular, the Midwestern German-American bishops, priests and lay journalists were altogether suspicious of any hasty attempts at an Americanization of the immigrants. In their eyes, it was difficult to see how a Catholic faith could endure apart from the cultural trappings which had sustained it in Germany; and of special importance was the maintenance of the German language in the schools and churches. Nor were they at

<hr/>

[14] The best account of the whole Americanist episode is contained in McAvoy, *op. cit.* Cf. also Robert D. Cross, *The Emergence of Liberal Catholicism in America* (Cambridge, 1958), *passim.*
[15] *The Church and Modern Society* (Chicago, 1896), p. 73.

all inclined to look upon American life as a rich soil for religion. The very notion of accommodating the Church to the spirit of the age, to American values, was to them a dangerous idea, certain to bring harm to the eternal truths of the faith. Like the Irish before them, they saw religion and culture as inextricably bound together; and even more than the Irish they thought that only rigidity and stout opposition to the times could preserve them. Sharing the German-American attitude were Bishop Michael Corrigan of New York, his suffragan bishop in Rochester, Bernard McQuaid, a number of important Jesuits and Monsignor Joseph Schroeder of Catholic University. Though the fortunes of this group waxed and waned, they continually found some friendly ears in Rome. Both in Rome and in America it was easy to find many who were ready to agree with the sentiments of one influential German-American priest, Father Anton Walburg of Cincinnati. America, he said, was a "hotbed of fanaticism, intolerance and radical ultra views on matters of politics and religion. All the vagaries of spiritualism, Mormonism, free-loveism, prohibition, infidelity, and materialism, generally breed in the American nationality."[16]

The details of this controversy need not detain us. What is of particular relevance here is that it grew out of the first genuine attempt to come to grips with a whole gamut of important American values: democracy, pluralism, cooperation between religions, state neutrality toward the churches and the problem of the relationship of religion and culture. It was a confrontation that was bound to occur once the initial hurdles of caring for the first swarms of immigrants had been cleared. And it came, not surprisingly, at a time when the Church was beginning to regain some of the confidence and dynamism which it had possessed prior to the 1830s. Put in its sharpest fashion, the question posed by an English priest commenting on the American scene goes to the heart of the issue: "If Democracy, which has learned in its own order the secret of self government, is to be reconciled with Rome, can the temper, the methods of the sixteenth century avail under circumstances so novel and unprecedented?"[17] Ireland, Gibbons and Keane gave one answer; the Germans, Jesuits, Corrigan and McQuaid another.

Eventually (as I will discuss below), those suspicious of an Ameri-

---

[16] *The Question of Nationality* (St. Louis, 1889), p. 43.
[17] William Barry, "The Troubles of a Catholic Democracy," *Contemporary Review*, LXXVI (July, 1899), p. 78.

canized Catholicism were to triumph. Yet while the Americanists were in the ascendancy, from approximately 1885-1893, there took place a remarkable lay renaissance. This parallel development was hardly coincidental: they both sprang out of the same spirit of confidence, creativity and vigor engendered by the more favorable position of the Church and its people. Just as some of the bishops were coming to see new possibilities of American Church development, so too a number of laymen were seeing the need for a new place for themselves within the Church and for the Church in society.

At first glance, there was little to suggest the possibility of a lay revival. Certainly the Third Plenary Council in 1884 contained nothing in its formal decrees to encourage the layman. Nor for the most part were the bishops during the eighties concerned about opening up new avenues of lay participation and activity. Moreover, the ultramontanist movement in Europe, both preceding and following the First Vatican Council in 1870, was notably fearful of lay encroachments on clerical privileges. Finally, the American bishops had long since accustomed themselves to providing complete leadership in the Church; the absence of any genuine lay cultural leadership both before and after the Civil War served only to confirm their own tendencies to shape and direct the Catholic masses.

Nonetheless, a lay renaissance did take place. One important reason was that the more favorable social milieux of cities like Chicago, St. Louis and Detroit made it possible for at least some lay Catholics to turn their attention from mere survival to an active consideration of their newly-won cultural and civic freedoms, as well as to the kind of role they could play in the Church. For those who did, there were a few bishops ready to encourage them: Ireland of St. Paul, Gilmour of Cleveland, Foley of Chicago, Spalding of Peoria and Kain of Wheeling.[18] Moreover, in the pages of the *Catholic World,* steeped in the progressive spirit of the Paulist fathers, the laity could find an outlet for their new probings. And even behind the scenes, in the Third Plenary Council, there were strong efforts, of mixed success, not to bind the laity on such matters as parochial school attendance and membership in secret societies.[19]

The resurgence of lay aspiration took a number of forms. In St. Paul,

[18] McAvoy, *op. cit.,* p. 51.
[19] Cf. Cross, *op. cit.,* pp. 170ff.

Minnesota, a group of laymen formed a Catholic Truth Society with the aim of responding to attacks on the Church and of spreading information about the Church. It also took the form of a continuing effort by a few laymen to form a federation of Catholic benevolent and civic societies, an effort dating from the founding, by a New York lawyer, of the "Catholic Union" in 1871. But the most important manifestations of renewed lay vigor were the efforts of a number of Midwestern laymen to hold a Catholic lay Congress and the spate of articles which appeared in the *Catholic World* in the late eighties and early nineties.

The April, 1888, issue of the *Catholic World* contained a remarkably candid piece on the laity.[20] It was, perhaps understandably, anonymous, with the author identified simply as "A Layman." He begins by noting that there are a considerable number of Catholics who do not practice their religion, especially, he implies, among the educated classes. He then goes on to point out that, compared with the early Christian Church, the laity do not take an active part in the life of the Church. Observing that there is much complaint both about the passivity of the laity and about widespread losses to the Church, he suggests that these two problems are closely related to one another: "One flagrant error of Protestantism is that it reduces religion to a purely personal and private matter . . . the logical end of which tendency is the denial of the objective reality of religious truth. . . . The query is: Would not a tendency towards the same lamentable end arise from a condition of things which more and more had the effect of separating the great body of the Catholic laity from active participation in the institutional phases of religion?"

In this vein he asks, "Is there not a certain exaggerated feeling of condescension toward the laity, a certain feeling of exclusive possession in the Church, displayed among a large number of the priesthood?" Allowing that there is some danger "of merging priest and people into one," which would be a "perversion" of the rights of the Church, he nevertheless states that the time is ripe for a return to a "more normal state of things, granting that the present state may be a relic of abnormal conditions." At the end he calls for a greater participation of the laity in the liturgy as a necessary first step; the people, he says, are mere spectators at Mass.

[20] "The Laity," *Catholic World*, XLVII (April, 1888), pp. 12-18.

Another article, in 1889, calls for the laity to be organized and utilized by the Church:[21] the laity have an intrinsic place in the Church; they can be given responsibilities; the Church can only be a center of attraction for the laity if they have a vital role to perform; they have talents which ought to be taken advantage of in the parishes. And from a slightly different angle, Father E. B. Brady deplores the sluggishness of the laity: "We do not ask them to enter within the sanctuary rails . . . but we do insist they take their full share in the public action of the Church, and assert their convictions in season and out of season."[22] During this period as well, numerous articles appealed for congregational singing and deplored the muteness of the people.[23]

If to a mid-twentieth-century reader these *Catholic World* articles suggest some remarkable parallels to the kinds of appeals being issued today, let him also listen to the words of a San Francisco priest in the early nineties: "It would add new life to the Church in America were the laity to take an interest in Church affairs, and to express their opinions thereon. . . . Clerical diplomacy has several centuries of mistakes to its account; free speech can hardly hope to break the record. . . . It is far better to make a mistake in acting, than never to act at all."[24]

Still another sign of the lay resurgence could be found among the numerous lay editors of diocesan newspapers. Some, such as Arthur Preuss of the St. Louis *Fortnightly Review* and Condé Pallen of the St. Louis *Church Progress*, were outspoken opponents of any liberalizing movement in the Church, often taking the side of the German-American bishops against the Americanizing ones. On the other hand, John Boyle O'Reilly of the Boston *Pilot* and Thomas Preston of the Brooklyn *Examiner* were notable for their devotion to liberal causes. But whether liberal or conservative, many editors of this period felt free to take a position opposed to that of either their own or other bishops. In addition to the diocesan papers, the *American Catholic Quarterly Review* provided still another forum for lay voices—and often in such uncommon areas as philosophy and comparative religion.

[21] Albert Reynaud, "Organize the Laymen," *Catholic World*, L (Dec., 1889), pp. 285-291.
[22] "Catholic Progress, Old and New," *Catholic World*, LI (Jan., 1890), p. 433.
[23] Cf. Alfred Young, "Shall the People Sing?" *Catholic World*, XLV (July, 1887), pp. 444-453.
[24] Cross, *op. cit.*, p. 170.

Lay Congress in Baltimore

The most notable instance of the new stirring of the laity was the Catholic Lay Congress held in Baltimore on November 11-12, 1889. The idea of holding a Catholic congress was not a new one. As early as 1868, Isaac Hecker had called for regular general congresses with lay and clerical participants to discuss social and economic problems.[25] Both Hecker and those who took up the idea in the late eighties were impressed with the success of the periodic lay congresses (under clerical direction) held in Mainz, Germany, beginning in 1848, and the mixed congress held in Malines, Belgium, in 1863. But it was not until the mid-eighties that the idea could find support in America. By then, there were some influential laymen prepared to work hard and persistently to bring about a lay congress. Not surprisingly, the most important of these laymen were from the Midwest. Though William J. Onahan of Detroit, already well-known for his social thought, was eventually appointed chairman of the organizing committee, the real initiator of the congress was Henry F. Brownson of Detroit, the son of Orestes A. Brownson.

In Brownson's eyes, a Catholic congress would serve to "unite Catholics, giving them an opportunity to see and know one another, of proclaiming to the world that the laity are not priest-ridden, and of ratifying the declarations of the clergy."[26] Sharing Brownson's enthusiasm were such distinguished laymen at Charles J. Bonaparte of Baltimore, Patrick Donahoe of Boston, Henry Spaunhorst and Peter Foy of St. Louis and Maurice Egan of Notre Dame. As a group, they were perhaps the most eminent laymen of their day. Only John Boyle O'Reilly of Boston and the historian John Gilmary Shea, among outstanding lay figures, had their doubts, and these resulted as much from a fear of an unfavorable non-Catholic reaction as from anything else.

The major problem the organizers encountered was not a lack of lay enthusiasm; it was to convince the bishops of the need, the value and the safety of a lay congress. At the outset, the only enthusiastic episcopal supporter of the idea was John Ireland. But Ireland was able to gain

[25] "Shall We Have a Catholic Congress?" *Catholic World*, VIII (Nov., 1868), pp. 224-228.
[26] "The Catholic Congress," *Michigan Catholic*, Dec. 12, 1889. Quoted by Sister M. Sevina Pahorezki, O.S.F., in *The Social and Political Activities of William James Onahan* (Washington, D.C., 1942), p. 109n.

the support of a few other bishops and, with their aid, to convince Cardinal Gibbons that such a congress posed no danger to the Church. Gibbons' initial reaction had not been favorable. Not only did he doubt the value of anything as short as a two-day meeting, but he was also fearful that "in the atmosphere of American freedom, unrepresentative men are prone to utterances which may be misinterpreted."[27] Fortunately, his objections were not strenuous, and Ireland and the other bishops were able to convince him that, properly supervised, the organizers could be trusted.

In order to make sure that the laity did not step out of line during the congress, the hierarchy quickly appointed an episcopal commission to work with the laymen in making preparations. At a preliminary meeting of this commission it was decided, on the suggestion of Bishop Foley of Detroit, that all papers to be read at the Congress should be submitted in advance to the commission. The ostensible reason for this decision was that the printing and distributing of the papers in book form would be facilitated. In fact, however, as Bishop Foley was to write to Cardinal Gibbons, "That was the reason I assigned but in my own mind was the idea that we should get hold of all the papers and have a committee of bishops to be here at that time and pass upon the character of the papers."[28] Another Bishop, Patrick Ryan of Philadelphia, urged in the letter to Gibbons that, "Only the safest men should be selected to write, and they had better be left entirely free, after some preliminary advice."[29] As might have been expected, not all the lay organizers were happy about this hierarchical incursion. Only William James Onahan readily cooperated with the bishops; Brownson and Foy were annoyed that Onahan had proved so suppliant and Foy in particular was indignant about hierarchical control.

In the end, these annoyances proved to be unimportant. The congress opened in Baltimore on November 11, 1889, at the same time that the hierarchy was meeting in that city to commemorate the centenary of their establishment. In all, 1500 lay delegates were present, including Negroes and Indians, as well as many bishops and priests. As far as can be judged, the only effect of the episcopal caution was to ensure orderli-

[27] Allen S. Will, *Life of Cardinal Gibbons* (2 vols.; New York, 1922), I, pp. 198-200.
[28] Quoted in Pahorezki, *op. cit.*, p. 112n.
[29] *Ibid.*, p. 114.

ness. The hierarchical ruling that there would be no floor discussion of the papers read was added insurance that things would not get out of hand; but that was unlikely in any event since the cards of admission, by committee agreement, had been given to the Ordinary of the various American dioceses to whom application had to be made.[30] Thus protected from the unexpected or unacceptable, the clergy and laity present were given two days of the most enlightened lay thinking of the day. If the back-stage preparations of the papers did not altogether bear out Archbishop Ryan's claim that the congress proved that the laity were not "priest-ridden," they did show that the clergy and laity could cooperate effectively.

In the opening address, William J. Onahan sounded the main themes of the papers which were to follow. The most characteristic note, incessantly reiterated by almost every speaker, was that Catholics joyfully accepted the First Amendment to the Constitution. Indeed, the separation of Church and State, he said, sounded "the keynote of our future prosperity."[31] But no less prominent, if somewhat less high-pitched, was the theme of the pressing need for a Catholic confrontation of the social problems of the day: the welfare of the immigrants, the rights and needs of the working classes, the support of social justice. What Onahan touched on, other speakers developed. A Washington, D.C., lawyer, William Richards, in an address on "Labor and Capital," delivered a blistering attack on the evils of "untrammeled capitalism," defending the rights of workers to form associations to protect themselves against exploitation. Peter L. Foy speaking on "The New Social Order," while not as sharp in his indictment of capitalism, nevertheless saw the poverty of the workers as springing from social injustice and not from personal failings. The plight of the worker required state aid and intervention, an interplay between public and private charity, and, finally, "a more equitable distribution of the joint production of land, labor and capital." It was little wonder that the resolutions of the congress were hailed by many Catholics as well as non-Catholics for their progressive social thinking.[32]

[30] "The Call for the Congress," in *Proceedings of the Catholic Congress* (Detroit, 1889), p. xii.

[31] *Ibid.*, p. 6.

[32] Cf. Abell, *op. cit.*, pp. 104ff., for an excellent discussion of the social thought of the congress and its reception.

Of equal significance were the papers given by John Gilmary Shea and Henry F. Brownson. In Shea's eyes, the main concerns of American Catholics were their relationship to the Holy See and to the American government. With respect to the government, Shea had some complaints. Not only did it on occasion invade the rights of Catholics, but Catholics did not have the legal talents available to fight for their rights in the courts. The only way to correct this situation was for Catholics to organize their legal strategies more effectively. Generally, Shea saw a great need for a wider distribution of Catholic literature, both to inform Catholics and to combat anti-Catholicism by providing the non-Catholic with information about the Church. The over-all stress of Shea's remarks was on the necessity of greater Catholic solidarity in the face of threats posed by American society. Thus his concern with the role of the laity turned on the problem of how the laity could better be used in defense of the Church. "The Catholic laity of the country," he said, ". . . can thus prepare to devise and plan concurrent action so as to give strength to the whole body. Keep alive attachment to the Church, and secure from the designs of latent or overt proselytism the rising generations, that the faith may be handed down intact from sire to son."[33]

If Shea articulated what was perhaps the most common attitude to the new responsibilities of the laity, Brownson struck a bolder note. He laid far less stress on the laity as a bulwark for the Church, and instead expressed his concern with the relationship between clergy and laity. Urging the layman to take a more vigorous place in American society, he held that the layman could neither serve the Church effectively in the world nor defend its rights if he was not given the opportunity to speak freely within the Church and in his everyday secular life. If after the Reformation it had been necessary for the laity to "repress all expression on their part in connection with religion," it was no longer possible, in a mixed society, for the Church to demand this of them. "To pretend to keep them [the laity] from error by the restriction of free speech in these days is as idle as to blow against the wind. Those within the Church who are likely to say anything to the injury of religion can no more be repressed by ecclesiastical supervision than those without."[34] Calling for a greater mingling of Catholics with non-Catholics, a joining with them in good civic works, Brownson argued that the laity must

[33] "The Call for the Congress," op. cit., pp. 24-25.
[34] Ibid., pp. 27-28.

have the confidence of the clergy in their work in the world. "If they," he put it directly, "are only to repeat what is dictated to them, never think for themselves, or dare utter their thoughts, they can have no energy or freedom, and can produce no effect."

The two most important episcopal speakers supported Brownson's thinking, though less energetically. Cardinal Gibbons, after alluding to his early doubts about the congress, could say of it that, "It emphasizes and vindicates the important fact that the laity have the right, and have also the duty, of cooperating with the clergy in every good measure affecting the interests of society, of the country, and of the Church at large."[35] Speaking of the clergy and the laity, he added that, "I think that in some respects they have been too far and wide apart." Even so, Gibbons made it clear that he expected the laity to await the direction of the clergy before venturing out on their own.

Bishop Ireland was more open. Making clear by a frequent metaphor where the final authority lay—"priests are officers, laymen are soldiers" —he exhorted the laity to take an active role in the Church and society. "There is, on the part of the Catholic laymen, too much dependence upon priests. . . . Lay action is today particularly needed in the Church. Laymen in this age have a special vocation."[36] But the only way lay leadership could be developed, Ireland held, was by improving Catholic education. In particular, it was up to the colleges to provide a lay elite, men who could hold their heads up in American life and who could serve Church and country in the highest and most influential capacities. His final words to the delegates were: do not "go home and slumber, as in the past—go back to work. . . . I assure you, in the name of the bishops and priests, that we will lead, but I shall be very glad to see you get ahead of us in something."

In the aftermath, the congress was judged from almost every side to have been a success. Some complained that its brevity had curtailed its effectiveness. But even the early doubters had to admit that it had not brought any dire consequences upon the Church. (One priest, reportedly, "went home thanking God that the Church escaped unharmed."[37]) A sign of success was the decision to hold further congresses and, specifi-

[35] *Ibid.*, p. 15.

[36] *Souvenir Volume of the Centennial Celebration and Catholic Congress* (Chicago, 1893), p. 18.

[37] Cross, *op. cit.*, p. 169.

cally, to hold a second congress in Chicago in connection with the World's Fair of 1893.

Though it opened in Chicago on September 4, 1893, with some 2500 delegates in attendance, the Columbian Catholic Congress was not the great success that the 1889 congress had been. It had more opposition from the conservative bishops and clergy, and many of the original lay leaders were less enthusiastic. However, Onahan, Spaunhorst and Bishop Ireland, whose interest remained undiminished, were again able to prevail. What was notable about this second congress was the even greater stress laid on the Church's social teachings and the urgent need of social justice; the publication of Pope Leo XIII's Rerum Novarum in 1891 provided much of the impetus. But also important were the efforts of Ireland and a few other bishops to let the world see the Church's concern for the welfare of all men. Indeed, Ireland rejected the desires of the conservative members of the organizing committee, who were in the majority, that such subjects as religious education and the temporal power of the Pope in Italy be stressed. The latter viewed the congress as a great occasion for making clear to the world and to America some of the Church's worries about its own rights and those of the Pope. Moreover, as the arch-conservative Condé Pallen saw it, the Church was already in the vanguard of social progress. It was unnecessary for the Church to take greater lead in social reform efforts for it was already supplying the individual with "truth" and "with the necessary sacramental strength to walk the narrow path of justice and virtue."[38] Pallen and his supporters could gain little support from Ireland for this viewpoint.

The papers read at the congress were a notable example of the most advanced Catholic social thinking of the day. On the question, for instance, of labor-management bargaining three out of four speakers supported compulsory government arbitration. Others called for expanded insurance programs for workers, greater governmental protection of workers' rights and associations, and state intervention to secure, when necessary, just wages for the working man. By and large the American Catholic community had received Rerum Novarum with disinterest or downright hostility, but the speakers at the congress saw it for what it was—a magnificent document opening up whole new vistas for Catholic social thought.

[38] "The Catholic Church Progressive," St. Louis Church Progress, January 9, 1892.

With the Columbian Catholic Congress, the lay renaissance reached its apex. The fortunes of the laymen may be said to have begun ebbing toward the middle of the last decade of the nineteenth century. The difficulties attendant on the organization of the Columbian Congress suggested a spent force—an impression that was to become increasingly confirmed in the opening decades of the twentieth century.

Before turning to the reasons for this decline, we should note that the upsurge of the laity was paralleled by a re-examination among the clergy of their seminaries, their intellectual life and the efficacy of their work. The drive by many of the liberal bishops, led by Bishop Spalding of Peoria, for a Catholic university was the most prominent sign of the clerical renaissance. Although the idea was first discussed at the Second Plenary Council in 1866, it took a considerable and persistent effort over more than a generation to bring it to fruition. The opening of Catholic University in Washington in 1889 marked a milestone both in Catholic higher education and also in the efforts of a minority of bishops and priests to provide the clergy with a genuine university education.

There can be no doubt that such an effort was necessary. While there were a few good seminaries—St. Charles' in Philadelphia, St. Bernard's in Rochester, St. Joseph's in Dunwoodie, N.Y., St. John's in Boston and St. Paul's in Saint Paul—their primary aim was to graduate pastors. In speculative theology, much less the social and physical sciences or the liberal arts, there was no great interest. "The ecclesiastical seminary," Bishop Spalding said, "is not a school of intellectual culture. . . . Its methods are not such as one would choose to open the mind, to give it breadth, flexibility, strength, refinement and grace."[39] The bishops who recognized the weakness of the seminaries were not able to do much about it—even Catholic University was weak for many years after its foundation—but they did at least raise the question. What they did not foresee clearly was that as the twentieth century advanced, the gap between the education of the clergy and that of the college-trained laity would widen. If the priest himself was not getting the best education for his own development, he was getting a far worse education in understanding the world in which the laity lived. As the *Catholic World*

[39] *Means and Ends of Education* (Chicago, 1895), p. 212. Cf. also John Tracy Ellis, *John Lancaster Spalding* (Milwaukee, 1961), pp. 40ff., for a helpful discussion of Spalding's thinking on education; also Cross, *op. cit.*, pp. 173-175, for a discussion about seminary reform.

complained in 1896, the general opinion of the priest was an "estimate of clerical excellence which actually concentrates everything praiseworthy in the high title of a 'safe man.' It means that priestly happiness consists in being let alone by the people and promoted by the bishop."[40]

A Loss of Vigor

The question to which we must now turn is why, after a promising decade from around 1885 to 1895, the lay renaissance lost its vigor. The reasons are obscure. What is strikingly clear, however, is that after the Columbia Congress there were no more lay congresses, there was little discussion of the laity in the Catholic press (even in the *Catholic World*), and there were hardly any exhortations such as those issued earlier to the laity by Ireland or Gibbons. The opposition to the Columbian Congress had been enough to discourage Onahan and his group from trying for still another. Though not aimed at lay congresses specifically, a letter sent on September 15, 1895, from Pope Leo XIII to Francesco Cardinal Satolli, the Apostolic Delegate to the United States, forbidding Catholic participation in inter-faith religious congresses, was surely no source of encouragement to the laity. Moreover, it would appear that the hierarchy and even Bishop Ireland became increasingly disinterested in promoting large lay gatherings which would discuss major social and cultural problems.

The most likely reason, however, for the general decline of the laity after 1895 was the fate of the movement, led by Bishop Ireland, to harmonize Catholicism and American life. As suggested above, the lay renaissance coincided with the rise to prominence of those bishops and clergy who urged a more rapid Americanization of the immigrant, a fuller entering of the Church into American life, and an adaptation, wherever doctrinally possible, of the Church to the American scene. It coincided as well with a new optimism about the Church's future progress, stimulated by success in solving many of the problems which had been a legacy of the first heavy immigrant waves.

But by the middle of the last decade of the nineteenth century, a growing opposition to the Americanist program became noticeable. The condemnation of three secret American societies in 1893 against the

40 "The Ambassador of Christ," *Catholic World*, LXIV (March, 1897), p. 826.

wishes of Gibbons, Ireland and Archbishop Riordan of San Francisco, the denial by Pope Leo XIII in his encyclical *Longinqua Oceani* that the relationship between Church and State in America was necessarily "the most desirable state of the Church," and the forced resignation of Bishop Keane as rector of Catholic University in 1896 were all hints that the tide was turning. But the most devastating blow came in an apostolic letter, *Testem benevolentiae,* on January 22, 1899. This letter, addressed to Cardinal Gibbons, praised the American hierarchy and the American people but, at the same time, condemned certain opinions which the Pope took to be entertained by some American Catholics, e.g., "that, in order more easily to bring over to Catholic doctrine those who dissent from it, the Church ought to adapt herself somewhat to our advanced civilization, and, relaxing her ancient rigor, show some indulgence to modern popular theories and methods."[41] Moreover, the Pope said, "the followers of these novelties judge that a certain liberty ought to be introduced into the Church, so that, limiting the exercise and vigilance of its powers, each one of the faithful may act more freely in pursuance of his own natural bent and capacity." Whether or not there were any American Catholics who held such views in the sense in which the Pope understood them is a point which cannot be discussed here.[42] For their part, the Americanizing bishops and priests denied to a man that they held such views; and in reality, the actual occasion for the apostolic letter was not anything in particular that Americans had been saying but, instead, the views indirectly imputed to them in an overly enthusiastic preface to a French translation of Walter Elliott's *Life of Father Hecker* written by Abbé Felix Klein, a professor at the *Institut Catholique* in Paris. The fact that the ideals of many of the American liberal bishops and priests were being fervently espoused by a number of French priests for transplantation to Europe was still another cause, as were the conservatives' protestations to Rome.

In any event, *Testem benevolentiae* dealt a blow to the Americanist movement and to the optimistic, progressive spirit which had permeated it. "To have hoped," Father McAvoy has written, "that the conservative and more traditional—as some might say sacristan—Catholicism of West-

---

[41] *Documents of American Catholic History,* edited by John Tracy Ellis (2nd ed., Milwaukee, 1962), p. 320.

[42] The "Americanist heresy," as many called it, has been dismissed by most historians as a "phantom heresy."

en Europe would accept the practical, rough, and democratic notions of American Catholicism in the closing decades of the nineteenth century, probably was too much."[43] Yet the problem of the way the Church ought to relate itself to American society had by no means been solved. If *Testem benevolentiae* did not necessarily amount to a repudiation of the ideals of Gibbons, Ireland and the Paulists, it did bring about an effective silencing of discussions and debate; the question was not resolved, it was simply left hanging in mid-air. Only in our day has it been reopened. In addition, what little vigor and daring were able to survive the condemnation of Americanism were further stifled by the condemnation of Modernism in 1907. The combined effect of the two condemnations was devastating for the speculative and experimental side of the American Church.

In the end, the great contribution of the Americanist movement to the renaissance of the laity was the very direct manner in which the questions were raised of the place of individual initiative in the Church, the role of the Catholic in a democratic and pluralistic society and the responsibility of the Church and its members to the temporal order. For as soon as one raises these questions, the problem of the layman comes immediately to the foreground. To go one step further: it would appear that the laity are only taken seriously when the Church feels itself either in a period of strength or on the verge of such a period. It seems reasonable to suppose that at such times—and the peak years of the Americanist movement provide a prime example—the hierarchy is prone to be more optimistic about the value of freedom, more hopeful about the value of pluralism and religious freedom to the Church, and less likely to press its authority to its absolute limits. When, on the contrary, Church leaders are fearful of society, excessively worried about the maintenance of the faith of the people, wary of contemporary thought, they will be very reluctant to encourage activity, freedom and initiative in the laity. As the way of safety, they will want to keep the layman on short reins.

Unfortunately, then, once the American Church began to waver in its optimism around the turn of the century, the lay renaissance slowly withered away. Concretely, of course, this renaissance depended in part on some outstanding laymen to give it strength and direction—and some outstanding and influential bishops to support it. Yet the question must

---

[43] McAvoy, *op. cit.,* p. 366.

arise as to why, in the early decades of the twentieth century, the American Church languished in its over-all development almost until the time of World War I.

There is no simple answer and there can be no pretense here of giving one. Surely the condemnations of Americanism and Modernism were, taken together, one cause. They stifled effectively any adventurous spirit, any encouragement of independence and initiative on the part of either laity or clergy. Caution and excessive prudence became the dominant spirit, not only in the American Church but in the Church throughout the world. Another likely factor was the absence of any genuinely powerful figures in the Church. Archbishop Ireland was, after the turn of the century, no longer the dynamic leader he had been before; and in 1902, Bishop Spalding was to say, "Our great sees are largely in the hands of men who have lost their vigor of mind and body."[44]

Nor were there, among the laity, leaders to take the place of some of those of an earlier generation. Just why this should have been the case is not clear. In Father McAvoy's judgment, it was an important weakness of the seminaries "that they did not produce the Catholic lay scholar so necessary in the secular fields of knowledge which are becoming the major interest of the modern American university."[45] Similarly, it was probably a mistake for Catholic University in its early years to limit itself to theology students, for in America "the leadership in the intellectual world was fast departing from clerical direction."[46] In the Catholic colleges, intent on preparing their students for the various professions, there was little interest in either intellectual excellence or the training of lay leaders. American Catholic intellectual culture after the turn of the century was mainly the product of scattered individuals, usually unattached to any university that might have nourished their growth and development.

Finally, advanced lay thinking on social questions was in short supply after the Columbian Congress. Growing alarm over the advances of socialism after 1900 was undoubtedly one reason for the continuing Catholic coolness toward social reform. The work of the German Central Verein, which tried to interest Catholics in social questions, was

[44] McAvoy, "The Catholic Minority after the Americanist Controversy 1899-1917," *Review of Politics*, XXI (Jan., 1959), p. 58.
[45] *Ibid.*, p. 69.
[46] *Ibid.*, p. 70.

perhaps an exception, but it had an uphill struggle on its hands—against the indifference of many of the bishops, the apathy of the laity and a general worry about the influence of radicalism among Catholics. Only in the second decade of the twentieth century was Catholic social thought able to make some major advances. Even then, the leadership came mainly from clerics: Fathers William Kerby and John A. Ryan at Catholic University and Father Peter Dietz of Ohio provided the main part of it.

One good index of the fate of the layman between 1900 and World War I is found in the struggle to form and sustain the Federation of Catholic Societies. That Federation was the outgrowth of the same idea that had motivated Richard Clarke in 1871 to form the Catholic Union: the desire to have a national organization which would unite the various charitable and fraternal groups. While Clarke's efforts had only a moderate success, partly because of the opposition of Archbishop Martin Spalding of Baltimore, the idea was one which did not die. It seemed apparent to many that a Federation which could coordinate the efforts of such organizations as the St. Vincent de Paul Society, the Ancient Order of Hibernians, the Central Verein, the Irish Catholic Benevolent Union, the Knights of Columbus, as well as the numerous smaller parish societies which had sprung up as an alternative to the condemned masonic organizations, would be able to bring great weight to bear in the service of the Church. Moreover, a union of these societies would enable them to defend each other as well as the Church from outside attacks.

After many years of effort, the American Federation of Catholic Societies was formed in 1901.[47] In theory, the Federation was a lay organization. At its founding convention it did not ask for hierarchical approval nor did its constitution provide for clerical officers in its official positions. In its early phases, however, it did gain the backing of a number of bishops, notably Sebastian Messmer who was influential in urging that the Federation have a social program and be prepared to cooperate with non-Catholics. As it turned out, the Federation was never a great success. Even though much of its work consisted in defending Catholic rights, it never gained full episcopal support. Without that

[47] A full account of the Federation is to be found in Sister M. Adele Francis Gorman, O.S.F., *Federation of Catholic Societies in the United States, 1870-1920* (unpublished Ph.D. dissertation, Department of History, University of Notre Dame, 1962).

support, and lacking also dynamic lay leaders, the Federation suffered a continual financial problem—so much so that it was never able to afford a national headquarters. Nor did it ever actually function as a *lay* organization: interested bishops formed an advisory board and priests served on its various committees.

Still, despite inherent weaknesses, the Federation did some important work in supporting the formation of various permanent Church organizations: the Layman's Retreat Movement, the Federation of Catholic Alumnae, the National Catholic Educational Association, among others. By the time the Federation was absorbed into the National Catholic Welfare Conference shortly after World War I, and eventually disappeared with the formation of the National Council of Catholic Men, it had provided some precedents for future cooperation between clergy and laity. And, through the inspiration and leadership of Father Peter Dietz, some early advances were made in bringing Catholics and non-Catholics together in non-sectarian organizations.

What, finally, was the meaning and significance of the dramatic resurgence of the laity in the 1880s and 1890s and the subsequent decline after the turn of the century? In answer to that question, let me simply assert some general propositions which seem amply confirmed by the broad trend of events, both theological and social. First, a viable and significant lay movement depends upon the support and encouragement of the hierarchy. However much the layman may desire a meaningful place within the Church, and responsibilities and freedoms to support that place, he cannot achieve it without the active assistance of the hierarchy. Second, a lay renaissance presupposes a general Church renaissance. In this sense, a lay renaissance is not an isolated event in the life of the Church: it must be accompanied by a general rethinking of the Church's function in society, a rethinking of the value and effectiveness of its organizations, its universities, its intellectual life, its clergy and its social thought. Third, a lay renaissance is impossible unless the Church faces the world with a sense of confidence. If the Church feels harassed or endangered, it will not give the layman much leeway; on the contrary, the more threatened the Church feels itself to be, the more the hierarchy will tend to centralize all power and responsibility in its own hands. Fourth, a lay renaissance will depend upon lay leaders who have come to terms with the society in which they live— who have achieved some general social status and acceptance, some economic stability, some sense of identification with society. A lay movement would be most unlikely among Catholics who feel themselves alienated from American life. Fifth, any lay movement will show the effects of the layman's attempt to reconcile the demands made upon him by Church and society; it will reflect not only his dedication to the Church, but also the influence which the values of society have had upon him. Sixth, the freer the layman finds himself in society and the more integrated he is in the community, the more he will look for many of the same privileges within the Church.

CHAPTER 4

Emergence from the Ghetto:

1917-1960

IN RECENT YEARS, perhaps no subject has so exercised the American Church as the "emergence of the layman."[1] Even the most cursory glance at the Catholic diocesan press shows this to be a theme which has thoroughly captured public interest. At the same time, there have been numerous signs that the layman is coming into his own. There have been significant indications of episcopal enthusiasm for a more active and effective laity; a proliferation of lay organizations and a rapid growth in the number of those taking part in them; an intensified effort to clarify the theological role of the layman in the Church; and a new receptivity to lay complaints and desires among the clergy. Given this ferment, it is only natural to believe that something entirely new has made its appearance on the American Church scene, something which by a magical transformation has suddenly and unexpectedly burst forth.

The truth of the matter is that the layman has "emerged" before in the American Church. During the heyday of trusteeism he emerged in a fashion far more dramatic (and disastrous) than anything we can see today. In the life and work of Orestes A. Brownson the American laity had a prophetic figure as forceful and vigorous as anyone now living. In the agitation and enthusiasm during the 1880s and 1890s, culminating in the lay congresses in Baltimore and Chicago, "emergence" was the order of the day. And that highly charged expression "the age of the laity," which many think of as one newly coined, is at the very least seventy years old. In short, if we are to speak accurately, we must say that the layman is emerging—again. The question which this new emergence poses—and it is unanswerable at present—is whether it will endure and bear the fruits which are latent in it.

[1] Cf. Donald Thorman, *The Emerging Layman* (New York, 1962).

79

If the past is any clue to an answer, it shows at least that little can be taken for granted. A genuine lay emergence, as I suggested in the last chapter, depends upon many things: a combination of favorable social conditions, vigorous lay leadership, an interested and optimistic hierarchy, a spirit of experimentation and confidence within the Church, and a general absence of fear and cultural separatism. To these conditions—if we recall the lay trustee disputes and the Americanist controversy—should be added the absence of any tendencies toward lay excess (or at least the belief that any excesses do not tell against a whole movement).

For it seems almost axiomatic, in America as well as the rest of the world, that progress in the Church is a very tortured matter. The Church's capacity to expand its horizons, while very great, is matched by an equal capacity to panic and retrench abruptly when reformation seems to be getting out of hand. It takes far more effort and persistence to induce the Church to make changes than it does to get the Church to back off and assume a defensive posture; panic spreads more quickly than enthusiasm—and the Church is more easily able to implement a reactionary spirit than a progressive one. This is by no means a necessarily bad trait. More than once in the history of the Church, the progressive spirit has needed to be sharply and swiftly curbed; the fact that the Church has been able to do so has been one important reason that it has endured and maintained its unity throughout the ages. But it is a trait to be kept well in mind, no matter how widespread enthusiasm for a new cause may be, no matter how much support a new trend may seem here and now to have from the teaching authority of the Church.

With these cautions and qualifications mentioned, we can now turn to the immediate background of the contemporary "emergence of the layman." For the present emergence is, in an important sense, only one phase of a general upheaval in the American Church which actually began with the end of World War I. One cannot grasp the full import of the layman's place in both Church and society today unless it is seen as part of an entire spectrum of social, cultural, educational, and theological change whose roots can be traced back many decades.

It would be no exaggeration to say that the Church after World War I underwent a remarkable transformation. A change was clearly in order, for the time between the opening of the twentieth century and World War I had been unproductive, overshadowed by the condemnation of Americanism, the absence of notable laymen or churchmen, and the theological strait jacket imposed by the Church's reaction against Modernism. The Church grew, but as Father McAvoy has put it, "only in numbers." What brought about the change was, in great part, the war itself.

On the one hand, it had the effect of hastening the process of the Americanization of the newer immigrants. What urban life and urban ghettos could not bring about the war did: the mixing of Americans of all creeds, nationalities and races, opening the vista of a new and different way of life, less dominated by old ethnic attachments and more imbued with the spirit of America as an open society. The restrictive immigration laws enacted in the years between 1921-1924 furthered the process of breaking down the isolated cultural worlds of the immigrants. What all this was to mean is now clear: a genuine American Catholic Church was about to make its appearance, a Church which was to become something more than a rough union of differing and often disparate Catholic ethnic groups. With the end of immigration, as Will Herberg has argued, religious association rather than ethnic bonds were to become the means by which Americans achieved their self-identity.[2] Yet this point overlooks the liberating effect the loss of ethnic identity had on Catholics—the Church was now free, if not forced, to find some genuinely American sense of Catholic self-identity. This was the task the Americanist bishops had set themselves in the 1880s and 1890s; but it required World War I and the end of immigration to establish the necessary base to re-open more successfully their passionate case.

On the other hand, the war served as a major force in galvanizing the hierarchy to act more boldly and vigorously. There was, of course, the initial need to pledge the support of Catholics to the war effort—and this was done in the usual manner with all the by-now familiar pledges of Catholic loyalty to the American flag. But more important was the need to create the means by which that support could be organized and implemented. In 1917 the bishops established the National Catholic War Council to coordinate Catholic war activities. The success of the Council led, shortly after the end of the war, to a general desire that the American Church should have one major coordinating body. Consequently, with the approval of Pope Benedict XV, the bishops estab-

[2] Will Herberg, Protestant-Catholic-Jew (rev. ed., New York, 1960). I might say in passing that I think Herberg overstresses the place of religion as a means of achieving American self-identity. Among Catholics at least (and I suspect among Protestants as well) religious identification seems to me to take a second place to economic, regional or educational identifications.

lished in September of 1919 the National Catholic Welfare Council (N.C.W.C.). Shortly thereafter the word "Council" was changed to "Conference" because of a fear on the part of some bishops that it might weaken their diocesan authority. At the heart of the Conference were a number of subcommittees: for social action, education, and lay organizations, among others. They were charged with coordinating Catholic activities in specific areas, making recommendations to the bishops and providing them with information. Thus was laid the basis for an organization which in the years ahead was to channel and direct the activities of the American Church in an increasingly orderly and creative fashion.

But the formation of the N.C.W.C. was not the only sign of a new episcopal current. The Pastoral Letter of the bishops in 1919, which announced the formation of the N.C.W.C., was in many respects a remarkable document. Restating in forceful and vigorous language traditional pastoral concerns, it laid heavy emphasis on the necessity of social justice as part of the post-war reconstruction. Invoking Pope Leo XIII's *Rerum Novarum,* the bishops called for an intensified effort to shape a humane and just social order, stressing in particular the relevance of religion and morality to industrial problems.[3] Noteworthy in this respect was the bishops' support of trade unionism, collective bargaining and the right of labor to a living wage. Yet, however remarkable the bishops' emphasis on social justice, there was nothing particularly significant about their references to the laity. Addressed as "beloved children," they were commended for two things: their financial support of the Church's charitable and educational activities and "your correspondence with the intent of your pastors." If these words hardly constituted a special mandate to the laity to take a larger role in the work of reconstruction, the Pastoral Letter in its totality and the subsequent work of the N.C.W.C. —especially the latter's sponsorship of regional and national conferences on industrial problems—clearly established the Church's concern for the temporal order. One way or another, the implementation of this concern would increasingly have to involve the active cooperation of the laity. Indeed, Father Peter Dietz' "Militia of Christ," an organization of Catholic union leaders during the pre-war years, was already a foreshadowing of such cooperation.

The N.C.W.C. and the general impetus provided by the Pastoral Letter promised better things to come. For the time being, however, the

[3] *The National Pastorals of the American Hierarchy, 1792-1919,* ed. by Peter Guilday (Westminster, Md., 1954), pp. 266-340.

Church still had a vast number of problems to cope with. In the ten years or so prior to the passage of the restrictive immigration laws, over five million immigrants came to this country, with well over half estimated to be Catholics. The Church was faced with all the heavy financial problems these great numbers entailed for education, assimilation and the most basic kinds of charitable assistance. Moreover, anti-Catholicism was still a force to be reckoned with, as the candidacy of Al Smith for the Presidency was to show in 1928. At the same time, there can be little doubt that the closing off of massive immigration was a blessing in disguise. It meant that finally the Church would have a chance to catch up with its task and slowly come out from under the burden of attempting to do the impossible for a Catholic population which had for nearly a century grown at a prodigious rate.

It was during the twenties that Catholics showed the first signs of a renascent cultural and intellectual life. The one thing which did not yet appear was a renewed sense of the necessity of theological excellence. "In the general American ignorance of theology, Catholic theologians were content to reassert the principles of the *Cathechism* of the Council of Baltimore."[4] The one exception to this generalization was the work of a number of priests at Catholic University in the area of moral theology, especially relating to social and economic matters. In the thinking of Fathers John A. Ryan, William J. Kerby, Francis Haas and John Maguire, Catholic social thought was to receive a solid and scholarly basis. In addition, the Rural Life Conference formed in 1922 was a sign that new avenues of pastoral theology were opening up. But on the whole the great religious advances within the Church were in the devotional rather than the theological spheres; the twenties saw a great surge in more frequent communions, increased devotions to the Eucharist, a growth of devotions to the Sacred Heart, the Blessed Virgin and St. Joseph, and an upsurge of missionary fervor and interest in devotional literature.

Intellectual Awakening

However important this latter development was to be for the spiritual life of American Catholics, the increasing indications of a cultural and intellectual revival were to be no less important for the future of the

[4] Thomas T. McAvoy, C.S.C., "The Catholic Church in the United States between Two Wars," *Review of Politics*, IV (Oct., 1942), p. 416.

layman. For at the same time that a number of Catholics were beginning to worry about the lack of Catholic intellectuals, they were also beginning to manifest a spirit of self-analysis and self-criticism about Catholic leadership in America. This new spirit was comparatively mild—particularly in comparison with that of the 1950s; nonetheless, its significance was great. It could only be a matter of time before the self-criticism reached into the matter of the laity's passive place in the Church.

But first an intellectual revival was necessary. In the twenties it took a number of forms. In the first place, a group of important magazines came into being: *The Commonweal, Thought* and *New Scholasticism* were the most notable. Secondly, the decade witnessed the formation of some important scholarly associations, especially the American Catholic Historical Association (1922) under the inspiration of Peter Guilday and the American Catholic Philosophical Association (1926). Thirdly, Catholic colleges began to expand rapidly, though there was as yet comparatively little sense of the value of these colleges for producing an intellectual elite. Fourthly, there began to appear frequent complaints about the paucity of Catholic intellectuals and the unpleasant reality of a strong streak of anti-intellectualism among Catholics. In 1921, Patrick Scanlan, managing editor of the *Brooklyn Tablet*, could complain of a "lamentable apathy toward higher education," and go on to say that, "At the present time our lay leadership is well-nigh bankrupt. . . . Although we are one-fifth of the population, we do not furnish one-fiftieth of the higher intellectual life of the country."[5] So too Professor Carlton J. H. Hayes of Columbia said in 1922 that, "The greatest need among Catholics . . . is of intellectual leaders"; and *The Commonweal* in a 1926 editorial lamented that "we have no John Dewey, no Elihu Root, no Ralph Adams Cram, no H. L. Mencken, no Edward Arlington Robinson—and we have not seemed particularly to care about having them."

It was in the twenties as well that Catholics first began to play the *Who's Who* game, a game that has since become a regular feature of intellectual revivals. What percentage of those distinguished men listed in *Who's Who* are Catholic—and the inevitable second question, why

[5] *American Catholicism and the Intellectual Ideal,* ed. by Frank L. Christ and Gerard E. Sherry (New York, 1959), p. 72. Oddly enough, in his later years Scanlan was among the first to decry the complaints during the late 1950s that Catholics were not providing intellectual leaders.

aren't there more? In 1927, for instance, it was estimated that only 7 out of every 100,000 Catholic men were in *Who's Who* but nearly 20 out of every 100,000 Jews. Even the Seventh-day Adventists had a higher representation. Similarly, there was much lamenting of the fact that there were no distinguished Catholic scientists and very few Catholics who were members of the faculties at secular colleges. Such studies were also a common feature of the thirties—and the depressing results were about the same.

Here and there amidst these laments could be heard a call for a greater number of laymen on the faculties of Catholic colleges, expressing in the most delicate of terms a conviction that an intellectual revival could only come from the laity. Yet during the twenties and early thirties little hope existed for a genuine raising of intellectual standards. Catholic colleges were overcrowded, under-endowed, and the general attitude of the hierarchy and clergy toward them was that they were meant to provide an education for as many as possible instead of to produce intellectual leaders. For all that, it was significant that the agitation for intellectual leadership came mostly from laymen, and a striking amount from those few, such as George N. Shuster at *The Commonweal* and Jerome Kerwin at the University of Chicago, who were themselves known and respected outside of Catholic circles.

Perhaps the most representative instance of the thinking of this new generation of Catholic laymen is found in Shuster's book, *The Catholic Spirit in America*, published in 1927.[6] While showing a clear and a sympathetic understanding of the great handicaps of the American Church—its poverty, its great number of still unassimilated immigrants, its pressing and first-priority material needs—he could still hold up some high cultural ideals and point out important portents for a cultural awakening. Though he could say, "A kind of terrible contempt for thought and loveliness has settled upon American Catholicism,"[7] he could also feel confident that "the future Catholic cultural revival . . . will be an enterprise in which clergy and laymen frankly join hands. . . . Less of an apologist than he is now . . . the layman will manifest a spirituality which (to borrow the language of philosophy) is less logical and more ontological."[8] Before that happy state of affairs could come

[6] New York.
[7] *Ibid.*, p. 170.
[8] *Ibid.*, p. 201.

about, however, Catholics would have to change their attitude toward American society. "Catholics," he wrote, "even today live in something like an armed camp,"[9] able through their numbers to veto many things in American society but without the power to exert any positive influence.

Despite these criticisms, Shuster's tone was calm, the book positive and hopeful; compared with the writings of present-day Catholic intellectuals, his words had few sharp edges. The same was true of most of the Catholic self-criticism which came out of the twenties. In part, no doubt, this was the result of some degree of timidity—criticism of things Catholic was still something new—but it may also have been symptomatic of a generation which saw unlimited horizons ahead. Then, too, the twenties were a time in America of hope and prosperity, and Catholics were affected by the general sense of well-being.

With the advent of the depression all this changed. No realistic person could entertain the notion that America would be spared the economic and social ills that were the common lot of mankind. For those within the Church who were still wary of social reform, the fear of Communism and socialism was a stimulus far more powerful than were exhortations during times of prosperity. And for those already concerned with the problems of industrial society, the decade of the thirties spurred them to increased efforts. Over and above the new sense of social urgency, the thirties also saw the first real development of "Catholic Action," which Pope Pius XI defined as "the participation of the laity in the apostolic mission of the hierarchy."

The total impact was, if not electrifying, still considerable; it marked the real beginning of the American lay movement. Now it is possible, I believe, to chart two sides to this lay movement: an "official" side, by which I mean those movements which arose under the direct guidance and inspiration of the bishops through the agency of the N.C.W.C.; and an "unofficial" side, by which I mean those organizations which, while accepted by the bishops (or at least not hindered), arose more or less spontaneously among scattered groups of individuals and did their work independently of the official agencies of the hierarchy.

The official lay movement, which was called at first "Catholic Action," was very much the work of the N.C.W.C. As the result of Pius XI's

[9] *Ibid.*, p. 118.

calls for greater Catholic concern with the temporal order and especially because of his encyclical "On the Reconstruction of the Social Order" in 1931, the N.C.W.C. embarked on a broad program of activities, directed mostly toward the enlightenment of the Catholic population on the great needs of the day in Christian education, decent movies and literature, the Catholic press, and social and economic justice. In addition, massive Eucharistic congresses in Omaha, Cleveland and New Orleans were seen by the hierarchy as an occasion for the laity to express their devotion to God and loyalty to the Church. Working closely with the N.C.W.C. and the bishops were the Knights of Columbus, the Holy Name Societies and various other of the older lay and fraternal organizations. Although this emphasis on Catholic Action in fact touched comparatively few Catholics, it introduced the Church's social teaching for the first time on the popular level; henceforth it would at least become increasingly difficult for all but the most uneducated to think of religion as solely a private, sacramental matter, centering exclusively on personal morality. It was during these years too that the National Council of Catholic Men, an agency of the N.C.W.C., began to gain in strength; it would soon provide social action programs for mass lay organizations and establish international lay contacts.

Although much more could be said about these "official" Catholic Action movements, there is good reason to think that the most important spur to the lay apostolate was to come ultimately from the "unofficial" movements which began to appear during the thirties and forties, and which made a great leap forward just after World War II. Undoubtedly, the most notable and influential was the Catholic Worker movement, begun in 1933 by Dorothy Day and Peter Maurin. They put their voice and pen to work in exposing the great evils of the age: the sufferings of the unemployed, the homeless, the exploited minorities, the brutalized industrial worker, and the migrant laborer. Strongly agrarian in emphasis, pacifistic, and anti-industrialist, the Catholic Worker movement rapidly caught the imagination of a large number of Catholic intellectuals who were impatient with the more moderate work of the official lay movements, and especially such organizations as the Holy Name Society and the Knights of Columbus.

In this respect, the thirties saw the beginning of a very self-conscious sense of alienation on the part of intellectuals and social reformers from the more popular manifestations of American Catholic culture and conservative social thought. Not only did this group feel that the Church's social thinking was being paid mere lip-service, but it was influenced by non-Catholic thought and willing to take seriously the Church's oft-repeated claim of openness to truth from whatever quarter it would come. How much the Catholic Worker movement appealed to this segment of the Catholic populace is suggested by the fact that its publication, *The Catholic Worker,* rapidly achieved a circulation well over a hundred thousand and that within a few years some thirty-three houses of hospitality had been opened throughout the country to give content to the conviction that feeding the hungry, clothing the naked and giving shelter to the homeless was of the essence of the Christian life. Among the many offshoots of the Catholic Worker spirit was the formation of the Association of Catholic Trade Unionists in 1937 and of innumerable discussion and social action groups throughout the country. But the most important result of the Catholic Worker and its allied houses of hospitality was the great number of Catholics who came under its spell and then went on to form new organizations, or to introduce a heightened sense of zeal in older ones.

In the late thirties came new and accelerated efforts to shape a lay apostolate in the Midwest.[10] In particular, Monsignor Reynold Hillenbrand, the rector of St. Mary of the Lake Seminary at Mundelein near Chicago, was beginning to educate a whole generation of priests in the social thought of the Church, the lay apostolate and the liturgy. At Notre Dame, Father Louis J. Putz and others were working along the same lines. The result of these efforts was to make the Midwest the center of creative thinking on the place of the Church in society and the effective utilization of the laity in the Church's apostolate to the world. Just before and immediately after World War II this creativity gave rise to a variety of specialized organizations: the Christian Family Movement (C.F.M.); the Young Christian Workers (Y.C.W.), patterned on the famous French *Jeunesse Ouvrière Chrétienne* movement; the Young Christian Students, The Grail, and the Cana Movement.[11] Coming out of the same milieu were also the Catholic Interracial Council, the Catholic Labor Alliance and *Integrity* magazine.

[10] A good, brief survey of these developments can be found in "The Apostolate" by Father Louis J. Putz, C.S.C., *Perspectives* (Sept.-Oct., 1962), pp. 12-15.

[11] The best general description of these organizations is in Leo Ward, *Catholic Life, U.S.A.: Contemporary Lay Movements* (St. Louis, 1959).

Although each of these groups was formed for some specialized task, they all shared a number of common values: a devotion to the social encyclicals, a dissatisfaction with the work already being done in their areas, an intense, activist zeal to make their religious convictions count in the world around them, and a persistent search for a spirituality which would uniquely express and shape their interior and exterior religious life. Of special importance as a common bond was the liturgical movement. While a new interest in the liturgy first appeared during the twenties under the inspiration of Father Martin Hellriegel of O'Fallon, Missouri, Father William Busch of St. Paul Seminary and the monks of St. John's Abbey in Collegeville, Minnesota, it was not until the thirties that it began to have a general impact. Part of this was due to the work of Father Virgil Michel, O.S.B., who in 1926 founded the journal *Orate Fratres* (now called *Worship*) as well as the Liturgical Press, thus providing for a continuing source of information and guidance on the liturgy; and part of it to the establishment of a number of workshops and summer schools devoted to liturgical subjects.[12] At Notre Dame especially, the liturgical movement and the lay apostolate benefited each other, and it became common to view a fuller participation in the liturgy as central to the apostolic life.

It would, of course, be misleading to suggest that all of these new signs of life in the thirties and early to mid-forties were very widespread or met with instant acceptance among the great mass of clergy and laity. On the contrary, they formed only a small part of the overall activities of the Church. They were, properly speaking, splinter groups which could not claim any kind of widespread support until at least the mid-fifties. The further one went from Chicago and a few other Midwestern centers, the less one heard of these things. On the East Coast they were hardly heard of at all. But their importance did not lie so much in the number of supporters as it did in the fact that they represented a fresh approach to individual spiritual life, the work of the Church in the world, and the duties and responsibilities of the layman.

Moreover, in actual practice, these groups brought about a far richer relationship between clergy and laity than was customary. One reason

[12] See "The Liturgical Movement in the United States," by Sister Jane Marie Murray, O.P., and Paul Marx, O.S.B., in *The Catholic Church, U.S.A.*, edited by Louis J. Putz, C.S.C. (Chicago, 1956), pp. 301-314. Cf. also Paul B. Marx, *Virgil Michel and the Liturgical Movement* (Collegeville, Minn., 1957).

for this was the sense the interested clergy and laity had of being a minority in the Church, of having more values and aims in common with each other than with their more stagnant clerical and lay brothers. Another reason was that since these groups and movements were small, there was at first no bureaucratic machinery to stifle an easy and informal lay-clerical relationship. Still another reason was probably the fact that most of them had comparatively little contact with chancery offices and official archdiocesan centers. Though in most instances episcopal permission (or at least permissiveness) was necessary, these groups remained out of the main stream of diocesan activities, thereby avoiding many of the handicaps to private initiative which prominence and official importance inevitably seem to breed. One might except Chicago from this generalization: Samuel Cardinal Stritch did much to encourage the great variety of organizations which sprang up in his archdiocese, and chancery contacts were more common.

Though care must be taken not to exaggerate, it would be reasonably accurate to assert that a good number of those most active in these movements felt a strong sense of antipathy for much that passed for Catholic life in the United States. Among the laymen, there was often a feeling of frustration and annoyance in the face of indifference or suspicion among the conservative clergy. The complaint was not primarily that the run of the clergy were not interested in zealous and socially conscious laymen; instead, it was that the clergy ignored papal social thought and those progressive trends which represented an attempt to make Catholicism relevant to the age. In contrast to the situation today, there was far less talk then of giving the laity independence and a special role than there was of finding ways to stimulate the clergy to provide better leadership for the laity. The sense of distance between these laymen and the clergy was heightened by frequent lay rejection of most of the popular devotionalism, of political conservatism (taken to be an occupational trait of the clergy), of excessive attachment to middle-class values and an anti-Communism indifferent to pressing social ills and human injustices. The fact too that so much of the theological inspiration behind these early lay activities and orientations could be traced to European sources, mainly French, was still another source of separation. The few priests allied with these laymen shared most of their complaints and often felt a comparable estrangement from popular Catholicism.

The Impact of the War

With the end of World War II some important changes were on the horizon. Their first impact was to make more of a difference to the Catholic in American society than to the lay renaissance within the Church. The years immediately following the war saw an intensification of efforts to develop the lay apostolate rather than any new change in direction. Many lay groups sprang up in the late forties, but most of them had their genesis in pre-war thinking. If, as it turned out, they were received more enthusiastically than before, this had as much to do with the changing social role of the Catholic as it did with the intrinsic merits of the movements themselves.

As we have perhaps only lately come to realize, World War II set in motion a whole train of social developments, the full force of which Catholics are now feeling in all aspects of their lives. It was not so much that World War II itself brought about any upheaval in the Catholic community; in that respect, World War I and the end of mass immigration were probably felt more directly. Its real effect was rather to speed up very abruptly the whole process of assimilation and Americanization which had been going on for some decades. To the various Catholic ethnic groups that had already been in the process of decomposition, the war dealt a decisive blow. And whereas even prior to the war Catholics had been participating in the economic, geographical and status mobility of American society, the war served to redouble these trends, mixing Americans in a way they had hardly dreamed of even in the palmiest days of the twenties. Adding to these forces of acculturation, powerful enough in themselves, was the post-war prosperity. More and more, Catholics were coming to live among non-Catholics and, at the same time, to possess the money and goods that had enabled the Anglo-Saxon Protestants to maintain cultural dominance for generations.

Yet it must be emphasized that while these social changes were taking place, they co-existed with many visible remnants of older attitudes; little thought was at first given to the way Catholicism should relate to the new social opportunities. In this sense, the American Catholic religious mentality appears to have lagged behind the changing sociological position of Catholics; not until at least the mid-fifties would the full implications be seen.

It is useful to take a brief look at the more important social changes—

and at some of the controversies attendant upon them. A useful point of departure is Kenneth Underwood's book, *Protestant and Catholic*,[13] which represents the results of an intensive study of Catholic-Protestant relations in Holyoke, Massachusetts, in the years 1947-48. Underwood's study has a double significance. On the one hand, it tells us something about how one predominantly Catholic community behaved socially and politically just after the war. On the other hand, it presents an image of Catholicism in action which a great many Catholic intellectuals and lay leaders themselves had of the Church in America.

What was the image which emerged from that study? Perhaps the most characteristic note was that, given the slightest opportunity, Catholics would not hesitate to ride roughshod over non-Catholics. In an incident involving Margaret Sanger, Catholic pressures led to the cancellation of a talk she was scheduled to give at a *Protestant* church and the shifting of the talk to a union hall. Underwood discovered not only that many of the clergy and laity felt they had a full right to use any type of coercion necessary to prevent their consciences from being violated, however remotely, but also that there was so little contact between the Catholic majority and Protestant minority that it was impossible to adjudicate disputes by informal discussion and cooperation. Nor was there, by and large, any desire among Catholics to break down the cultural barriers which separated them from Protestants.

Underwood found that Catholics felt they had a perfect right to shape the moral consensus of Holyoke; accordingly, they evinced little interest in minority rights. Further, he discovered that some eighty per cent of the Catholic pastors saw no moral issues for the Church in such problems as low-income housing, tax and welfare policies, labor-management relations, political reform and economic stability. In the light of these findings, it is not surprising that Underwood concluded that the Holyoke clergy offered the laity little in the way of social or moral leadership.

Yet even in this study a portent of the future was clear. For Underwood noted that the higher the educational level of Catholics, and the higher their income, the more likely they were to resist certain kinds of clerical thinking; it was the most highly educated who were the most critical of Catholic pressure exerted against Margaret Sanger. The more educated "appear to be less rigid in their doctrinal content and less dependent upon Catholic moral teaching for their judgments of 'correct'

[13] Boston, 1961.

action. On basic religious matters . . . they respect the Church deeply and support its demands with enthusiasm."[14] What Underwood did not say, though his conclusions suggest it, was that, lacking social and moral guidance from the clergy, the more educated laity were prone to shape their own values. Moreover, and this Underwood did suggest, their higher income brought them into much closer contact with Protestants. Consequently, they were "much more appreciative of the role of the Protestant churches in supplementing or correcting Catholic action."

At the same time, it is well to bear in mind that Underwood did find a basic loyalty to the *Church*; but this did not necessarily mean a rigid adherence to the demands of the local clergy. Such a pattern has, by now, become much more common. Significantly, one of the major aims of the various lay groups which were rapidly growing in the late forties was to combat the discernible dissociation of religious and social values among Catholics; and one of their basic criticisms of the clergy was that their indifference to the religious implications of social problems fostered that dissociation. (Presumably, none of these newer groups existed in Holyoke during those years.) If the town Underwood chose was an exceptional one, there seems little doubt that the mentality of the Catholics he found there could be duplicated in lesser degrees elsewhere.

Inevitably, though, a change had to come. At the end of World War II, perhaps sixty-five per cent of the Catholic population were members of the lower classes. But with the post-war boom, the G.I. Bill, and the progressive move of great numbers of Catholics to the suburbs, the old urban patterns were rapidly becoming a thing of the past. In particular, the move to the suburbs had a special place in the break-up of earlier urban ways. As Father Andrew Greeley cogently points out in *The Church and the Suburbs*,[15] the mass exodus to the suburbs created new and complex problems for the Church: prosperity, the sometimes harmful effects of pluralism, a change in lay-clergy relations marked by more criticism of the clergy, a confused role for the priest, a less rigid attitude toward authority—and the very real possibility of religious indifferentism. Yet, despite all the problems, there were also many positive effects, notably the opening up of new possibilities for a vigorous laity. Both priests and clergy accepted the challenge of the suburbs in a more confident manner than had marked the Catholic response to urban life.

[14] *Ibid.*, pp. 94-95.
[15] New York, 1959.

Indeed, if Robert D. Cross is correct, one of the important shortcomings of the American Church has been its fearful and defeatist attitude toward city life.[16] In contrast, the suburbs have become a new frontier where Catholics and non-Catholics together are responsible for the shaping of the moral and cultural climate. If one can blame the suburbs for some of the obvious ills of American society, Catholics at least cannot claim that they came to them as aliens and outsiders forced to resist pre-established hostile forces.

As important as all these changes were in the late forties and early fifties, Catholics had not yet escaped from the effects of their background. Almost all surveys made in the early and mid-fifties showed that, as a group, Catholics lagged behind both Protestants and Jews in economic attainment, civic prominence and educational achievements. Even those Catholics who graduated from college were, by economic standards at least, less successful than members of most other American religious groups.[17] Whatever occupation one might choose—with the possible exceptions of law and medicine—Catholics were notably absent from positions of leadership and influence; they were rising, but it was still too early to say that they had arrived at a level of full economic and social equality.

Partly because of this Americanization, partly because of the urbane anti-Catholicism represented by a Paul Blanshard and partly because of the sharp division of opinion which the McCarthy era introduced into Catholic discussions of "the American way of life," the fifties saw the re-emergence of an analysis of the place of Catholics in American life. For the first time since the Americanist crisis, the question of the compatibility of American pluralism and Catholic principles became a live, indeed burning, issue. On the one hand, as a result of an increased incidence of Catholic boycotts against objectionable films and books, of Catholic pressures to keep birth-control laws on the books in some states, of the resistance by political force to changes in the divorce laws in other states, and of many other community conflicts, Catholics were

---

[16] "The Changing Image of the City Among American Catholics," *Catholic Historical Review*, XLVIII (April, 1962), pp. 33-52. Cross sees this defeatist attitude as helping to "account for the tendency of Catholic Churchmen to concentrate upon resisting the city's impact on the Church instead of developing the Church's impact on the city" (p. 52).

[17] Cf. John J. Kane, "The Social Structure of American Catholics," *American Catholic Sociological Review*, XVI (March, 1955), pp. 23-31.

once again challenged to prove their full acceptance of the First Amendment to the Constitution and the right of free speech, a free press and a free electorate. On the other hand, the writings of Father John Courtney Murray, S.J., published in *Theological Studies* between the late forties and early fifties, re-opened on the theological plane the question of the Church's teaching on the relationship of Church and State. Thus both the necessity of self-defense on the civic and political level and the positive efforts by a few theologians to settle once and for all the theoretical compatibility between Catholicism and pluralistic democracy engendered a mass of writings, lectures, and symposiums on American Catholic manners, mores and community goals.

To these more obvious causes of Catholic debate and discussion must be added still another: the presence on the American scene of a growing number of articulate laymen and priests who, accepting without question the general compatibility of their faith and American principles, were intent on discovering the precise relationship between the two. Beginning with the national debate over the methods and aims of Senator Joseph McCarthy in the early fifties, the terms "liberal" and "conservative" came into play to designate different Catholic approaches to social and political questions.

On the liberal side, men like James O'Gara, John Cogley and William Clancy at *The Commonweal*, Father Robert Hartnett, S.J., at *America*, Donald McDonald at the Davenport *Messenger*, and Joseph Cunneen at *Cross Currents*, began to urge their fellow Catholics to abandon ghettoism and separatism; to embrace the cause of social and political reform; to oppose the kind of political coercion and national fear engendered by McCarthy and his followers; to urge internationalism in place of jingoistic nationalism; to press for racial justice, civil liberties and academic freedom.[18] In particular, the Catholic liberal urged his fellow Catholic not to be overly zealous in the manipulation of political power—to think first of the common national good before pressing to legislate his beliefs on non-Catholics. So too the Catholic liberal was passionately devoted to the idea of inter-faith goodwill and cooperation. When Christian ecumenicism and the concept of "dialogue" appeared during the mid-fifties, it was the Catholic liberals who first hailed and publicized them.

[18] A useful book on the characteristics of this group is *Catholicism in America*, by the editors of *The Commonweal* (New York, 1954).

On the conservative side, a different emphasis was apparent. In the pages of diocesan newspapers such as the *Brooklyn Tablet*, in the national weekly paper, *Our Sunday Visitor*, and in the writings of such men as Fathers James Gillis and Richard Ginder, almost all of the values expressed by the liberals were violently rejected. The Catholic conservative was prone to choose national security over civil liberties, to oppose inter-faith contacts and movements, to urge Catholics to preserve their values at all costs in the face of a rising secularism, to see in the agitation for social justice an occasion for Communist subversion, to suspect Catholic liberals of temporizing with Catholic principles, and to support any effort which would enable divine law to be fully backed by the sanctions of civil law.

In the eyes of the Catholic liberal, the conservative was tainted by the fears and worries of bygone ages and excessively pessimistic about the course of American culture and opinion. In the eyes of the Catholic conservative, the liberal was selling out Catholicism to the secularism of the age and was all too willing to elevate civic harmony and peace above timeless verities which admit of no compromise. For both, Catholicism and American values were perfectly compatible—as long as one understood which values were genuinely American. Moreover, each had recourse to the teachings of the Church to support his reading of the American system. The liberal saw in contemporary papal social teaching the basis for a rich, progressive and happy relationship between Catholic values and American institutions. The conservative, less inclined to defer to contemporary papal teachings (unless they referred to the evils of Communism) than to older theological tracts, saw America as at bottom dependent upon Catholic moral teachings for its ultimate survival. If, at first, the Catholic liberal was on the defensive, by the end of the fifties it was the Catholic conservative who was losing ground; by then, papal social thought, ecumenicism, internationalism and social justice were becoming accepted parts of the American Catholic consensus. Yet pockets of conservative resistance remained strong.

An End to Complacency

While it is hazardous to draw sharp boundary lines, the year 1955 seems to have marked the beginning of a new direction in Catholic self-analysis. In the fall of that year the Jesuit quarterly *Thought* published an article by Monsignor John Tracy Ellis entitled "American Catholics and the Intellectual Life."[19] The substance of Monsignor Ellis' article was not unfamiliar: that, in proportion to their numbers, Catholics were notably deficient in producing their share of scholars and intellectuals. Similar complaints had been made in the twenties and thirties. What distinguished Monsignor Ellis' study from earlier ones, however, was his sharp indictment of American Catholics. Granting the many sociological and historical reasons which helped in part to explain the lack of a strong American Catholic intellectual tradition, he nevertheless could say that, "The chief blame, I firmly believe, lies with Catholics themselves. It lies in their frequently self-imposed ghetto mentality which prevents them from mingling as they should with their non-Catholic colleagues, and in their lack of industry. . . . It lies in their failure to have measured up to their responsibilities to the incomparable tradition of Catholic learning of which they are the direct heirs."

The effect of Monsignor Ellis' indictment was profound. In the years immediately following the publication of his article a flood of literature appeared on the subject of American Catholics and the intellectual life; almost all of it, in its direct inspiration, could be traced to Monsignor Ellis.[20] In the most obvious respect, then, his article touched off a major debate in American Catholicism, initiated an historically important period of highly intensified self-criticism, and opened a new quest for Catholic intellectual excellence.

But it had a still more profound effect, one which has gone unnoticed. For as the above quotation makes clear, Monsignor Ellis had to a great extent repudiated the traditional line of American Catholic self-analysis, that is, economic disadvantages, immigrant difficulties and anti-Catholicism as providing the sole explanations for Catholic deficiencies. Instead, while granting the great importance of these influences, he said that Catholics were themselves directly—and culpably—responsible for their shortcomings. To be sure, scattered individuals had said the same thing before, but none had the same effect on American Catholicism; none

[19] *Thought*, XXX (Autumn, 1955); the essay was also published as a book: *American Catholics and the Intellectual Life* (Chicago, 1956).
[20] Cf. especially Thomas F. O'Dea, *American Catholic Dilemma* (New York, 1958); Gustave Weigel, S.J., "American Catholic Intellectualism: A Theologian's Reflections," *Review of Politics*, XIX (July, 1957); Justus George Lawler, *The Catholic Dimension in Higher Education* (Westminster, Md., 1959); Leo Ward, *New Life in Catholic Schools* (St. Louis, 1958); and Christ and Sherry, *op. cit.*

could command the same audience as that distinguished American Catholic historian. With one blow, the direction and tone of Catholic self-criticism was changed. While considerable respect was still paid to sociological conditions, the real culprit was rapidly accepted to be the American Catholic mentality. In earlier generations, society, poverty and oppression were taken to be the villains; after Monsignor Ellis' attack they were taken to be the manners, mores and values of American Catholics—and their institutional manifestations and causes.

Once this period of self-criticism was under way, three distinct themes could be seen in the literature and speeches which appeared from every side. On one level—the most widespread and popular—the question of Catholics and the intellectual life was seen as concerning the effectiveness of Catholic higher education. Were the Catholic colleges instilling in their students a genuine love of learning and respect for things of the mind? Were the Catholic colleges producing graduates who could hold their own in comparison with graduates of non-Catholic colleges? By and large, the most common answers were in the negative. And the most common explanations were that the Catholic colleges were overly concerned with preserving the faith and morals of their graduates at the expense of reverence for intellectual values; that the Catholic colleges were cut off from the main stream of American intellectual life; that they were excessively interested in athletics, new buildings and vocationalism; and that they aped the worst aspects of American higher education instead of the best.

A second theme which appeared with great frequency was that American Catholics showed a depressing and disconcerting strain of anti-intellectualism. Whatever the historical and sociological reasons, it seemed to many observers that Catholics were all too quick to join in the condemnation of "fuzzy-minded intellectuals" and "eggheads" which was a feature of the McCarthy era. Far from respecting the work of scholars and thinkers, Catholics were inclined to see them as posing threats to American and Christian values. Moreover, along with this distrust of intellectuals, Catholics appeared to be obsessively interested in middle-class American values: the accumulation of wealth and status symbols, social respectability, conformity to the manners and mores of popular culture. In sum, too many Catholics were in practice denying the great intellectual traditions of Catholicism; in place of these traditions American Catholics had substituted all the worst aspects of contemporary culture.

The third theme was that American Catholics were burdened with a number of attitudes which were a distortion of intellectual and Catholic values. Though far less commonly stressed in the popular forum, this theme was in the long run to have the most significant and revolutionary implications. Perhaps its clearest expression was found in Thomas F. O'Dea's book *American Catholic Dilemma*. Mature intellectual activity among Catholics, he wrote, was hindered by "the basic characteristics of the American Catholic milieu": formalism, authoritarianism, clericalism, moralism, and defensiveness.[21] No sooner had O'Dea's themes been introduced than the problem of Catholic intellectualism became merely one of a far broader spectrum of questions: What is the role of the Catholic in the world? What is the nature of authority and obedience in Catholicism? How ought the Catholic to relate himself to non-Catholic values? How much and what kind of freedom does the Catholic have in the Church? To what extent and in what ways is the Catholic free to make up his own mind in matters of politics, ideologies, intellectual and scientific trends—and faith and morals?

In the aftermath, the discussion about Catholics and the intellectual life turned out to be only a useful point of departure for a discussion about the nature and direction of contemporary American Catholicism. It was not, surprising, then, that specific discussions about the initial subject of debate—Catholic intellectualism—ran a relatively short though fiery course. Once that subject was vigorously confronted it was not difficult to come up with some solutions: the raising of academic standards, the acceptance of excellence as a goal of the colleges, curriculum changes, a more urgent quest for good faculties, higher endowments, and so forth. But when it came to confronting the broader issue of what it meant to be a Catholic in the modern world, and in the contemporary Church, it was far harder to formulate specific goals. For those questions, unlike the ones narrowly related to Catholic higher education, were not so amenable to solution.

It was one thing to decide, as many Catholic colleges did, that honors programs for the brighter students would be a fruitful venture. It was quite another to decide how free the Catholic ought to be to inquire into the teachings of the Church, how independent he ought to be as a citizen of the Church's social teachings, how much freedom he had to differ with his parish priest, his bishop or the pope. But these were

[21] O'Dea, *op. cit.*, pp. 155ff.

exactly the kinds of problems which were to come out of the great debate on Catholics and the intellectual life; and they were also the great problems which were at the root of much of the earlier but continuing discussion of Catholicism and American society. The greater the success of the Catholic community in solving its lesser problems, the more formidable and pressing became the larger ones.

The role of the laity in Church and society is precisely one of those larger problems; indeed, it occupies the very center of the stage, raising in a direct way all the most pressing issues of contemporary Catholicism: the nature and extent of ecclesiastical authority; the relationship of the priestly and prophetical elements in the Church; the question of self-determination and independence for the individual Catholic—the problem of conscience; the relationship between man as believer and man as citizen, between Catholic values and democratic values. In the end, the way the Church solves the problem of the laity will be an index of the way it has chosen to work out many of its other broad problems. That the laity should emerge as a central concern in our day seems, in a sense, inevitable. It bespeaks the increasing maturity of the Church; but it also bespeaks the fact that the Church, for all its success in coping with lesser problems, has barely touched the larger ones.

Part Two

Part Two

CHAPTER 5

Changing Church, Changing Layman

In CERTAIN ERAS, the Church seems to create its own problems; in others, it is the society in which it is immersed which thrusts them upon the Church. In our era, however, no such easy distinction is possible. Both Church and society have been on the move; society has created problems and dilemmas for the Church, but the Church too has been busy raising its own fresh questions and recognizing new demands which the times have pressed upon it.

The problem of the laity is a perfect illustration. On the one hand, the nature of the society in which we live has placed on the shoulders of the layman many moral and social burdens undreamed of by earlier generations. That these burdens are the fruit, in many instances, of successful assimilation does not alter that fact. Inevitably, both the lay Catholic and the Church have to confront American society. On the other hand, the Church itself, in its modes of worship, in its theology, in its social thinking, has been changing rapidly—the fruit of the work of a new generation of thinkers ever more intent upon plumbing the mysteries of the Christian message. From the outside, then, society is pressing upon the Church. From the inside, Catholics themselves are pressing.

That this dynamic interaction of inner and outer forces should have come to bear so heavily on the problem of the laity is hardly surprising. When one surveys the broad period from the end of World War I up through the present, the inevitability of this development becomes apparent. For that was a time which saw the final breakdown of ethnic Catholicism and the final phases of assimilation. It saw Catholics, after generations of explanations, excuses and sometimes evasions, finally put their minds to work on their own failings rather than those of their non-

103

Catholic neighbors. It saw, finally, the emergence of an educated and increasingly outspoken body of Catholics no longer content to accept the mediocre in Catholic life, no longer content with Catholic separatism and ineffectiveness—no longer content, in O'Dea's terms, with authoritarianism, clericalism, formalism, moralism and defensiveness.

At the same time that all these great social and cultural changes are taking place among American Catholics, the Church universal is changing. New currents of theological thought are slowly being felt by all Catholics: the biblical revival, the liturgical and ecumenical movements, the accelerated pace of Catholic social thinking, the new emphasis on human freedom, the impact of existential and personalist currents, the idea of unity and brotherhood of all men. Rarely in the history of the Church have so many creative, genuinely probing, genuinely progressive trends emerged in such a short time. Rarely have so many theologians, on so many fronts, thrown themselves so vigorously into the task of renewing Catholic life and thought, into finding new paths and rejecting outworn ones. Rarely too has a general theological ferment filtered down so rapidly among the people; the time lag between the creative work of theologians and its direct influence on the lives of ordinary Catholics is becoming shorter. Among the educated and theologically informed laymen, the impact is now felt almost immediately. What is avant garde one year may be common coin the next.

Nor can one fail to notice the increasingly great influence of non-Catholic thought among Catholics. Not only are the theologians coming to adapt non-Catholic terms, concepts and modes of thought to Catholic purposes and aims, but the educated layman himself is more prone than ever to give a serious hearing to intellectual trends originating outside of the Church. It is sometimes said that one great glory of the Church is that it can assimilate to itself truths discovered by those not of its fold. But it might just as fairly be said that the great triumph of non-Catholic thought is that it has been able to influence even so conservative a body as the Catholic Church. In any event, even the most cursory examination of recent Catholic writing reveals the influence of contemporary Jewish thought (Buber's "I-Thou" relationship); of contemporary probing into the mysteries of evolution; of Freudianism; of the cultural anthropologists; of the philosophical existentialists. It would, in fact, be no exaggeration to say that many of the most vital intellectual currents in contemporary Catholicism could be traced to some initial source outside of the Church.

Three general forces are, then, having a powerful impact on the Catholic: the social confrontation with American society, the rapidly evolving thought of Catholic theologians, and the powerful force of non-Catholic intellectual currents. At the focal point of these forces is the Catholic layman. His is the steadily more complex task of finding a way of harmonizing the values of the society in which he lives and the Church of which he is a member. As if this task were not difficult enough, he must attempt this harmonization at a time when the Church itself is in a state of rapid change. He is a member of a society which is changing, a social minority which is changing, and a Church which is changing. Given such a variety of changes, given such powerful forces at work on him, who can be surprised that he should show all signs of both heady excitement and enthusiasm—and profound confusion and bewilderment? By turns, the layman today is heartened and depressed, confident and apprehensive, passive and rebellious, defensive and belligerent, honest and evasive. Amidst all these stresses and strains, the tasks of the layman have become clear. He must find out how he is to use his new social freedom. He must find out what his place and function is in the Church. He must find out how and in what ways he is to express his values in society. Of all these tasks, that of finding his place in the Church has become the most urgent.

The question I want to look into now is this: where does the layman stand in the American Church? This can only be answered by asking and answering a number of other questions: where does the layman *think* he stands? where does he *want* to stand? where does he think he *ought* to stand? There is, to be sure, a "problem of the laity." But what exactly is this problem? The trouble, of course, with all of these questions is that they admit of no decisive answers. Too much, in the end, depends upon individual circumstances, geographical location, social and educational background to make any neat generalizations; one must rely on rough indications. I make then no pretense at offering a complete account of the layman's present place—or his thinking about that place —in the American Church. What follows is an interpretation of a variety of facts, a welter of confusing and sometimes contradictory clues.

Sources of Lay Vigor

We may look first at some of the more obvious reasons for the prominence of the lay question in the American Church today. As suggested in the previous chapter, it was the history of the American laymen in the past four or five decades which set the stage. But there are, beyond the tide of history, some more immediate causes for the lay emergence.

First, there can be little doubt that the exhortations, encouragement and pleas of recent popes for a more effective and active laity have had a major impact on Catholic thinking. There have been at least two specific motives for these exhortations, one which could be called practical and the other theological. In his important address to the Second World Congress of the Lay Apostolate in 1957, Pope Pius XII said: "One of the reasons for this call to the laity is undoubtedly the present shortage of priests. . . . We need only mention the important contribution of Catholic teachers and religious to the teaching of religion. . . . On the other hand, even independently of the small number of priests, the relations between the Church and the world demand the presence of lay apostles. The *consecratio mundi* (consecration of the world) is in its essence the task of laymen, of men who are intimately involved in economic and social life, who take part in government and in legislative assemblies."[1]

Underlying these two specific motives, however, is a still broader one: "It would be a misunderstanding of the true nature of the Church and her social character to distinguish in her a purely active element, the ecclesiastical authorities, and on the other hand, a purely passive element, the laity. All the members of the Church, as We Ourselves have said, in the encyclical *Mystici Corporis Christi*, are called to collaborate in the building and perfecting of the Mystical Body of Christ. All are free persons and must therefore be active." Almost all recent papal and episcopal statements on the laity have incorporated at least one of these motives, and frequently all of them. Significantly, each of them reflects contemporary trends in Catholic life and theology. Both the concept of *consecratio mundi* and the Church as the Mystical Body of Christ mark, in particular, new directions in modern Catholic theology.

Second, there has been a marked increase in recent decades in the number of educated Catholics. Today, more than at any time in the history of the American Church (or the Church universal, for that matter), there are thousands of Catholic college graduates, thousands

---

[1] "The Lay Apostolate," translated in London by the Catholic Truth Society, 1957. An excellent general collection of papal statements on the laity can be found in *The Lay Apostolate* (Boston, 1961).

of Catholic graduates of non-Catholic universities, and many well-in-formed Catholic high school graduates. Even granting the many failures of Catholic education, there can be little doubt that there is a strong and vital spiritual zeal among a vast number of Catholic laymen. The main characteristic of this new generation is its unwillingness to limit its religious life to a minimal observance of Church laws or a purely in-terior, private spiritual life. Unavoidably, such widespread zeal has made the problem of the laity's role in the Church a central one. For the new zeal reflects, in great part, those trends in Catholic thought which em-phasize the active part all must play in the Church and the specific task of consecrating the temporal world. If the popes had not emphasized the relationship of the laity to these trends, it is likely in any event that the laity itself would have seen the connection. One way or another, wide-spread Catholic education would have brought into sharp relief the question of the laity.

Third, along with the growing number of educated Catholics has come an increasingly sophisticated and critical turn of mind. While a critical turn of mind is a natural characteristic of the educated man, it has a special relevance for the educated Catholic. He has cast a sharp eye not only on the society in which he lives but on the Church as well. "There has inevitably appeared," Monsignor John Tracy Ellis has said, "a closer scrutiny of all that pertains to the Church, a sharper and more critical turn of mind which makes the educated Catholic layman of the second half of the twentieth century a quite different person from his unlettered immigrant grandparents of two or three generations ago."[2]

Yet the importance of this latter development would not be so great were it not for two other trends which have strengthened it: self-criticism as an accepted part of Catholic life and a greater receptivity on the part of the Catholic press and Catholic publishers to controversial discussions and debates. The first trend has already been touched upon in the preceding chapter. It may, however, be said of the second that the soul-searching that preceded the Second Vatican Council, taken together with a widespread movement sharply to distinguish "official" Catholic thinking from personal opinions, has made controversy a part of Ameri-can Catholicism. And it may be added that the theologically sophisti-cated layman has shown himself increasingly adept at employing the

2 "The Catholic Layman in America Today," *The Commonweal*, LXXVI (June 22, 1962), p. 320.

kinds of subtle distinctions once used exclusively by theologians. That is, he is learning how to write and speak about delicate and fundamental matters in such a way as to avoid the charge of meddling in matters that don't concern him; or, when the charge is leveled, of avoiding its implications by a persuasive employment of the teachings of the magisterium itself. (The debates between liberal and conservative laymen over the meaning and importance of some recent papal encyclicals have been a prime instance of this adeptness.)

Fourth, the pioneering work of a few theologians, mainly European, on the layman's role in the Church has added a solid, if still incomplete, theological dimension to the discussion. Father Yves Congar's book *Lay People in the Church* has been the most influential. But Michael de la Bedoyere's *The Layman in the Church*, Msgr. Gerard Phillips' *The Role of the Laity in the Church*, Jacques Leclercq's *Christians in the World* and J. M. Perrin's *Forward the Layman* have also had a powerful influence. At the same time, numerous works on the parish, the social apostolate and lay spirituality have made their impression. A special place is held by those writings which stem from the liturgical movement, one of whose chief aims has been to bring about a more meaningful participation of the laity in the worship life of the Church.

Fifth, the mushrooming lay apostolate movements have brought the question of the laity far more sharply to the fore than previously. In the late thirties, the forties and in the early fifties, such specialized organizations as the Christian Family Movement, Young Christian Workers and the Young Christian Students involved a comparatively homogeneous group of people closely united with one another by a fairly clear understanding of their goals. But with size and growth have come a variety of new and sometimes conflicting influences and a variety of different conceptions of their methods and strategies; and not a few of these new divisions have turned on differing understandings of the layman's role. So, too, the growth of these organizations has brought them into much closer contact with the hierarchy; by entering into the main stream of American Catholicism they have had to submit their activities to closer official scrutiny. This has not only limited their organizational independence to some extent; but it has also led, in a few instances, to lay-episcopal clashes turning on the question of lay independence and initiative.

Sixth, there seems little reason to doubt that social and cultural freedom in American society have led the layman to seek greater freedom and equality within the Church. The layman of a hundred years ago, who was socially deprived and in a culturally subservient position, was understandably docile as a member of the Church. In Church or out, inferiority and the bottom rung of the ladder were his accepted lot. But in our day the layman is likely to have a considerable degree of social freedom: he can aspire to and achieve positions of leadership and control; he can criticize and reject those aspects of American life of which he does not approve; he can live where he likes, act as he likes, read what he likes; however remotely, he has a say in the way he is governed, a choice of those who are to govern him, a voice in the laws of the land, a bill of rights, and courts to judge his grievances impartially. As a layman in the Church he enjoys few of these privileges—and he cannot help noting the difference between his state as a citizen and his state as a Catholic layman.

It is hardly surprising, then, that the layman should on occasion seek within the Church some of the same rights as he has in society. In no way does this mean that he is intent on overthrowing the hierarchical, authoritarian structure of the Church; there is no evidence to support such an assertion. But it does mean that he is likely to be attracted to those quite legitimate theological developments which, of late, have stressed the value of lay consultation, free speech in the Church, the right of appeal against unfavorable hierarchical decisions and the acceptability of differing interpretations of the Church's teaching. It means, in short, that the layman today is prone to seek as much freedom for himself within the Church as is compatible with the nature of the Church, as much leeway for personal decision as is compatible with the divinely fixed authority of the Church. He has no desire to overthrow that authority. But he would, if possible, like the contrast between his role as citizen and his role as faithful Catholic reduced. If he is a free man in society, can he not have greater freedom in the Church? That is the question which his successful social assimilation has put before his eyes.

Now it may immediately be seen that these six causes are hardly of a single kind: some can be called theological, others sociological. Each, however, bespeaks change—in the Church and in the cultural characteristics of the layman. Just how influential each one is, just how each ought to be ranked in importance, seems to me unanswerable. What is clear is that no one of these causes could alone explain the present burning interest of the layman in his own situation. It is most common, of course, for Catholics to lay the greater stress on the theological and hierarchical exhortations, or on the newly awakened zeal of laymen to realize their faith more fully in their personal and public lives. Thus in most popular writing on the layman, emphasis is given to the appeals of the popes, the "challenges" before him, and the new spiritual vistas open to him who will respond to the call of the Church and the needs of the world. Undoubtedly, lay zeal has been of tremendous importance.

Yet theological explanations have tended to obscure the vital role played by the changing social conditions of the layman. Were it not for the fact of widespread economic security, social mobility and the breaking down of class and educational barriers, it seems highly unlikely that such vigor would be present—or at least would have taken its present form. For it presupposes in the layman a certain amount of leisure time, civic influence, political choice, surplus spiritual energy, and a desire to do something more than survive and raise a family. Moreover, it seems highly unlikely that he would be so concerned about his role in the Church if he were not living in a society which emphasized the value of personal responsibility and self-determination.[3]

In brief, then, the emergence of the problem of the layman is indicative of both a theological and a social upheaval in the Church and in the Catholic community; neither upheaval is by itself sufficient explanation. When seen in the perspective of earlier periods of lay renaissance in the American Church, it is clear how important the interaction of theological and sociological causes are. As previously indicated, a number of conditions appear necessary for a genuine lay movement: the support of the hierarchy; a general Church renaissance; a confident Church; lay leaders who have come to terms with the society in which they live; an educated body of lay leaders; the existence of a tension between the values of the Church and the values of society; and a desire on the part of the layman to achieve some of the same privileges within the Church that he enjoys in society. All of these conditions were present, for a small minority at least, during the late 1880s and early 1890s. They are

---

[3] It seems safe to suppose that one reason so little attention is paid to the influence of democratic values on the layman is a general fear, on the part of most lay leaders, of giving the impression that "secular" values have undermined their respect for the values and ways of ecclesiastical authority.

now present again—yet this time on a scale which far surpasses anything known to the American Church in the past.

Progress and Tensions

Unfortunately, the mere existence of favorable conditions is no guarantee that either the aspirations of the laity to play a more integral role in the Church, or the aspirations of the clergy and hierarchy that they do so, will be realized. Hopes, desires and ambitions are one thing, implementation another; theory one thing, practice another. As it has turned out, the stronger the lay movement has become, the more apparent have become the difficulties in bringing it to full realization.

Before examining these difficulties, it would be well to indicate some important signs of progress. For it is undoubtedly true that there has been progress. At no time in the history of the American Church have there been so many laymen actively engaged in serving the Church. There are thousands of laymen, for one thing, teaching in Catholic schools—from the grammar school to the graduate level. The growth of their numbers has been little short of spectacular. In 1948, for instance, there were some 7400 lay teachers in parochial and secondary schools. By 1960 there were at least 35,000. One in every three teachers is now a layman. In Catholic colleges and universities there are now two lay teachers for every one religious. And, with no signs of abatement, the ratio of lay to religious teachers continues to grow in favor of the layman.[4] Still another sign of progress is the number of laymen actively involved in lay organizations. Not only have the specialized lay movements such as the Christian Family Movement grown at a spectacular rate, but the older lay organizations have also registered tremendous gains. Taken together, membership in lay organizations now numbers well over five million. To be sure, this figure is greatly swelled by such massive groups as the Holy Name Societies and the Knights of Columbus, many of the activities of which are more social than spiritual or apostolic. Yet even these organizations are far more active and creative than at any time in the past and increasingly aware of the necessity of breaking from past orientations.

[4] William H. Conley, "The Lay Teacher in Catholic Education," in *Proceedings of the Fifty-ninth Annual Convention of the National Catholic Educational Association* (April, 1962), p. 27.

Of great significance too is the slow increase in the number of bishops attempting to give the layman a larger voice in diocesan matters. There now exist dioceses in which layman have been appointed to diocesan synods, ecumenical boards and educational commissions. In many instances they are charged with providing the bishop with information, recommendations and advice on matters of broad diocesan policy; no longer in some places are laymen asked merely to assist in money-raising campaigns or to make available only their business talents.

Membership in organizations is, however, not the only sign of lay vitality. Of equal importance is the proliferation of adult education courses devoted to giving the layman a more intelligent understanding of his faith and its meaning in the modern world. Every major American city has at least one program designed to provide the adult layman with an introduction to theology. Many cities have fully developed educational programs under diocesan auspices touching upon almost every aspect of Catholic life. With few exceptions, these programs are well attended and enthusiastically received. No less important is the fact that Catholic book publishers are finding the contemporary Catholic layman unusually eager for solid theological and spiritual writings; well over five hundred new books are published every year for Catholic readers. And Catholic magazine publishers are finding an equally receptive audience. At a time when secular journals have a difficult time gaining new readers, Catholic ones have been registering spectacular circulation gains. So too the dozens of diocesan newspapers have not only grown rapidly in circulation, but they have also felt themselves under great pressure to provide more sophisticated reading fare.

This catalogue could easily be expanded. One could add to the list the sudden growth of secular institutes, the formation of such new movements as the Papal Volunteers which have the aim of enabling young men and women to do apostolic-social work abroad, the numerous Bible study groups, Mass preparation groups, and many other lay activities. Yet few of these would exist were it not for the active support and encouragement of the hierarchy and the clergy. Hardly a week goes by without an episcopal sermon, address or pastoral encouraging the layman to be more active in the service of the Church, to take advantage of the lay organizations designed for his benefit, to read and think more diligently and creatively. And countless thousands of priests work with great energy to perfect their parish life, to entice or prod their parishioners into parish organizations, to educate and to invigorate their flock, to strengthen their spiritual life and love of the Church.

My main purpose here, however, is not to catalogue the great gains made by the laity or to list the various ways in which the hierarchy and clergy have attempted to give their support. These gains exist and cannot be ignored. In comparison with earlier generations, the picture is very bright. But it is not the whole picture. With these advances have come an equal number of problems and dilemmas—in many instances generated by success. Most importantly, the more advanced the lay movement has become, the more clearly have hitherto unsuspected difficulties arisen. Some of them are of a fairly simple kind; but others raise questions of very serious import for the Church.

Without intending to slight their significance, some of the obvious problems can be discussed briefly. Perhaps the most apparent one is that the vigorous activities of many lay organizations have demonstrated the disparity between the engaged, committed Catholic and the great mass of indifferent Catholics. Though the number of laymen involved in parish or supra-parochial groups is large, the fact remains that the majority stay away. Despite the exhortations of popes, bishops, and priests, and the work of countless lay leaders, most Catholics have remained untouched by recent developments. Even in the most advanced parishes, active participation in parish life is limited to a minority. Compared with those Catholics, say, who regularly watch television, the numbers who enroll in adult theology courses are small. Compared with those Catholics who regularly read secular magazines, books or newspapers, the numbers of those who read Catholic literature are very small. Even in cities with a population of over one million Catholics, those who read their diocesan newspapers rarely exceed one hundred thousand.

Lay apathy is, then, an inescapable reality. The success of many lay organizations has shown sharply how few laymen do, in fact, lead an active Catholic life. If it is easier than in the past to arouse and stimulate the layman, it is still a frustrating experience for most pastors to attempt to gain the support necessary to put into effect even the simplest kinds of lay programs. Ironically, the more ambitious the program, the more advanced its conception, the more difficult it also is to break through the barriers of inertia. The pastor who attempts to institute liturgical reforms, raise the intellectual level of the Holy Name Society or the Sodality, create new and challenging programs, is in almost every parish faced with resistance or indifference. The complaint of many priests that the problem of the layman is his apathy, is well founded. But it may be doubted that it is the crux of the matter; the roots of apathy lie deep and do not exist in isolation.

Another obvious problem is the existence of great regional disparities in the American Church. In the Middle West, vigorous lay activity is an accepted part of Church life. Along the Eastern seaboard, it is a fairly rare phenomenon (though hardly absent). With a different tradition of lay-clergy relations, a less defensive and insular clergy and hierarchy, a more solid place in the community, the Church in the Middle West has been more receptive to the experimental, less attached to the traditional, and more alert to the possibilities of lay initiative and responsibility. By contrast, in the East and in some parts of the South and Far West, the Church is comparatively rigid and fixed in old ways. Only with great difficulty can a pastor get permission to introduce liturgical changes, establish new lay organizations and find a body of parishioners eager for renewal. Just as traditions and attitudes are different from region to region, so too the rate of change varies. At the same time it can probably be said that these regional differences will diminish with time.

In the end, however, it is the less obvious problems which are the more important. A useful way to approach them is to look at the desires and goals publicly expressed by various lay leaders. Fortunately, the three years prior to the opening of the Second Vatican Council were remarkable for producing some outspoken comments on the role of the laity in the Church.[5]

The most common desire is that there be more dialogue *in* the Church. There should be more contact and discussion among clergy and laity, and what is even more important, a way must be found to make the layman's hopes, desires and criticisms known to the bishops and the teaching authorities of the Church. Even recognized lay leaders, so runs the complaint, have little chance to discuss their problems frankly with bishops; the latter live in a world isolated from lay cares and problems. In this respect, it is urged that laymen should be given a greater consultative voice in episcopal decisions, especially those touching upon

[5] Cf. *The Layman in the Church*, ed. by James O'Gara (New York, 1962), reprinted from a series in *The Commonweal; Looking Toward the Council*, ed. by Joseph Cunneen (New York, 1962); *The Sign* (October 11, 1962), pp. 11-15; *Eucharist*, I (October, 1962), pp. 33-40.

temporal matters—that they should receive some formal status in the Church's administrative and decision-making apparatus. Overarching these specific concerns is a general plea for greater freedom of speech: freedom for the laity to discuss the actual practices and policies of the Church; to debate openly its stand on social and political issues; to submit ideas in a direct fashion.

Closely related to freedom of speech is the wish that lay organizations be given greater scope to make their own decisions, to exercise their own initiative. Most lay organizations are "lay" in name only; it is the local bishop, or the chaplain of the organization who has the decisive power. Clerical or episcopal paternalism saps lay vigor, frustrates legitimate aspirations for lay responsibility and hinders the free progress of the layman. Still another criticism is that the clergy and the hierarchy do not give enough recognition to lay intellectuals—those men best able to provide intelligent leadership for the laity and to be of assistance to the clergy and bishops in solving some of the problems facing the Church and in meeting the challenges ahead.

A common criticism is that not enough of the bishops or clergy are making a vigorous effort to provide leadership on the moral and social issues of the day. They are not, it is said, confronting the pressing problems of Catholic family planning, the population explosion, the economic and social ills of the age, or nuclear war. In sum, the kinds of problems the bishops and clergy will emphasize are not always those which most concern the laity; on his most agonizing dilemmas the layman receives little real assistance. Again, many lay leaders emphasize the obligation of bishops and priests to promulgate widely and forcefully the social teachings of the Church. The great majority of Catholics do not know the Church's more advanced views on economic life, on civil liberty, on international relations, on nationalism and on social justice—and one of the main reasons for this ignorance is that the clergy have been remiss in promulgating and explaining the papal encyclicals and the work of contemporary theologians.

Touching directly on personal religious life are the frequent appeals for a greater use of the vernacular in the liturgy—that the layman will come to participate more fully in the Mass. The liturgical movement itself is a main point of discussion. Despite repeated papal directives, a great number of bishops and pastors have not taken advantage of the liturgical movement to make the liturgy more meaningful. It is also common to hear demands that theologians and devotional writers renew their efforts to develop a spirituality relevant to the layman's state in life. Too much religious writing, the complaint runs, is actually an adaptation of a spirituality originally devised for the clerical or monastic life; too much still dwells on the dangers and distractions of the world, too little on the necessity of the layman's accepting, and attempting to shape and revivify, the world.

Finally, and perhaps most importantly, the Church has been called upon to define in some precise theological fashion the place and status of the layman. Again and again it has been pointed out that only one canon in the whole of Canon Law specifically treats of the rights of the laity, and that one in a very vague and unsatisfactory manner.[6] Similarly, it has been noted that, with almost no exceptions, the official theological tracts used in seminaries make only passing references to the laity. What little work has been done remains as yet on the outskirts of traditional Catholic theology.[7] Even the numerous papal statements on the lay apostolate, while emphasizing the importance of the layman in the Church, offer comparatively little in the way of precise theological advances in clarifying such matters as "the priesthood of the faithful" or the "priesthood of the laity," however much they may suggest that some possible meanings of these expressions are compatible with Catholic doctrine.

It would be possible to extend this list of lay desires, hopes and criticisms. Yet the most salient points have been mentioned and the broad shape of the direction of lay thinking encompassed in the general comments just presented. A number of questions immediately arise. How representative is such thinking? How widespread are these desires and criticisms? A definite answer is not possible. Those laymen who have spoken or written in this vein are the most highly educated and articulate. In addition, they would most commonly be thought of as among the more liberal. In this respect, it is notable that a conservative publication like the *Brooklyn Tablet* has shown little interest in exploring the difficulties or frustrations of the layman in the Church. This is an attitude

---

[6] Canon 682: "The laity have the right to receive from the clergy according to the rules of ecclesiastical discipline, spiritual benefits and the helps necessary for their salvation."

[7] Cf. Jeremiah Newman, *The Christian in Society* (Westminster, Md., 1962), for a discussion of this question.

found among many conservative Catholic groups, few of which have thought it necessary to address themselves to such questions. At the same time, however, it seems safe to say that the issues raised by the more liberal laymen probably reflect the thinking of many younger Catholics and of the lay leaders actively engaged in the contemporary forms of the lay apostolate. The fact that these problems have been raised and considered in such a wide variety of periodicals as *America, The Commonweal, The Sign, Ave Maria, Cross Currents, Jubilee, Perspectives* and many diocesan newspapers makes it impossible to dismiss them as representing the thinking of only a negligibly small, overly critical or overly ambitious segment of American Catholics. Equally important, this is the segment which has been the most influenced by the progressive strains of Catholic thought; thus as harbingers of future trends they probably count more heavily than the conservatives.

The next question which might be asked is even more difficult to answer. What do these desires and criticisms reveal about the mentality of the contemporary educated Catholic layman? Put another way, what is the self-image which the layman has of his present role in the Church? The educated layman is, first, sharply aware of the discrepancy between the ideal of an active responsible laity and the concrete possibilities of realizing that ideal. The Church, as he sees it, is simply not organized or structured in such a way that the full utilization of lay talent and zeal is possible. He feels, second, that a gulf exists between him and the hierarchy and clergy. Not only do they not know of his deepest needs and desires, but they are for the most part so inaccessible as to make it impossible for the layman to make his views known. Third, he believes that the Church is not at all clear on the layman's potential contribution to the Church; and it sometimes seems to him that the teaching authority in the Church is far more intent on preserving the rights of the clergy than it is in defining the rights of the layman. He believes, fourth, that he is not in fact (despite what the popes have said) considered to be a full and active member of the Church; if trust, confidence and clear mandates for action are criteria of an active role in the Church, then his present state shows those conditions to be unfulfilled.

The self-image which emerges here is, broadly speaking, one of some degree of repression, frustration, disenchantment, mild cynicism and thwarted zeal and intelligence. The layman cannot speak when he wants to, cannot be sure anyone will listen when he does speak, is not consulted even when his thinking and experience could be of profit to the Church. That all American Catholic laymen do not see themselves exactly in this light is apparent. But a considerable number do—especially those most concerned with the general problem of the laity in the Church.

We can now confront the crucial question: Why does this broadly critical, frustrated and disenchanted state of mind exist among so many laymen? This question is particularly pertinent since, as suggested, the layman has made great progress in the Church; moreover, as any number of papal and episcopal statements make clear, the Church can hardly be called indifferent to the layman or uninterested in his welfare and possible contribution to the good of the Church. Nevertheless, despite recent gains, the laity's dissatisfaction with the present state of affairs is increasing rather than diminishing. Despite the great strides the Church is taking in granting him a fuller role, the layman himself is raising his standards at an even faster pace. From many signs it seems that the more interested the Church has become in the layman, the more dissatisfied he has become with his status. For many of the clergy this is a disturbing, and sometimes galling paradox. The reward for their efforts in behalf of the layman seems to be only increased criticism and rebuke. Faced on the one hand by an apathetic mass and on the other by a sharply critical minority, it is hardly surprising that many priests and bishops should find the contemporary lay mind fickle, erratic and puzzling.

Four Realities in American Catholicism

In actuality, there need be no great mystery—though many small puzzles and riddles will remain. One way to dissolve the mystery is to see it in the context of four realities of contemporary American Catholicism. The first reality is the existence of vast social, cultural and educational differences among Catholics. The second reality is the existence of sharply diverse understandings of Catholicism among different groupings of Catholics. The third reality is that the attempt to implement contemporary advances and principles has, in practice, proved to be far more difficult than originally envisioned; in many instances the attempt at application has shown that the principles themselves are vague and insufficient. The fourth reality is the existence of deeply ingrained mores, customs and traditions which a mere zeal for reform is incapable of changing.

At the risk of drawing somewhat artificial distinctions, we might usefully see how each of these realities comes to bear on particular aspects of the lay problem. We can first turn to the question of the vitality of parish life. A frequent complaint of zealous laymen is that contemporary parish life is insufficient to meet the spiritual needs of the educated, inquiring parishioner. In the average American parish both the sermons and the parish societies are directed to the "average" parishioner; that means to parishioners with, perhaps, no more than two years of high school education (and not necessarily received in Catholic schools). Moreover, in a great many parishes there is a considerable spread of class and cultural differences, ranging from the lower to the upper-middle classes. Inevitably in such a situation those who have been highly educated are going to suffer. Even if they want to, it is sometimes exceedingly difficult for parish priests to devise sermons and parish functions which will appeal to all. Some group will, unless the circumstances are exceptional, be neglected; since they are usually in the minority, it is likely to be the educated, informed laymen.

There are still more complications. Although Catholicism itself may (and ought) to serve as a bond of solidarity among parishioners, the weight of social and educational differences often erects more personal barriers than their common faith can surmount. Thus in those parishes (perhaps the majority) where lower or lower-middle class Catholics predominate, the college-educated layman is likely to find himself hard-pressed to work constructively and smoothly with the less educated. They do not form his normal circle of friends or acquaintances and they may not share his personal social values or tastes; these are differences which are almost as hard to surmount in local churches as they are in ordinary life.

In such a situation, it sometimes proves all but impossible to shape parish organizations in such a way that they will serve the needs of all. In addition, as Father Joseph H. Fichter, S.J., has argued very plausibly, the colleges appear to be pulling the educated layman away from his parish. "The bonds of friendship," he writes, "formed in college cut across parish and diocesan lines. The academic, cultural, economic, political and even religious interests of the college student help to reduce his parochial orientation and affiliation."[8] In particular, his religious education is likely to orientate him to a broad, universal Catholicism rather than to the local Catholicism of parish life. It is hardly surprising,

[8] *Social Relations in the Urban Parish* (Chicago, 1954), pp. 174-175.

then, that many recent Catholic college graduates find parish orientations narrow, constricted and disillusioning. The better his education, unfortunately, the more likely he is to find himself frustrated, unchallenged and uninterested in his parish. Social and educational differences —the first reality of American Catholicism—thus pose some important handicaps in the shaping of an effective, satisfied laity.

The impact of the second reality of American Catholic life—diverse understandings of Catholicism—can be seen very clearly in the complaint of many lay leaders that the clergy and hierarchy have been remiss in accepting and implementing recent liturgical reforms. Yet one good reason why the American Church has been so slow to encourage these reforms is that they overthrow the individualistic, subjective and devotion-centered spirituality common to older generations of American Catholics. For these Catholics, a religious life which lays strong emphasis on personal salvation, personal devotion, and personal morality receives a rude shock when confronted with the objective, community-oriented, public character of the liturgical movement. It is not only something new, and thus unsettling, but it also seems to deny the value of much taken to be central to Catholicism.[9] For the educated and theologically sophisticated layman, however, it is precisely the objective, communal character of contemporary liturgical theology which is most meaningful and most appealing. A conflict has proved to be inescapable, and those layman committed to the liturgical movement have clashed with adherents of the older view. Similarly, there is friction between those laymen devoted to the social teachings of the Church and those more narrowly concerned with private morality. The difference here is between two currents of Catholic moral theology, the former more recent in origin.

The power of the third reality in American Catholic life—the difficulties which have arisen in trying to apply new principles—can aptly be illustrated by observing the formal lay apostolate movements. In their early days the problems were comparatively straightforward: the great need was to educate the Catholic in a more apostolic form of Catholicism, to arouse him from his slumber, to win over, on a theoretical level, those unaccustomed to think of the layman exercising any special role in the Church. The task of arousing enthusiasm and combatting

---

[9] Cf. Gregory Baum, "Conflicts and the Council," *The Commonweal*, LXXVI (September 21, 1962), pp. 511-514, for an excellent discussion of the different theological emphases of the Marian and Liturgical movements.

indifference was enough to keep these movements occupied; the subtle difficulties appeared only when some of the initial battles were won. One difficulty has already been suggested: the larger these movements become, the more they tend to be involved in diocesan bureaucracy—and diocesan prudence and caution. Another difficulty is that, as they extend their influence, the more likely they are to tread on the toes of the older lay organizations.

But perhaps the most serious difficulty stems from the fact that it has proved very hard to determine precisely what relationship holds between the lay apostolate and the teaching authority of the bishops. In one sense, it is obvious that every layman has the duty of respecting the office and authority of the bishops; but it is far less obvious just what formal relationship should obtain between the bishops and the lay apostolate movements. At one time, beginning with the pontificate of Pope Pius X, the expression "Catholic Action" was used to designate "the participation of the laity in the apostolic mission of the Church." Yet by defining Catholic Action in this way, the lay apostolate became too closely tied to the specific work of the hierarchy and too subservient to the authority and direction of the bishop. "The bishops," one writer stated, "inevitably dealt with the laity as they did with their own priests and religious, in disregard of the whole idea of the lay apostolate and its responsibilities."[10] An essential part of this older notion of Catholic Action was that it required a specific mandate from a bishop. Little room was made for those laymen who desired to work informally in the world as individuals, rather than as members of formal organizations. Still less room was made for lay initiative, creativity and responsibility within supposedly "lay" movements. The very concept of the lay apostolate has proved to carry within it many contradictions and mutually exclusive impulses.

The fourth reality—the persistence of ingrained mores, customs and traditions—can easily be seen in its influence on Catholic education. Possibly no lay complaint has been more loudly uttered than that the lay teacher in a Catholic school is treated as little more than hired help, neither greatly respected for his contribution nor allowed to have a voice in educational policy or administration. No matter how few in number, or how lacking in professional competence, the charge runs, it is the clergy or religious who have the decisive power in the schools and uni-

[10] Robert A. Graham, S.J., "The Laity, the Council and the New Apostolate," *America* (May 6, 1961), p. 248.

versities. Yet it is hardly startling that this should be the case, for, despite the shortage of vocations, Catholic education is still primarily taken to be the responsibility of religious. Though rapidly changing under the pressure of circumstance, this attitude lingers on.

Moreover, it is an attitude which is reinforced by the fact (especially on the university level) that many schools are looked upon as the private property of bishops, parishes or religious orders. It is thus taken to be perfectly natural that the direction and administration of these schools should remain in the hands of their owners. The lay faculty member is not a member of these closed religious corporations which have rigid and old traditions antedating his very existence.[11] The lay teacher comes and goes; the school goes on. It is a tradition which can hardly fail to frustrate those professionally competent laymen who, if they were teaching in the public schools or secular colleges, would face no formal barrier to advancement. In most Catholic schools, colleges and universities no amount of competence is sufficient to win for them the highest policy-making positions.

The "realities," then, of American Catholic life bear heavily on the problem of the layman. Even a classification of the type presented here hardly does justice to the complexity of the situation. For one thing, whether it be a matter of parish life, the liturgy, the lay apostolate movement or the layman in Catholic education, each of the four realities will usually have some influence. The problem of the laity in parish life, for instance, is one of many dimensions and not only the one I chose to single out. It involves the educational and class differences among Catholics, the existence of differing and often competing conceptions of the nature of Catholicism, the conflict of new ideas with old customs, and the agonizing task of finding ways to translate theory in practice. The same can be said of the lay apostolate, Catholic education and the liturgical and social encyclical movements.

Thus any attempt to reduce the complexities of the lay question to some simple, manageable form runs into a host of difficulties. They can neither be formulated nor answered in any simple way. Those who emphasize that nothing more is needed than the putting into practice of the principles emphasized by the popes fail to recognize that the disparate cultural situation of different groups of Catholics makes it exceedingly troublesome to determine how this can be done. Nor do they often

[11] A discussion of this problem can be found in James Maguire, C.S.C., "A Family Affair," *The Commonweal*, LXXV (Nov. 10, 1961), pp. 171-173.

recognize that these principles themselves have not always proved sufficiently precise to be very helpful. At the same time, however, even those who emphasize that the prime need is to achieve a full theology of the laity often fail to realize that far more than theology determines the actual life of the Church.

There is no need to continue multiplying complexities; they are obvious enough. Yet it is important that they be recognized fully. A failure to do so in most discussions of the laity has been the prime cause of so many aimless and contradictory descriptions of the actual status of the layman in the Church. From the viewpoint of the layman steeped in recent Catholic thought, possessed of the critical faculties which result from a successful university training, zealous to use his talents in the service of the Church, eager to bring his faith to bear on his secular life, much of what he sees in the Church can only be depressing, frustrating and disillusioning. If he is fortunate to live and work in those parts of the country where the Church is open to lay initiative, then many of these tensions may be bearable or absent altogether. But if he does not, then the tensions may be unbearable. In both cases, however, it often turns out that lay aspirations far outrun even the comparatively rapid advances that have taken place. Those who complain that the educated laity sometimes seem unwilling to admit progress fail to see that lay standards are rising at a very rapid rate.

From the viewpoint of a hard-pressed parish priest or a bishop, however, the problem of the layman often appears in a very different light. Lay apathy and indifference are present in the American Church; many laymen have no desire at all to serve the Church, to understand their faith more intelligently, to assist the clergy or hierarchy; for every prodding and chafing layman there are many more who find it an effort to keep the most minimal laws of the Church. In such a situation, there should hardly be any astonishment that many priests find the complaints of the few unrealistic and unfair. In the face of the avant-garde layman pleading for a recognition of his insights and his enthusiasms, many a pastor can justly retort that the greatest obstacle remains the inert mass of laymen who resolutely refuse to tolerate any change in the *status quo* or do anything to improve their own lot in the Church. All too often the bishop or priest finds himself in an impossible position: forced, on the one hand, to satisfy zealots and, on the other, to arouse and strengthen the sluggish and the complacent. It is not easy to do both things at once.

CHAPTER 6

Concord and Conflict:
Clergy and Laity

SOONER OR LATER every discussion of any importance will take a personal turn. The abstract will give way to the human, the theoretical to the personal. In some instances, the shift may be a healthy one; in others, it merely complicates and confuses. For better or worse, however, one cannot talk for long about the place of the laity in the Church without talking about the relationship between clergy and laity. This is not to say that there are not any aseptic and impersonal ways of discussing this relationship; as the last chapter suggests, one can skirt the subject simply by turning one's eye elsewhere. But not for long.

For in the end those who must confront each other, the layman and the priest, are human beings. The fact that priests are ordained to administer the sacraments of the Church, to preach the gospel, and to preserve and extend the Word of God, does not annul their humanity. Not only the layman, then, but the priest and the bishop as well must wrestle with the gritty realities of human relationships, problems and temptations. Even when one has said all that can be said about the formal role of the layman in the Church, and the formal role of the priest and bishop, there is still much to add about the way in which these roles are exercised in daily life.

The temptation to avoid putting the relationship between clergy and laity in these terms has been strong in American Catholicism. It is far safer, far less unsettling, to pose the lay question as one turning on the elaboration of a detailed theology of the laity; or as one reducible to the need that the laity be more holy, more zealous, more understanding. Such things are surely important. But equally important is the fact that any meeting of the needs of the layman, any fulfillment of the papal

124

leads and directives, any realization of the potential of the layman must involve the quality of the personal bond which exists between clergy and laity. Nor can it fail to involve the mutual expectations which clergy and laity have of each other, the way they evaluate each other's work and the positive assistance they give to each other. However obvious these points may seem, both the clergy and laity have been at times reluctant to approach their relationship in direct terms.

The simple truth is, however, that the American Church has found it impossible to ignore the relationship between the clergy and laity and still deal with the question of the laity in a meaningful way. It has become apparent that the laity have many criticisms of the clergy; that many, indeed, hold the clergy in part responsible for the ineffectiveness of the lay apostolate and the failure of the layman to see the Church in its most dynamic and challenging reality. It has become no less apparent that the layman has only as much freedom and power of initiative in the Church as the clergy sees fit to allow him. Finally, it has been argued persuasively that no amount of papal or theological elaboration of the rights of the layman and his dignity in the Church will have any practical importance if the clergy and hierarchy are unwilling to take it seriously. Just as it has been possible for many bishops to ignore papal directives on church music, liturgical reform and principles of social justice, so it will also be possible for some of them to ignore or thwart developments in the Church's thinking on the layman.

What is the present relationship of the American laity and clergy? No one, it can flatly be asserted, can answer that question with any certainty. There are very few available empirical studies of the question (and they are difficult to devise in the first place), and there are few writings of any kind which do not tend to give a distorted picture. Perhaps the greatest source of distortion has come from those who believe that, for the good of the Church, it is a matter which ought not to become a subject of public discussion and debate. Nothing, they hold, is more important than to maintain the traditionally harmonious relationship which has existed between the layman and the priest. For that reason it is better that the "positive" side of the picture always be emphasized; it is better that any signs of tension and disaffection be minimized, if not ignored. After all, great progress is being made and that is the important thing. Unfortunately, such an approach is better suited to a theology of positive thinking than it is to the demands of healthy analysis. But there is some truth in the common complaint that those who emphasize only the dark side of the picture and dwell only on the sources of discord themselves distort the full reality of the American Church; what is true in one section of the country may not be equally true in another, what one layman finds a difficulty may not bother another, what one generation expects may not interest another at all.

It is difficult, then, to provide a balanced appraisal. The issue can be approached either in terms of the strength of the clergy-lay relationship (and it is normally very strong) or in terms of the shadowy and more unpleasant signs of a growing strain (and such signs do exist). The choice here falls on the latter. One good reason for this choice is that these signs of strain are something new on the American scene. Another is that those who are most critical of the clergy, and most concerned with effecting a fruitful and mutually enriching relationship, are often the ones most steeped in papal thought on the laity, most highly educated in current trends of theology and most intent on transforming the Church into a more effective force in private and public life. They are, in brief, the people whose impact on the Church in the years ahead is likely to be powerful and decisive; in great part, they represent the first flowering of the changes which have already taken place. If one can date the emergence of the lay question to the mid-thirties at the very earliest, then the present generation is the first generation of the new American layman. And to judge from the trend among recent Catholic college graduates, the second generation will be far more critical and will create far more problems for the Church than the first generation thought possible.

It is well first to inquire why the relationship between the clergy and the laity is changing, for the first and most obvious answer to the question about the present state of their relationship is that it is in a period of rapid change. One direct way to characterize the situation is to contrast the present role of the clergy with their role prior to World War I. The classic stereotype of that earlier role (but a well-attested one) is that of the priest as a charismatic, central figure in the lives of his immigrant charges. Not only did the priest minister to spiritual needs but he also guided social and economic progress. His opinions were respected, his education and knowledge praised, his community status exalted.

This is hardly the case today. The Catholic priest is still the object of considerable devotion and affection; he is still a highly respected person among the majority of Catholics. But he is no longer considered better educated or particularly well equipped to provide the layman with enlightened advice on coping with the economic, political and social problems of daily life. Where once the priest was looked upon for wisdom on the whole gamut of life's problems, he is now expected only to provide guidance on the more narrowly "spiritual" problems. In Church, the priest is indispensable; outside of Church, he is simply one more person with one more opinion.

The cause of this change is readily apparent. The contemporary layman is a different person from his unlettered grandparents. Inexorably, the status of the priest has diminished in the eyes of many laymen—not only because the priest's role has become a narrower one but also because the layman himself, in his general life, has far less need of his help. This by no means implies that his sacerdotal function is less respected; on the contrary, it is as highly respected as ever. But it does mean that the priest as a person is no longer a special object of unusual esteem. "It seems," one layman has said, "that the layman is taking his moral questions to a family counsellor, his personal problems to an analyst, and his social problems to the politician."[1]

Thus deprived of many of his earlier functions, and much of his earlier aura, the priest has become much more like an ordinary person, one specialist among many (however unique his specialty may be). And on the purely human plane the priest is apt to be looked upon as a person just as human and fallible as anyone else. Indeed, in recent years the priest as a fallible and struggling man has been the object of unusual attention on the part of Catholic novelists; and many priests and laymen have expressed a certain dismay at what has happened. "This sudden rash of realistic novels about the fallen priest," one Jesuit has written, "makes one wonder if it may be a sign of what appears to be a contemporary phenomenon: the attempted secularization of the priest, even by sincere and intelligent Catholics."[2] While there may be reason to

---

[1] Quoted by Father Joseph H. Fichter, S.J., in a letter to the author. Father Fichter himself added that "This meant that the multiple counseling functions of the priest in a simple society get to be spread among non-clergy specialists in a complex society."

[2] Father Daniel N. Dwyer, S.J., the Boston *Pilot* (February 18, 1961). Among many books pertinent to this observation may be cited: *Be Not Angry* by William Michelfelder (New York, 1960); *The Devil's Advocate* by Morris L. West (New

doubt any such "attempted secularization" of the priest, these novels do indicate that the priest is no longer someone set upon a special, and distant, pedestal. He has become fair game both for the inquiring and critical layman and the Catholic novelist.

Yet the changing image of the priest has not been accompanied by a lessened demand that the priest be a competent priest. On the contrary, it appears that far more is expected of the priest today than ever in the past—and the more advanced the education of the layman is, the more at home he is in contemporary theology, the more stringent these demands become. If the priest is not expected to be a guide to social mobility as in the past, he is expected to be a competent guide to the spiritual life and the implications of Catholicism in modern life. In particular, he is expected to have a high degree of perception into the psyche of the zealous layman and the world in which he moves. Unfortunately, this is precisely where laymen find him deficient. They find him a good administrator, a good money-raiser, a good organizer, a good builder; but they do not always find him a good spiritual director or a percipient observer of the layman's intellectual, cultural and religious struggles. Worse still, to the more critical-minded he seems to be unaware of papal statements on the importance of the laity, blissfully ignorant of recent theological advances and doggedly determined not to recognize contemporary changes in the Church and its members.

Such at least are the complaints and such are the standards and expectations of the present generation of educated laymen. But they are complaints which many priests themselves second. Father Louis J. Putz, already mentioned as an important leader in the specialized lay apostolate movement, has written of those movements that "the greatest obstacle to [their] growth and development . . . is still the lack of understanding on the part of the clergy as to the fundamental role of the laity."[3] And Monsignor George W. Casey, a columnist for the Boston *Pilot*, has observed that "the pastor who rules his parish with a rod of iron is still with us. By such a pastor I mean one who uses social pressures and *ad hoc* sanctions to enforce his rulings, arbitrary and otherwise. One who

York, 1959); *The Fountain of Arethusa* by Maurice Zermatten (New York, 1960); *Gemini* by William Kelley (New York, 1959); *No Little Thing* by Elizabeth Ann Cooper (New York, 1960); *Vessel of Dishonor* by Paul Roche (New York, 1962); *Morte D'Urban* by J. F. Powers (New York, 1962); *The Tiber Was Silver* by Michael Novak (New York, 1961).

[3] "The Apostolate," *Perspectives* (September-October, 1961), p. 14.

takes advantage of the immunity of his pulpit to beat down opposition, and advantage of respect for the cloth to enforce his own opinions."[4] Here Monsignor Casey puts his finger on a common lay complaint: despite the fact that the layman of today is a different person from his forefathers, many priests continue to act as if nothing has happened in the last fifty years.

It is unnecessary, at this point, to continue listing specific criticisms of the clergy. What they suggest is that the relationship between clergy and laity is changing very rapidly; and that the main causes of this change are the new place the present generation of laymen have in American society, the different image of the person of the priest, the force of the lay movement in the Church, and the rising expectations of clerical excellence common among a more sophisticated body of educated laymen. Not surprisingly, the sharpest criticisms of the clergy have come, in most instances, from those most clearly identified as active, vigorous and serious Catholics. If these laymen are, as yet, still in a minority they are nevertheless influential among their fellow laymen and significant as an indication of future changes among the greater mass of laymen.[5]

Clerical Formation

It is now pertinent to ask why, if the layman has made many advances and changed in many respects, the clergy have not kept pace? All things being equal, there would be no reason not to expect the clergy to change as rapidly as the laity. Are they not, after all, as much the product of the present age as the laity? In one sense, of course, they are. But in a more important way, the clergy and the laity inhabit different worlds within the same era; and even within these worlds, age, social background, intellectual interests and educational formation make a considerable difference. It is evident, for instance, that there are some important differences between those bishops, pastors and priests educated prior to World War II and those laymen educated since the Korean War. Not

---

[4] "The Parish Tyrant," the Boston *Pilot* (August 5, 1961).

[5] Cf. Sally Whelan Cassidy, *Some Aspects of Lay Leadership* (unpublished Ph.D. dissertation, Department of Sociology, University of Chicago, 1959). Though Miss Cassidy limited her study of lay leaders to those active on the diocesan level and higher, she found evidence of some important differences in attitudes toward the clergy among older and younger lay leaders. The latter tended to be less dependent upon the clergy and far more critical of them.

only have the latter been shaped in an America very different from that which existed when the older generation of priests were growing up, but they have been introduced to a Church in the throes of a variety of theological, pastoral and intellectual changes, many of which were hardly dreamed of before the last three decades.

No less important is the fact that the younger group has come from families much more at home in the American scene than the families of those who are their bishops and pastors. Today nearly half of the average freshman class at a Catholic college have parents who themselves had some college training; by contrast, very few of the present bishops had parents with any college education. Again, a sizable number of the most active, educated laymen have attended non-Catholic colleges and universities; by contrast, barely a handful of the present bishops (and doubtless few of the pastors) have had anything other than a totally Catholic education. It thus seems safe to say that few of today's pastors and bishops (those, in short, who exercise the most decisive leadership in the Church) have had the full experience of American Catholic assimilation and the direct contact with American cultural and religious pluralism that have been the lot of the post-war layman.

As Father Joseph H. Fichter has observed: "In the shifting American structure, the lay Catholic population is always 'ahead' of the Church professionals. . . . Until, if ever, the class structure becomes fairly stabilized, there will probably be both a time-lag and a class-lag between the ecclesiastical professionals and the laity they serve."[6] Given this "lag" and given the different backgrounds of the older clergy and the younger laity, it is not odd that many laymen should find their dilemmas and aspirations inadequately recognized. Yet if these differences help to explain some of the new tensions between clergy and laity, they do not do full justice to the situation. They do not, for instance, explain why many young priests receive a goodly share of criticism; nor do they explain why, even when there are good and obvious reasons for clerical decisions, many laymen still feel the clergy to be unable to understand the laity.

If there is any single adequate explanation, it is the fact that the clergy inhabit a different institutional world than the laity. It is a world slow to change, resistant to innovation and settled in its traditions, a world

---

[6] *Religion as an Occupation* (Notre Dame, 1961), p. 87.

which shapes the priest from his first day in a seminary and which, though less restricted after ordination, is not essentially different. It is marked, to be sure, by a continuing emphasis on the majesty of God, by a genuine sense of vocation and duty, and by a daily life given over to the service of others. But it is also marked by a great emphasis on many virtues and many attitudes different from those appropriate to a layman in the world. These are not virtues and attitudes to be scorned by the layman; nor are they to be exalted above all others as a *sine qua non* of the model layman.

One may begin with seminary education. In a 1959 letter of the Roman Congregation of Seminaries prepared on the Centenary of the Curé of Ars, the following ideal was urged: "Let discipline, therefore, joyfully embraced, be the touchstone by which superiors test the vocation of their students. Let them demand an obedience, not merely theoretical, but effective, single-minded, and complete in all things, great and small contained in the Seminary Rule." This passage speaks for itself: the great virtues of the seminarian are obedience and acceptance of discipline. While it may in fact be doubted that all seminary rectors would thus exalt these virtues, there can be little doubt that the ordinary Catholic seminary is a tightly-run, strictly-controlled and exceedingly formal establishment. In this country, only West Point and Annapolis offer any parallels. From morning to night the student's day is rigidly planned, the standards of conduct exacting and the possibilities of individual initiative limited. Over everything hangs the ever-present realization that the seminarian's vocation is being tested; and the main criteria are not intellectual distinction, personal devotion or the promise of pastoral imaginativeness, but the ability to accept discipline and display obedience. "Its style of life," one seminary professor has said, "fails to achieve a synthesis of liberty and authority. It does not make sufficient effort to address itself to the liberty of another. The attempt is made only to obtain an outer conduct that is objectively correct. . . . The seminary puts emphasis on the instincts of passivity and submission."[7]

One important object of this regimen, of course, is to weed out those seminarians who would not have the stamina, self-discipline or seriousness of purpose necessary for the priesthood. Another is to instill in semi-

---

[7] Father Sergius Wroblewski, O.F.M., "Formation of Seminarians Toward a Diocesan Spirituality," *Proceedings of the 59th National Catholic Education Association Convention*, LIX (April, 1962), p. 78.

narians a full awareness that their role is, essentially, that of a servant of the Church. Still another is to ensure that priests are submissive to their bishops and to the authority of the Church. These are understandable motivations. But it is not at all clear that this systematic erasing of many important and normally laudable human traits—initiative, self-direction and psychological independence—is actually the best way to produce a clergy capable of understanding contemporary spiritual needs or the modern world. Nor is it certain that a way of thinking which is prone to identify the will of God with the will of one's religious superior may not produce some dangerous threats to personal integrity.

Unfortunately, there are still other weaknesses in seminary training which affect even more directly the relation of clergy and laity. One important shortcoming is that the majority of seminarians, during their formative period, are systematically deprived of any significant contacts with the laity. Most seminaries are institutions isolated from university life, self-contained educational entities; it is a rare layman who even sets his foot inside their doors. There is thus little opportunity (with the exception of brief vacation periods) for the seminarian to learn how the layman is being formed, what expectations he is developing or how a mutually respectful relationship may be achieved.

No less important, the seminarian is given a very scant education in those disciplines which loom so large in the modern world. Unless he makes special private efforts, it is more than likely that the graduate of a seminary will have only the barest acquaintance with literature, psychology, sociology, economics, history and political science. He will almost surely not have wrestled directly with the thought of Hegel, Marx, Freud, Darwin, or Kant or, for that matter, any of those who have left their mark on that "secular" age of ours. To be sure, many priests are aware of contemporary modes of thought, important intellectual currents and the thought of important non-Catholic thinkers. But their awareness is more to their own credit than to that of their seminary education. Under such conditions, many priests undoubtedly find themselves handicapped when faced with well-educated, intellectually sophisticated laymen. However useful a heavy regimen of philosophy and theology may be for part of their training, the price paid in terms of a broad liberal education is very high. There is more to the world than the truths of metaphysics and theology.

From the viewpoint of the layman, even theology would have more value if it emphasized the importance of the layman in the Church. That is not the case. Despite the vast amount of writing, research and historical exploration on the lay problem in recent years, very few of its results have found their way into the formal seminary manuals and courses. Detailed study and discussion of the theology of the laity is all but nonexistent and there is normally only the sketchiest kind of introduction to the specialized lay movements, the concepts and aims of the lay apostolate, and the papal writings on the layman.

Yet there is more involved here than a mere omission of these subjects. What the seminarians do receive appears to make it hard for them, even under the best of circumstances, to see the laity as an integral part of the Church. In particular, their study of the nature of the Church is based on the use of traditional tracts which lay heavy emphasis on what Yves Congar has called "hierarchology": "The treatise on the Church is a particular treatise composed in answer to a Gallicanism, to conciliarism, to the purely spiritual ecclesiology of Wycliffe and Hus . . . Modernism, and so on. It follows that it is composed in reaction against errors all of which call the hierarchical structure of the Church into question. . . . But if theology de Ecclesia be practically reduced to a 'hierarchology' or, more generally, be made a theology only of the Church's structure . . . there is a risk of the laity being regarded as simply an accident, an appendage of the Church."[8] In such a situation, as Father Jeremiah Newman has aply observed, "it is very hard to expect seminarians to take the matter of the lay apostolates seriously, if it is not treated as part of their normal course in theology. And it is very hard to expect that lay efforts in the apostolate will be anything other than half-hearted as long as the attitude of the clergy is one of uncertainty if not of opposition."[9]

It is difficult not to conclude that in many vital respects seminary education is badly deficient. Whatever its other virtues, it is an education ill-designed to prepare a priest to cope with the layman; and the more educated the layman, the poorer by contrast appears the preparation of the priest. Ironically, one great aim of seminary life is to emphasize the importance and dignity of the priesthood, and one way this is done

---

[8] Lay People in the Church, trans. by Donald Attwater (Westminster, Md., 1957), pp. 39-45.
[9] The Christian in Society (Westminster, Md., 1962), p. 115.

is to stress the ascetical superiority of the clerical to the lay life. This is perfectly proper, of course. But it too often turns out that the priest is given an exalted image of his role without, at the same time, being provided the type and quality of education designed to make him a natural guide to the layman. This discrepancy is a major source of clerical bewilderment and lay disenchantment. In the end, the seminarian is far better prepared to live in the clerical than in the lay world; yet he can be an effective priest only if he knows both worlds.

Clerical Freedom

Now it might be hoped and expected that ordination would mark a decisive change in the life of one trained for the priesthood. In many ways it does: his vocation has been tested, his status secured, and the worst burdens of disciplinary restrictions lie behind him. But in some very important respects, the change is not too striking. Most pertinently, the standards of obedience and respect for ecclesiastical authority remain as high as ever. Not only is there a tight chain of command in most dioceses, but there is also little opportunity for the priest to exercise any personal initiative in his daily life. Whatever he does of any importance can only be done with the approval of his bishop; and the bishop must be consulted, through the chain of command, before and not after he acts. "It is probable," Father Fichter writes, "that the ordinary rank-and-file functionary in a large diocese or religious congregation sometimes thinks of himself as being caught up in [a] bureaucratic system. In varying degrees he has noticed how rules and regulations seem to be emphasized for their own sake, how he is sometimes treated like a child without responsibility or initiative or personal competence."[10] That many priests chafe under this system is undoubtedly true. But there are others who find it ideal: "We hear much today of reasonable obedience. Supe-

---

[10] *Religion as an Occupation, op. cit.,* p. 223. Cf. also the following conclusion from the chapter from which the above quotation was taken (Chap. 9, "Organized Social Relations"): "As a member of a diocese or a religious order, the religious functionary is under a bureaucracy that in some way manages all three phases of his life. It provides regulations of behavior touching upon his domestic, religious and professional roles and gives him training for the performance of all three roles. In a simple agrarian system, or in an ancient monastery, this may have been a satisfactory arrangement. In the complex and dynamic society of modern America, it poses many problems of inconsistency and dissatisfaction" (p. 233).

riors must give a reason when they command, and the reason must be convincing and satisfying. This is nonsense! Having vowed to God your life, it is reasonable to accept His authority unquestioningly, without compromise and without 'taking a vote.' "[11]

At first glance, it might appear irrelevant to stress the role of obedience in the priest's life. What possible bearing could it have on his relationship with the layman? Unfortunately, it does have considerable bearing, first, on the way it forms a priest's outlook toward the layman. If it leads him to see respect for authority as the greatest of virtues, then he is very unlikely to appreciate the layman's need for personal exercise of responsibility. If docility and passivity are seen as pre-eminent marks of the Christian, then self-initiated and self-directed acts are likely to be viewed only as signs of rebellion or sinful pride. If an orderly chain of command and an orderly bureaucracy are seen as models for all human organizations, then there will be very little room for small, flexible, self-sustaining lay groups or purely individual initiative. If paternalism is taken to be the surest way to maintain order and conformity of thought, then the whole idea of a lay apostolate becomes meaningless.

Second, the role of obedience bears on the degree of freedom which the priest may exercise in behalf of the laity. As the parish and the diocese are structured today, there is little opportunity for the individual priest to grant what he personally may recognize as a legitimate request. He cannot institute liturgical reforms without episcopal permission. He cannot delegate major responsibilities to laymen. He cannot restructure parish organizations as laymen might desire. He cannot institute building programs without permission. If he is a curate, he can do no more than the pastor will allow him to do. If he is a pastor, he cannot act without the consent of his bishop. To be sure, the degree of discipline exercised varies considerably from parish to parish, and from diocese to diocese. But in few dioceses is a priest allowed to forget that his first loyalty is to the bishop. Rarely does a priest live in fear of his parishioners; yet he commonly lives in fear of his bishop. The great merit of this system is a well-disciplined body of priests. Order and authority are served. But it is a system which makes it exceedingly difficult for a priest to respond quickly, flexibly and imaginatively to the changing circumstances of the

---

[11] Father Reginald Redlon, O.F.M., "The American Character and Formation in Religious Life," *Proceedings of the Second National Congress of Religious of the United States* (Notre Dame, 1962).

layman. If not by choice, then by necessity, the organization of the Church must be served first; after that comes the layman.

There is no desire to be harsh here. On the contrary, my aim is to show that the relationship between clergy and laity is greatly complicated by the nature of clerical training and clerical life. The clergy is shaped to live one mode of life, the laity another. And it is exactly the different outlooks shaped by these modes of life which help explain an increasing tension among clergy and laity. In our society the layman, by dint of his education and social position, has managed to carve out large areas of personal freedom and decision. He is now used to being judged in terms of his professional skills. He is now free to live where he likes, do the kind of work he likes, and change jobs if he likes. The world in which the layman lives is one marked by freedom and self-direction. These are not the marks of the clerical world.

Still, no problem might arise were it not for the increasing demands made upon the laity to cooperate in the work of the Church. As long as the priest was expected, without assistance, to run those affairs pertaining to the inner life of the Church and the layman was expected only to obey the laws of the Church and contribute his money for its upkeep, there was no cause for confusion or tension. Each had his neatly defined place with little overlapping. But when the Church begins to call for greater lay cooperation with the clergy, when the layman is expected to do more than give money to the Church, when the layman is educated to do more, then the earlier boundaries become blurred. There can be no genuine cooperation between laity and clergy as long as the clergy are trained to believe that their word is law, that they are never required to consult the laity, that their ideas and direction must in all instances be decisive in the Church. Nor can there be genuine cooperation when, because of his prior loyalties to bishop or pastor, a priest is not free to respond to the legitimate requests and needs of the layman. If the paternalistic and tyrannical priest is a dying breed, there still remains a basic discrepancy between the freedom the priest is trained and prepared to give and the freedom necessary to meet the needs of the emergent layman.

Thus those clerics who accuse lay critics of failing to recognize the great progress the Church has been making, disregard an essential reason for this criticism: the persistent gap between what needs to be done and what is being done. The Church and the clergy are responding to the contemporary layman—but this response is proceeding at a much slower pace than the rising expectations of the layman. Most importantly, while the attitude of the clergy is indeed changing, the structures and institutions which decisively determine the real role of the layman are not. It is one thing for the priest to adopt a more positive and open approach to the layman; it is another to translate this new attitude fruitfully into organizational procedures. It is hard to make rapid innovations in seminary training, in theological manuals, and in the parish structure. A change in attitude does not guarantee a change in structure; and ultimately that is where the problem lies.

Every institution, whether secular or religious, can stand a certain amount of stress and strain. Some measure of internal tension can produce creative and fruitful thinking. This is also true of the Catholic Church. So far, the intense debate on the place of the layman in the Church has been creative. Yet there are increasing signs of an incipient anticlericalism among the laity, on the one hand, and, on the other, of newly-awakened fears of the laity among the clergy. The danger in these developments is obvious: the possibility of destructive antagonism between clergy and laity.

Varieties of Anticlericalism

Considerable caution, however, is necessary in speaking about this possibility. In particular, the word "anticlericalism" can be very misleading. Used in its most extreme and common historical sense it can be understood as a rejection of any form of dogmatic or denominational Christianity; not only the clergy but the very idea of an authoritative, teaching Church is rejected. In its most benign sense it can simply refer to a dissatisfaction on the part of the laity with those practices and institutions which effectively exclude the laity from playing any decisive role in the Church. In this latter sense, neither the clergy nor the authority of the Church is rejected, but rather the complete domination of the Church by the clergy. Anticlericalism in the first sense need not detain us; historically it was part of the nineteenth-century attempt of European political revolutionaries to destroy the Church's political and temporal power. For obvious reasons, it does not apply in this country; only the second kind of anticlericalism does.

Yet even in speaking of the more benign form of anticlericalism, care is necessary. In one way, it is perfectly possible to see anticlericalism as a necessary and healthy development in the Church. The laity can have an effective and meaningful place in the Church only as long as there is, among clergy and laity alike, a general resistance to the idea that the Church is identical with the teaching authority of the Church, or that the laity are passive clients of the clergy, outside of the Church proper. In our own day, there are few who would defend such an idea of the laity or of the Church. Nevertheless, it still remains common to treat the laity *as if* that were the determining concept; and it is the practice of the local churches which is the chief object of lay complaints. The absence of a full theology of the laity is also criticized; but it is primarily the actual treatment of the laity which causes unrest. Thus understood, the whole lay movement can be seen as a form of anticlericalism in which the appropriate goal of the Church becomes an integrated community of priests and people, each with their own dignity and proper function.

This very broad kind of anticlericalism poses no special difficulty; it is the legitimate offspring of an enriched conception of the Church supported by recent popes. Instead, the problem is posed by the way in which lay rights and freedoms are to be interpreted. For at the same time as recent popes and bishops have called for a more vigorous, responsible laity, they have not failed to emphasize their own decisive authority.[12] What has not been made clear, particularly in the face of the tensions noted above, is the extent to which the layman is free to dissent from the judgment of the bishops on social and political matters, to criticize particular decisions of the clergy, bishops and popes, or to chart his own prudential course in meeting particular problems. This lack of clarity, and the uneven acceptance among the clergy and the bishops of papal guidance and exhortations on the development of the laity, have produced considerable confusion.

What one group may consider a sign of rebellion against clerical authority another may take to be a legitimate use of lay freedom. The discussion in recent years of "anticlericalism" in the American Church can be seen in great part as a reflection of the confusion.[13] For it is by

[12] Cf. the characteristic statement of Pope Pius XII in an allocution to the leaders of Italian Catholic Action, May 3, 1951: "In one point all its members must be equal: in thinking with the Church, in devotion to the cause of the Church, in obedience to those whom the Holy Spirit has established as Bishops to govern the Church of God." *The Lay Apostolate* (Boston, 1961), p. 529.

[13] Among many others, Monsignor John Tracy Ellis has commented on the signs of anticlericalism: "It would be a disservice to the Church to deny the presence in our midst of symptoms that suggest an anti-clerical sentiment hitherto unknown to American Catholics." "The Catholic Layman in America Today," *The Commonweal*, LXXVI (June 22, 1962), p. 321.

no means obvious what should be taken to count as genuine anticlericalism. Though there have been accusations that the laity are overstep-
ping the bounds of criticism of the clergy, these charges have been
scattered and have aroused little support.[14] The few studies that have
been made almost all point to a laity basically satisfied with the clergy
and not at all prone to reject their authority.[15]

The question of anticlericalism cannot, however, be dismissed simply
by noting that there are no important signs of flagrant rejection of the
authority of the Church or the clergy. More pertinently, one can inquire
whether there are signs that, in subtle ways, the laity are evading or
minimizing the authority of the Church or negating by their practice
the status of the priest. These evasions or negations could take many
forms: a disposition to ignore the authority of the Church where that
authority conflicts with private predilections, a tendency to ridicule the
clergy and ignore their words or desires, a pattern of relying exclusively
on a vague lay consensus to solve difficult moral questions, and so forth.
Father Yves Congar has called attention to the dangers of a laity overly
intent upon asserting their rights; these dangers occur "when, for example, lay people think and say that matters of marriage or social morality
are *their* affair, and have nothing to do with the clergy; or when they
exclude their priest from this meeting or that Bible-study circle; or
when, rather disregarding the common and ordered character of ecclesial
life, they themselves choose a priest to suit the group they have
formed."[16]

No one, at least no layman, at all familiar with educated groups of
American Catholic laymen could deny that some of these tendencies
exist. There are some laymen who find it possible and preferable to
keep their contacts with the clergy to a minimum—to turn to them only
for the reception of the sacraments. At worst, there are some laymen

---

[14] Perhaps no episcopal statement in recent years was so widely denied as that
of one Eastern bishop: "There has been in recent months a vast volume of ill-
considered, badly-advised and poorly-defined talk about the place of the laity in
the Church. . . . This talk has already resulted in ignorant, insolent and arrogant
criticism of the bishops of the country by certain laymen. . . . Such talks sow the
seeds of anticlericalism." (Bishop George W. Ahr of Trenton, April, 1962.)

[15] Cf. Joseph H. Fichter, S.J., "A Comparative View of the Parish Priest," a
paper read to the Fifth World Congress of Sociology, September 7, 1962, Washington, D.C.: "Catholic Lay people are by and large satisfied with their parish
priest. They make use of his services, express high esteem for him, and are fairly
cooperative when the need is manifest."

[16] *Lay People in the Church*, op. cit., p. xxx.

who have a positive aversion to the clergy, quite independently of the personal merits or attractiveness of any particular priest. Of the two alternatives, the latter group appears too insignificant to be worthy of comment; they represent the unreasonably disgruntled. But the former may be growing, especially among recent graduates of Catholic colleges. In neither case, however, does the present situation warrant any immediate alarm on the part of the clergy.

Yet what should be borne in mind is that an imbalance between lay and clerical education, and a discrepancy between theory and practice with respect to the Catholic layman, easily breed alienation from the clergy. It is possible today for the perceptive and diligent layman to keep abreast of the most advanced theological thought. It is possible for him to have a far greater awareness of the problems facing the Church than some of the clergy. It is also possible for him to find attempts at cooperation with the clergy a frustrating and ill-rewarded venture. When these conditions develop, it is an almost irresistible temptation for the layman to chart his own course within the Church. In America, it is common to find laymen who are familiar with European theological thought; for them it is almost insupportable to be subjected to ecclesiastical thinking well behind that of the more advanced members of the Church universal. For anyone who is well-versed in the liturgical movement, the Church's social teaching, and recent Catholic ecumenical theology, the realities of many a parish can only come as a profound shock; it is hardly surprising, then, that some laymen should deny any special responsibility toward what they see around them.

Still, it would be misleading to give the impression that these tendencies represent a genuine rebellion against the clergy. In the great majority of cases, nothing of the kind is involved. To speak accurately, it must be observed that a considerable part of the criticism of the clergy and of the withdrawal from active involvement with the clergy represents the clashes of different age groups, different experiences of parochial Catholicism, and different appropriations of conflicting intellectual currents in the Church. Often the lay rebel is a person who has rejected the piety and practices of, say, Eastern seaboard Irish-American Catholicism, and has turned instead to the French or German theologian for a more congenial understanding of the Church. It is also important to recognize that the recent trend toward more outspoken criticism and free discussion of controversial questions—matters formerly reserved for the pages of professional theological journals—has simply brought out into the open some very old complaints. When these previously subdued complaints now receive the support of many theologians, it serves as further encouragement to speak directly, frankly and at times even harshly.

It is not surprising that some priests and bishops should find this new spirit of frank talk alarming. Despite the work of a theologian like Karl Rahner in his book *Free Speech in the Church*[17] there exists no consensus on the limits of criticism or even on the proper mode of criticism. Moreover, the fact that there exist so many diverse approaches to Catholicism in the contemporary Church makes many ecclesiastics accept criticism only as it accords with their own outlook. What one bishop or priest may find a desirable and justifiable criticism another may take as a personal insult. And on occasion it happens that a bishop or priest who champions one stream of Catholic thought finds himself criticized by laymen who champion another. In such instances, it sometimes looks as if laymen are challenging the authority of a bishop or of the Church when actually nothing of the kind is involved.[18] Such conflicts, notable for their confusion, usually bespeak different theological loyalties, different expectations and sometimes a difference between one generation and another; rarely can they be reduced to a simple clash between clergy and laity.

Clergy and Laity: Some Complexities

Indeed, it is in the end extremely doubtful that a casting of the lay-clergy problem in terms of clericalism or anticlericalism is very illuminating. At best, it is only momentarily helpful, a preliminary way of approaching the problem. In the long run it must give way to the complexities of contemporary Catholicism—complexities which, if they do not essentially alter the pattern of lay-clergy relations so far sketched, place it in a different light.

[17] New York, 1960.

[18] One of the most celebrated cases of conflicts of this sort came with the criticism, by a group of laymen, of an address delivered by the Apostolic Delegate to the United States, Archbishop Egidio Vagnozzi, at a Marquette University commencement on June 3, 1961. In his address, the Archbishop voiced many of the worries of conservative theologians with the biblical, liturgical and intellectual movements. For their part, the laymen denied the existence of the dangers and excesses he noted. Cf. the Davenport, Iowa, *Catholic Messenger* (June 22, 1961) and *The American Ecclesiastical Review*, CXLVI (Oct., 1961).

First, it is by no means clear that the contemporary educated Catholic layman knows exactly what he wants. Most commonly he will speak of the need for more communication between laity and clergy; for greater freedom to exercise personal judgment and responsibility; for freedom from clerical paternalism; for a clerical recognition that the temporal order cannot be scorned or degraded or the world denied; for the layman to be free to speak in the market place and bring the Church to that secular world in which he lives. Yet at the same time he may complain that the clergy do not tell him what to do in the world; that neither priests nor bishops provide him with sufficient guidance and direction to enable him to cope with the modern age. This ambivalence—between a desire to be free and a desire to be led—is rarely absent from even the most sophisticated writing and speaking by laymen. The clergy are condemned if they provide too little help—or too much. A most curious instance of this anomaly lies in the complaint, on the one hand, that the clergy do not concern themselves enough with the social and political problems of the day, and, on the other, that the clergy meddle too much in social and political matters which ought, properly, to be left to laymen. Again, it is often said that it is the task of the clerical theologian or bishop to provide broad, guiding principles for the laymen to work out in detail according to concrete circumstances. Yet, simultaneously, it is said that the clergy ought not to attempt to establish such broad principles unless they have been informed by the laity of the concrete facts of life.

In the face of these contrarieties, the clergy may feel justified in finding the contemporary layman hard to please and hard to fathom. Dissatisfied with his present role, caught up in swirling theological eddies and sociological change, the layman has yet to sort out the possibilities open to him and to achieve a clear idea of what he would like his role to be. In the meantime, he is apt to lash out erratically at the more obvious targets, leaving the real ones untouched. As long as he is a problem to himself, he is likely to be a problem for the clergy.

Second, it is becoming steadily more difficult to draw any hard and fast line between the desires and viewpoints of the laity and those of the clergy. One obvious reason, of course, is that much of the impetus for a more effective and vigorous laity has come from the clergy, and by no means simply because the clergy could use some help. Compared with the insights and leads provided by some clerical theologians, the layman's contribution to both the theoretical and practical problems of the laity have been very slight. Similarly, on any given issue—be it birth control, the intellectual life, or free speech in the Church—it is hard to find a clearly clerical and a clearly lay camp. The clergy are as divided on most important issues as are the laity; and the groupings of opinion in the Church cut decisively across lay-clergy lines. Without exception, every important movement in the contemporary American Church has both its lay and clerical leaders and followers; normally, they are joined together in very close alliances. It is now common for priests engaged in controversies to look upon articulate laymen as their best allies and spokesmen. Similarly, a sizable number of priests find their best friends and their closest confidants among laymen rather than among their fellow priests.

There is still a third consideration, one which has been ignored publicly by priests and laymen alike—clerical freedom. As noted earlier, many priests apparently chafe under the bureaucracy and discipline of ordinary parish and diocesan life; and one untoward effect is their inability to respond as freely to lay needs as they might desire. But to say this is only to touch the surface. Without desiring to raise the specter of what prevailed in the French Church on the eve of the French Revolution, where the lower clergy and laity formed an estate separate from that of the episcopacy, it is nonetheless possible to say that the lower clergy in the American Church are in very much the same position as that of the laity. In the larger American dioceses, access to the bishop may be as difficult for them as for the laity; their individual voices may count for as little in the formation of diocesan policy as those of active lay leaders. Above all, they probably have a good deal less freedom of speech and action than the layman. As much as he, they suffer from all the liabilities of a long tradition stemming from the days of trusteeism and the early immigration waves, of being treated with a certain wariness and rigor by the hierarchy.

Unlike the layman, however, the place of the lower clergy in the modern Church has not been the subject of close analysis and widespread discussion. Though it is commonly said by seminary professors and rectors that the contemporary seminarians are far more critical and inquiring than those of earlier generations, little has been done to explore the implications of this change. There seems little doubt that many of the changes in attitude and practice in the Church requested by the laity would, *mutatis mutandis*, be of value to the lower clergy: a greater freedom of public expression in the Church, less restrictions on private initiatives, a re-examination of the concept of obedience and authority in the Church.[19] The complaint of many priests that most laymen do not seem to realize that the clergy have no more freedom to speak or act independently than the laity is a very legitimate one. Their common problems produce a much closer bond between laity and clergy than has yet been recognized. Finally, the few studies of the clergy made in recent years show some significant differences between the priest's own self-conception and what the laity assume that self-conception to be.[20] The lay question is unlikely to be resolved without a parallel analysis of the theological and sociological status of the priest—and not just for the sake of clarifying his relationship to the laity but for the sake of his own well-being and satisfaction.

Fourth, amidst the various complexities which make tidy generalizations about the clergy and the laity suspect, the place of the bishop cannot be ignored. As successors of the Apostles, the bishops, together with the pope, have the ultimate duty and responsibility to preserve, clarify and proclaim the teachings of the Church. In America, unlike many European countries, the bishops have never been cut off from the people by education or social differences; they have been close to their flocks and admirably solicitous for their spiritual and material welfare. With few exceptions, they have been circumspect in the expression of their political views, taking great care not to coerce the political judgments of the laity. Yet, because they have been faced with vast financial and administrative problems, they have at times been forced to give a disproportionate amount of their time and energy to the purely temporal welfare of the Church.

The common image of the American bishop as, primarily, an administrator has much to support it. Doubtless this is an image which few of them relish; yet, so far there is little they have been able to do about it. As long as schools and churches need to be built, money raised and

---

[19] For one attempt at such a re-examination, see Karl Rahner, "Reflections on Obedience," *Cross Currents*, X (Fall, 1960), pp. 363-374. Cf. also Michael Novak, "The Priest in the Modern World," *Review for Religious*, X (1961), pp. 265-271.

[20] Father Fichter, for instance, has found that the role which priests most prefer is that of spiritual father, confessor and counselor. Despite this preference, they are usually forced by circumstance to give a disproportionate part of their time to financial and administrative matters. As a consequence, many laymen have an image of the priest as an administrator. Cf. Fichter, "A Comparative View of the Parish Priest," *op. cit.*

dioceses organized efficiently, they will have little leisure to cope with the more rarefied theological, spiritual and moral needs of the mid-century layman. This has given rise to still another image of the American bishops: they are neither theologically nor pastorally creative but are, instead, cautious and timid. In comparison with the German, French or Dutch hierarchy, they have left few marks on the liturgical or theological developments of our day. Although the Second Vatican Council has shown that they are hardly as conservative or reactionary as many Americans and Europeans take them to be, their influence has been felt more in the support they give to European groupings of opinion than in the leadership they themselves provide.

The whole orientation of the bishops toward American Church life cannot fail to have some bearing on the situation of the laity. In the past, the patent administrative needs of the Church tended to pre-empt the desire to offer the best possible spiritual guidance. But today when for many laymen the great need is not buildings or financial solvency, but the spiritual challenges and exigencies of a confused and disoriented society, some tensions and mutual dissatisfaction have inevitably developed. To a generation of laymen heartened by the work of contemporary theologians the concerns of the American bishops often appear to be excessively prudent and even anachronistic. This is an unfortunate situation, partly because it has led many laymen to despair of getting the help they need from the hierarchy, and partly because it places the bishops in an unnecessarily unfavorable light. For they are, as much as ever, fully committed to the good of the laity. Yet because they have inherited one set of major problems—those of administration, finances and efficient organization—and the contemporary laity are confronting quite different ones, it may easily appear as if they do not care about the laity.

At the root of this misunderstanding is, once again, the different pace of change between clergy and laity. As a body, the bishops have fallen heir to a tradition, going back to the immigration period, which conceives of the Church as socially beleaguered, constantly threatened with spiritual dangers, and ever pressed by a need for money and organization. What the great immigration waves showed the American Church was that the spiritual needs of the people could not be met without first establishing a firm base of efficiency. It is a tradition slow to die—especially since there is still an inadequate number of churches, greatly overcrowded schools and many Catholics without the service which the clergy and religious could provide. It is a tradition, in sum, which sees the real needs of the layman as best met by a solid institutional structure in the Church. The best bishop, consequently, is the one who is skilled at providing and maintaining this structure; however uninspiring the effort may seem, he is the one who does the most good for the laity. When one considers the great strength this tradition has given to the American Church it is difficult to deny its value.

Unhappily, this tradition is becoming an increasing liability. Its weakness is that it presupposes an underprivileged, uneducated and unassimilated Catholic layman. Insofar as there are still millions of Catholics who can be thought of in this way, the tradition still retains some justification. But it is singularly inadequate to meet the needs of the vast numbers of privileged laymen—those who have a decent Catholic education, who want to serve the Church more effectively, and who are fully engaged in living as accepted members of the American community. It is not that these laymen do not need better schools for their children and better churches for themselves; but they need much more. They need bishops today who are far more theologians than canon lawyers or administrators; far more anxious about the spiritual problems of the educated and loyal laymen than about the unceasing need for better buildings in which to serve and educate them; far more sensitive to the moral dilemmas of conscientious Catholics trying to live a Christian life in trying times than to budgets and clerical manpower.

It is easy, of course, to urge these things; and it is doubtful that many bishops would disagree. What is important is that the force of these conflicting pressures on the bishops should be understood. They account both for the dissatisfaction of many laymen with the bishops and also for the latter's justifiable belief that they are honestly and fully attempting to do their best for the layman. Both have a point. The layman who sees the bishop as indifferent to him is unfair; the bishop who believes that the tradition of which he is a part is still appropriate for today's layman is mistaken.

There are as many ways of playing pollyanna as there are ways of playing the alarmist and the pessimist. In the instance of the relationship between clergy and laity both of these extreme stances are common in the American Church today. There are bishops and laymen who find the present bond between clergy and laity to be ideal; what problems exist are those created by the misinformed, the rebellious and the uncharitable. At the other extreme are those who believe that things could hardly be worse, that the laity are an oppressed and misunderstood majority, the victims of blind and hide-bound priests. Neither extreme can be supported. If one can find one parish or one diocese where there is a cordial bond between clergy and laity, one can easily find another where discontent and mutual suspicion are common. If one can find some bishops who look upon an educated and critical layman as someone to be kept in his place, one can easily find others who bemoan the lack of lay vigor and interest. If one can find many laymen who have no difficulty shocking and scaring a conservative clergy, one can just as easily find whole parishes of laymen who find their priests radical, dynamic and quite unsettling to their own time-worn ways. Hence it is easy to find an exception to any broad generalization. For a Church in the midst of change, this is all the more true.

Yet the future must count; and one must look to the present to see the potential difficulties. The one great and very possible danger would be a laity which, in the main, achieved a level of education (theological and secular) and of social assimilation superior to that of the clergy. Where this discrepancy exists today, there is almost always tension and friction between clergy and laity; and there is almost always some mutual suspicion and fear. Significantly, there has been a steadily widening social and intellectual gap between priests and people; so far, there have been few signs that the clergy have recognized this gap, and few signs that the laity realize that many of their difficulties stem from that cause rather than from clerical resistance to the layman as such. If this gap continues to widen and if the clergy and the hierarchy do not realize the impact this can have on the traditional good will between laity and clergy, then widespread anticlericalism would be a distinct likelihood.

In our society, the Church must depend very heavily upon the laity to sustain it as an active force; it can hardly afford to allow a situation to develop which would lead the laity to believe that their energies and talents could best be directed elsewhere. One special attraction of our society for many laymen is that they can remain practicing, devoted Catholics and yet choose to have no more than minimal contact with the Church and the clergy; it is even possible for them to believe that one can serve the Church better precisely by avoiding direct service. In the end, there is no use holding up the past happy relationship between clergy and laity as a model for the future, or even measuring the present against that past. Times are changing; it is the problems and difficulties now emerging which demand attention.

CHAPTER 7

The Layman as Citizen

THE ELECTION of John Fitzgerald Kennedy to the Presidency in 1960 meant many things to many people. For Republicans it meant the end of the Eisenhower era and a return to the more familiar role of the political minority. For Democrats it meant, by however slim a margin of victory, that nothing is so unbeatable as an attractive candidate and a well-oiled political machine. But for one segment of the electorate, it was more than an ordinary victory. For Catholics the election was a special triumph. At long last, the refrain went, Catholics had "arrived" in American society; one of their own had made it as President. If all doubts about the compatibility of American democracy and Catholicism had not been exorcised from the American mind, a decisive number of voters apparently thought the issue of little consequence. Those who retained their doubts and voted accordingly were more than offset by those Catholics who flocked to Mr. Kennedy in large numbers.[1] One way or another, the great symbolic citadel of Protestant America had been stormed. No longer would it be possible to think of the Presidency as the exclusive preserve of the Anglo-Saxon Protestant. One could forget Al Smith and even, in the flush of triumph, the nature of Mr. Kennedy's interrogation by a group of Houston ministers. All that remained, it seemed, was for Catholics to savor the victory.

But what does one see when one looks a little deeper? If Catholics have "arrived," just where then do they now stand? The election itself is a good reason to hesitate. True, Mr. Kennedy won and overcame the religious issue. Yet it is hardly likely that he would have won had he been a graduate of a Catholic college rather than Harvard; had he come from

---

[1] A useful analysis of the impact of the religious issue in the 1960 election can be found in Theodore H. White, *The Making of the President 1960* (New York, 1961), Chap. 14.

148

an ordinary middle-income Catholic family; had he married a South Boston Irish girl—although, to be sure, he might also not have won had he not been the heir of all the practical wisdom of Irish-American politics.

In any event, John F. Kennedy can hardly be seen as a typical American Catholic. In great part, his victory was evidence that the first requirement for American Catholic social and cultural ascendancy lies in triumphing over one's cultural origins. Americans can forgive a man's personal religious beliefs far more easily than his cultural identifications and attachments. John F. Kennedy was not to repeat Al Smith's mistake. Yet it is doubtful, in this respect, that Mr. Kennedy taught American Catholics anything they did not already know. For some decades now they have known that while it may be no great disadvantage to be a Catholic, it can be a distinct disadvantage to be known as an Irish-Catholic or an Italian-Catholic or a Polish-Catholic.

They know how difficult it is to be thought of simply as an American-Catholic. An identification of Catholicism with certain ethnic minorities goes too deep to be easily uprooted. Like many other Americans, especially the Jews and the Negroes, Catholics are apt at times to wish that their past could be forgotten. Any attempt, however, to erase an ethnic or cultural past is beset with immediate difficulties. Other people, for one thing, find it hard to forget. For another, if by historical accident one's religious beliefs are interwoven with one's cultural origins, it is extremely difficult to know *how* to separate them.

It is this latter problem which has, historically, posed perhaps the greatest difficulty for American Catholics. For the key to successful assimilation has been found to be the creation of an image of the Church which is thoroughly American; or, more precisely, the creation of the image of the Catholic as a citizen as fully American as anyone else. This has been no easy task. In the past, when the Catholic was in fact a first- or second-generation immigrant, he depended very heavily on the immigrant community to sustain and fortify his religion. More often than not, he found it extremely difficult to imagine a purely American Catholicism; it was only natural to identify genuine Catholicism with the mores and folkways of his own ethnic group. For many, a break with the religious ways of the Old Country was tantamount to a breach of the faith itself.

Yet in time the break was made. Today it is likely that a majority of

American Catholics have only the dimmest ancestral recollection of their grandparents' ways. Unfortunately, this momentous change does not necessarily mean that Catholics have yet solved the problem of relating their Catholicism to American life. To be certain, they have found that a good income, a house with furnishings like those of one's neighbor, an accent-free language—and a Catholic president—are of great assistance. Such things make it easy to forget that difficulties still exist. But they do not, in the end, solve precisely how Catholics ought to relate their religion to their daily, their political, their civic, and their cultural life.

The very phrase "American Catholicism" suggests the central dilemma. If Catholicism is, as a religion, universal and transcends particular nationalities, how can there be such a thing as a Catholicism which is "American"? There is a common Catholic answer to this question. The Church is universal, but it is also imbedded in diverse cultures and national traditions; the task of the individual Catholic is to relate his faith to the concrete culture in which he finds himself; thus the Church is open to an American or French or Japanese expression—and it is the task of the Catholic to manifest this expression. This is a good answer—but a very abstract one. When faced with a society as diverse as our own, the Catholic can find it exceedingly difficult to know just how to relate his faith to the temporal order.

Insofar as it is simply a question of accepting the American constitutional and political system there is no difficulty. But when it comes to matters of social ethics, economic and welfare programs, religion and national life, education and foreign relations, no easy solutions appear. Buffeted, from the inside, by a wide variety of Catholic opinions about the proper relation of his faith to his civic duties and, from the outside, by an even more varied array of socio-political currents, he is often as muddled as any other member of our society. Similarly, in his private moral life it is by no means always easy to determine just which popular values he is free to accept and just which he must oppose—or how, should it come to that, he can best express his opposition. What needs to be pointed out, then, is that by the very fact of his new place in American society, the Catholic layman has had thrust upon him a new set of opportunities, risks and conflicting possibilities of choice. Naturally, these dilemmas are not wholly new; they bear at least a family resemblance to those of his grandparents. But they are new in the sense that broad social acceptance has considerably altered their quality and placed them in a different perspective.

Between Church and Society

To understand the nature of these new dilemmas, it is above all necessary to recognize that the American Catholic layman today lives his life in the midst of a complex web of religious, social and political relationships. As a Catholic he holds a specific body of religious beliefs. As a layman he stands in a certain relationship to the hierarchical authority of the Church. As a citizen, he participates in the American constitutional system. As a political being, he possesses certain opinions on the ideal direction of American society and a set of ideological commitments. As a member of some particular class—lower, middle, or upper—he will share many of the problems and values of that class. As a human being he is exposed to all the values and eddies of taste and mores which permeate American life.

By one means or another, the Catholic has to make some sense of this web. He must relate his role as citizen to his role as believer; his role as voter to his role as moral being; his role as free citizen to his role as one subject to the authority of the Church. In brief, the Catholic plays many parts; the task that confronts him incessantly is to find some meaningful way to relate them to one another. Inevitably, this task of integration or harmonization is a difficult one, and more so today than ever. Compared with a time when the Catholic's first challenge was to prove his loyalty, to work his way up the economic ladder, to achieve basic community acceptance, to preserve his faith in the face of overtly hostile social pressures, the situation in our day is far more complex. With the achievement of these initial goals, the fact of acceptance and social success requires the recasting of those basic questions that the Catholic has always had to put to himself. Once arrived, what then?

Two problems must be distinguished here. The first is that of determining the way the Catholic should resolve the conflicts of values which his dual role as Catholic and as citizen often entail. In speaking of "conflicts" here, I do not mean only those posed by theoretical questions of the relationship of church and state or those posed, for the Catholic, by the nature of authority in the Church. More importantly (for my purposes here at least), I mean the kinds of problems which arise from the difference between the values which a Catholic accepts as integral to his faith and those values, often very different, which are common in America.

The second problem arises from the kinds of tensions generated by

Catholic membership in two communities, the broad community of American citizens and the smaller community of Catholic believers. The basic conflict here can be seen as one of competing *loyalties*. Ideally, at least as argued in much Catholic writing, no genuine conflict is possible. In fact, however, the Catholic is often called upon to support the Catholic community in its efforts to sway other Americans, to defend the interests of the Church, or to contribute his time, energy or money to support some institutional aim of the Church which many non-Catholics deplore. The fact that, in the vast majority of instances, neither a person's faith nor his loyalty to the country is at stake need not lessen the difficulty of his dilemma. For the Catholic, as for every other member of some minority religious group in our society, there always seems to be a difficult choice between the common good of all Americans and the special needs of his particular church. Since the wishes of churchmen and the experiences of the institutional needs are not always identical with the needs of society, loyalties must be weighed and decisions made. That it is possible to be loyal to the teachings of the Church and yet, at the same time, to be disloyal to the goals of the Catholic community merely makes the choices all the more complex—especially when the relationship between the two different kinds of loyalties is hard to ascertain.

It is vital that these two problems—fidelity to the Church's doctrines and loyalty to the goals of the Catholic community—be seen as distinct from one another. A failure to see the difference accounts for a good deal of confusion on the part of the layman concerning his obligations and role as a citizen; a considerable amount of unnecessary friction between clergy and laity; and much misunderstanding on the part of the non-Catholic about the nature of the obedience the layman owes to the teaching authority of the Church. The layman's obligation to adhere to the dogmatic and moral teachings of the Church is very different from his obligation to the Church as a sociological group with a particular set of temporal needs and problems. The obligation, for instance, that a Catholic accept the Church's teaching on divorce is clear; he cannot be a Catholic if he does not accept it. Yet he has no similar duty to support, say, a local chancery office's desire to have zoning laws changed in order that an extension may be built on a parochial school. In the first instance, should he dissent, he will be in direct conflict with the authority of the Church; in the second, he will not be disloyal to authority but

may, should he oppose the zoning change, be disloyal to the Catholics
in that civil community. Put another way, the kind of personal conflict
he may feel if he is tempted by the ease of civil divorce will be different
from the one he will feel if, for the sake of civic principles, he opposes
the chancery office's desire to change zoning laws. In the former case,
the tension is between religious and secular values; in the latter, it is
between institutional and civic loyalties.

The reason for dwelling on this distinction can be stated directly. On
the one hand, as a result of his abandonment of the physical ghetto
which marked much early American Catholic life, the layman is more
than at any time in the past exposed to the full force of values different
from his own—as given him by his Church. He is thus forced to make
many more personal decisions than were his grandparents. On the
other hand, with the breakup of the ghettos and the consequent loss of
clear group identity as a Catholic among Catholics, and with, in addition, his natural identification with the broad American society, he is
faced more than ever with conflicts between institutional and civic
loyalties.

In the end, the quality of the layman's Catholicism will be determined
by the way he coordinates the demands made upon him by Church and
society; and his quality as a citizen will be determined by the way he
balances his civic loyalties and his institutional loyalties. In fact, the very
place of the Church in the life of the layman will be determined by the
way he reconciles its values with the secular values to which he is exposed; and the place of the Church in American culture will be determined by the way the layman reconciles his Catholic group allegiances
with his civic allegiances. Where choices are clear, any conflicts can be
resolved with dispatch. But they rarely are clear. The layman is, at one
and the same time, a member of an authoritarian—but not monolithic—
Church and a member of a democratic society mediating a pluralism of
values. Therein lies the difficulty of his position; but therein also lies
the great challenge before him.

Precept and Practice

With a skeletal description of the layman's situation as believer and
as citizen now in hand, it is useful next to take a look at the various
ways in which he is responding to his new status. First it must be said,

though, how very little is actually known about the American Catholic. He has been the subject of comparatively few sociological studies and even these have been very limited in scope.[2] This lack of empirical knowledge is especially evident when one attempts to determine the fidelity of American Catholics to the basic teachings and laws of the Church. How faithfully do Catholics observe the Church's commandment to attend Mass every Sunday, to receive communion at least once a year, to abstain from the eating of meat on Friday? On questions of this sort, most studies indicate a fairly high rate of observance. But when one inquires about the more difficult demands of Catholicism, or about those which might serve usefully to measure the effectiveness of Catholic training and education, one can say very little with any great confidence.

In the area of marriage, for instance, Catholic values are patently at odds with the non-Catholic consensus. Quite clearly, certain basic teachings of the Church can pose great difficulties for the contemporary Catholic: the Church's position on the necessity of sacramental marriages, the ban on divorce and most particularly the ban on the use of artificial contraceptives. How faithful are American Catholics to the Church's doctrines on marriage? No one knows for sure. What little is known, however, suggests that a fair proportion of Catholics do not observe the Church's teaching in one important respect or another. Some studies, for instance, show that 15-25 per cent of all marriages involving Catholics are invalid—mainly those before civil magistrates or Protestant ministers.[3] In some parishes the figure runs as high as 35 per cent. In addition, despite the Church's opposition (though there is no flat ban), perhaps one-fourth to one-third of all valid Catholic marriages are mixed.[4] (However, most studies indicate that their relative proportion is very closely correlated with the size of local Catholic populations. In the South, where Catholics comprise only a small portion of the population, the rate is very high. In New England, on the other hand, it is much lower.)

On the difficult problem of the proportion of Catholic couples who use

[2] A vivid discussion of the inadequacies of most sociological studies of American Catholicism can be found in Andrew Greeley, "Sociology of Religion," *The Critic* (Aug.-Sept., 1962).

[3] John Thomas, S.J., *The American Catholic Family* (New York, 1956), p. 165. On these figures, Father Thomas comments that "we have sufficient evidence to suggest that invalidity looms as a major problem for the Church in America."

[4] *Ibid.*, p. 154.

contraceptives there is little reliable evidence. It is generally acknowledged among parish priests that the Church's prohibition of artificial methods of birth control constitutes a major stumbling block; many believe it to be the cause of a considerable loss from the Church or of the non-reception of the sacraments of Penance and the Eucharist. The few attempts to find an empirical basis for these pastoral worries have been inconclusive, but they do show that *possibly* three out of ten married Catholics practice artificial birth control—and one study in North Carolina found that nearly half the Catholics there did.[5] There is little reason here to dwell on such inadequate statistics. They hardly indicate that American Catholics, by and large, are weak and indifferent. On the contrary, given the pressures upon them, they probably do remarkably well. Nonetheless, they suggest that a sizable proportion ignore some important parts of Catholic moral teaching; and one can safely assert that even more find themselves, at some point, caught in very painful ethical dilemmas.

Perhaps a more significant question concerns the effectiveness of Catholic education and training. One glaring omission in almost all studies of the American Catholic, especially those touching on his fidelity to the Church's moral laws, is that they do not distinguish between the weak and the strong Catholic, or the religiously educated and the religiously illiterate. Nor do they give any inkling about the early influences on a person's life. For instance, the different implications in the use of contraceptives by a Catholic who has had a solid background of Catholic education and one who has had little or none are obvious; but we are, statistically, still ignorant on these matters.

For generations, the policy of the Church in this country has been to create and support a system of parochial and secondary schools and to encourage the founding of Catholic colleges and universities. Theoretically, this makes considerable sense: the best way to ensure an integral, effective and faithful Catholic is to provide him with a Catholic education during his formative years. This is an assumption which has rarely been questioned; and one which has been fortified by a common hierarchical, clerical and sometimes lay suspicion about the "secularism" of the public school. Oddly enough, however, the Church has never

[5] Cf. Thomas Casey, S.J., "Catholics and Family Planning," *American Catholic Sociological Review*, XXI (Summer 1960); and John Thomas, S.J. *Religion and the American People* (Westminster, Md., 1963), pp. 76-77.

made any serious attempt to measure the success of its efforts—indeed, it has sometimes strenuously resisted any such investigation.[6]

The few random studies that have been made seem invariably to suggest one thing, that the Catholic educational system has by no means decisively proved its value in producing stronger, better-informed or more effective Catholics. This is not to say that the schools have failed to achieve their end. Instead, it is that when compared with the Catholic graduates of public schools and secular colleges, it is difficult to find any significant evidence that the graduates of Catholic institutions are notably stronger or more faithful or more apostolic Catholics.[7] Even if we can assume (at least for the sake of argument) that this is a valid conclusion, it is by no means clear why this should be the case. One can simply suggest some reasons: that the religious education given in Catholic institutions is inferior and ineffective (which many believe); that the forces of non-Catholic values in our culture are strong enough to overcome the advantage of a Catholic education; that family influence is the most decisive factor in the quality of one's religious life; and that both the intrinsic merits of an exclusively religious education and the dangers of a non-Catholic education have been over-estimated. Perhaps the reason which has been least considered by Catholic leaders is the last-mentioned one. It is likely that Catholic apprehensions about the dangers of a non-Catholic education may be exaggerated.[8]

In any case, there seems little to guarantee that a Catholic education will greatly assist the layman in confronting and dealing with the kinds of moral, social and spiritual problems which he is bound to confront in

[6] Only in 1962, under a grant from the Carnegie Foundation, was a serious study of the parochial school system begun at the University of Notre Dame. Upon the completion of that study, possibly in three to five years, both the critics and the defenders of parochial schools may be in a better position to know with some certainty what they are talking about.

[7] For some studies which tend to support this conclusion, see: Joseph H. Fichter, S.J., *Parochial School* (Notre Dame, 1958); the same author's article "Catholics and High Schools," *America*, CVII (1962), pp. 718-721; Peter H. & Alice S. Rossi, "Some Effects of Parochial School Education in America," *Daedalus* (Spring, 1961), pp. 300-328; Thomas Harte, C.Ss.R., "Catholic Education as a Factor in Catholic Opinion," *American Catholic Sociological Review*, X (March, 1949).

[8] Despite the many warnings given to Catholic high school students about the dangers of secular colleges, there are few data available to support their fears. Cf. Andrew Greeley, *The Influence of Religion on the Career Plans and Occupational Values of June 1961 College Graduates* (unpublished Ph.D. dissertation, Department of Sociology, University of Chicago, 1962), p. 126.

modern-day America. It may (and certainly should) assist him to some extent, but so many other influences will be at work on him that education alone is hardly sufficient to offset any disadvantages of family background or attitudes which he may bring with him. Nor will it guarantee the Church a better witness to Catholicism in the world.[9] This conclusion, if valid, implies an urgent need that American Catholic education be subjected to a close and careful scrutiny—myth and theory no longer suffice.

In the absence of reliable data, then, it is safe only to conclude that on the level of his personal morality and the integrity of his Catholicism the American layman presents a mixed picture. One cannot assert either that he is a model for Catholics throughout the world (except in his sacramental practice and in his financial support of the Church) or that his faith is only skin-deep. The truth lies somewhere in between. And if it cannot accurately be said that the Church's success in developing acutely sensitive, spiritually alert laymen has been outstanding, neither can it be said that the Church has failed in its most minimal tasks of education. What the Church has done is to retain the spiritual loyalty of the Catholic masses; what it has not done is to raise the religious ideals of the American layman much above the level of observance of elementary Church laws. One can usefully cite here an observation of Father Fichter: "Catholics share in the anti-Semitism of the Northeast, in the isolationism of the Midwest, in the prejudices against the Mexican in the Southwest. . . . On this level we are dealing with the moral and social problems on which the American people are confused, and on which Catholics demonstrate their achieved Americanization by sharing in that confusion."[10]

Politics and Ideology

With some sense of relief, it is time now to turn from the cloudy waters of the private moral and spiritual life of the American layman to his more public life in the community. The waters here, if not less

[9] For some disheartening statistics (hopefully outdated), see: Br. Dominic Augustin, "The Catholic College Man and the Negro," ACSR, VIII (Oct. 1947); John Kane, "Anti-Semitism Among Catholic College Students," ACSR, VIII (1947). Both studies revealed a pattern of prejudice.
[10] "The Americanization of Catholicism," in Catholicism and the American Way of Life, ed. by Thomas T. McAvoy, C.S.C. (Notre Dame, 1960), p. 124.

murky, are at least more accessible to public inspection. As already suggested in Chapter 5, one of the most important events in recent American Catholic social history was the re-opening during the fifties of the debate on the relationship of Catholicism and American life which had been abruptly terminated with the condemnation of Americanism in the last year of the nineteenth century. What brought this about was the fact of a generally successful integration into American life. That made the question a fresh and very real one.

Once Catholics in large numbers began to abandon the ghetto (whether in a real or figurative sense) and to repudiate the old ethnic ways of defensiveness, they were faced with a bewildering variety of political and social choices. On the most superficial level, they were able to choose, more consciously than in the past, among the political parties which dot the landscape. On a more basic level, they had to select also from among the various political and cultural ideologies which competed for their support. In the reality of American politics, where ideologies often cross party lines as frequently as do voters, a party allegiance is not tantamount to the acceptance of an ideological allegiance. The choice of a party in this country normally has little bearing on one's religious values. The support of an ideology, on the other hand, can reflect very directly the way an individual attempts to relate his deepest religious values to temporal values and institutions.

There is good reason to make use of this distinction between a party and an ideological choice in attempting to understand the kinds of dilemmas which the dual role of believer and citizen places before the layman. On the one hand, the past political history of American Catholics has seen a heavy support of the Democratic Party. Yet this support, as suggested earlier, has resulted more from an identification of that party with minority groups (and especially Catholic immigrants) than from Catholic support of the liberal ideology which has characterized Democratic theoreticians. Indeed, Catholics have normally been somewhat suspicious of many of the tendencies and assumptions which have been common coin among Democratic intellectuals: support of government intervention in the economic order, the use of federal power to effect social justice, and so on. Nor, culturally, have they had much personal contact with those social groups most responsible for Democratic theorizing: liberal Protestants, secular Jews, reform-minded American patricians.

Today, however, though many vestiges of instinctive Democratic leanings still remain, the Catholic increasingly finds it as natural to support the Republican Party as the Democratic. In fact, perhaps the most striking American political change during the fifties was the marked shift of Catholics from Democratic to Republican ranks, a change which most likely reflected the Catholic move to the suburbs, a greater sense of identification with Main Street America and a recognition that the Republican Party stood for many values congenial to Catholics. Presumably, too, the discovery by many Catholics that they were acceptable to Republicans—if not courted—brought their political conservatism into greater harmony with their voting practice. The candidacy of John F. Kennedy, of course, made a momentary difference, but it is likely that increased Catholic prosperity will mean an even heavier Catholic support for the Republicans in the sixties than in the fifties.

On the other hand, concurrent with a trend to Republican voting, American Catholic social thinking has moved closer to a liberal ideology than ever in the past. To be sure, the thinking of Catholic social theoreticians has proceeded from different premises than from those which inspire non-Catholic liberal ideologues. But one can find a sizable number of Catholic academicians, intellectuals, and journalists (joined by many of the clergy) who now support with enthusiasm liberal causes and values. The cumulative effect of the papal social encyclicals, a lessening of traditional Catholic fears about the use of federal power for social ends, and greater Catholic contact with those groups normally responsible in America for the shaping of liberalism have all contributed to this trend. The term "liberal Catholic," once employed as a weapon of character assassination by one Catholic against another, has now lost most of its force.[11]

Now there may appear in this conjunction of a Catholic movement toward the Republican Party and a growing acceptance of American liberalism something of a paradox. Yet one's puzzlement quickly disappears with the realization that party allegiance is no sure guide to ideological alignment. This is all the more so considering the slight differences between the two major parties in this country and the fact that the choice of one party or another is as often as not merely a func-

[11] The untiring effort on the part of Catholic liberal publicists to distinguish Catholic liberalism from nineteenth-century secular liberalism has undoubtedly played a part also.

tion of class and income. If one is to search for the decisive point of contact of the Catholic layman with the ideological currents in our society one must look elsewhere. Clearly, the old debate about whether a Catholic could (or ought) to be a liberal or a conservative has become almost meaningless. Neither American conservatism nor American liberalism is incompatible with Catholicism, whether in its dogmas or in its social teachings. If for no other reason, the flexibility (if not ambiguity) of much recent Catholic social thought makes either choice possible in theory; and the fact of large numbers of Catholics on both sides of the fence has validated it in practice.

Catholics and Pluralism

The decisive point of contact between American Catholicism and American society now lies in the new problems of religious pluralism posed by the disintegration of a traditional American consensus, of Protestant origin, on the relationship of religion and American society. In very rough terms this consensus involved three ingredients: a firm belief that America is a religious nation dependent upon Christian values to sustain its national life; that "Christian" is to be understood in a Protestant sense; that minority religious rights exist because the right of freedom of conscience and worship are an essential part of the Protestant understanding of man. This consensus no longer exists. At the roots of its disappearance are a number of contemporary social realities. The most basic is the existence of massive non-Protestant minority groups; Protestants no longer have the numerical strength or the social cohesion necessary to sustain a Protestant-American national ethos. Nor, consciously at least, do they appear to have any great desire to do so.

But it is necessary to understand the dynamics of this disintegration; and here the previously hidden social realities are now appearing in the open. For one thing, there now exist a large number of Americans— among them many Jews, unbelievers and Protestants—who believe that the laws, public institutions, perhaps the very signs, seals and symbols of the nation, should be scrupulously neutral concerning religion. In practice, this means a basic challenge to the belief that this is a "religious" nation. For another, Catholics, while supporting a Christian tradition, are now in a position to reject any assumption that "Christian" is to be understood as "Protestant Christian." Finally, both Catholics and those in favor of a purely secular basis for American public life reject any theory of religious freedom which presupposes a Protestant theological understanding of constitutional or civil rights. Thus, of the three ingredients of the traditional religious consensus mentioned above, at least two are rejected by Catholics and all three by those favoring a secular society. The very size and power of these two dissenting minorities make these rejections a potent social force.

It is beyond my province here to discuss the general implications of this change in the consensus. What is germane, however, is to inquire into its implications for the Catholic community. For what is now apparent is that Catholics, because of their newly-achieved social assimilation and their potential political power, are now in a position to help shape whatever new consensus will emerge from the ruins of the old. At stake is the kind and quality of the contribution which Catholics will make to the heated debate on religion and the aims of American life which has recently erupted. Its main elements are the challenge of Communism; federal aid to parochial schools; recent Supreme Court decisions on Sunday Blue Laws; disagreements over the place of religion in the public schools; and issues of public policy which have arisen out of conflicts over abortion and state-supported birth control programs.

With the exception of Communism, each part of the debate has turned on the meaning of pluralism. Does pluralism, which all ostensibly support, mean a plurality of values only within a religious framework? Does it imply the right of any one group to attempt through legislation and political power to impose its values on other groups or have its institutional needs recognized as long as this is done in a constitutional way? Does it imply the necessity of a rigid understanding of the separation of church and state or an understanding flexible enough to allow some forms of government encouragement of religious values? Along with these pressing questions, however, the problem of Communism has come to have a special importance. Is the best way to strengthen this nation against the threat of Communism a re-affirmation of America's religious heritage? Or would it be better to recognize honestly that such an approach is bound to be offensive to many who prefer to see American values grounded in non-religious beliefs? These are the questions which now exercise the Catholic community—and divide it; though they overlap the older debate on liberalism and conservatism, the ground of discussion has shifted to the more acute problems of pluralism.

Yet it is important to note that they have arisen not only for Catholics as individuals but also, and perhaps more acutely, for Catholics as members of the American sociological community of Catholics. To ask how Catholics as individuals ought to respond to these questions is not the same thing as to ask how they ought to respond as a body—or whether they ought to respond as a body at all. The distinction can be made clear by one prominent example. In the effort to gain federal aid for parochial schools under any broad education bill, different approaches have been employed by different bishops. Some, in arguing the merits of the case for such aid, have urged the laity to study the question personally and, if convinced, to support it as individual citizens. Others have made a conscious appeal to group loyalty; they call upon the laity to join together as a cohesive body to exert massive political pressure. In the one instance, the stress is laid on the layman as a discrete, assimilated citizen; in the other, it is on the layman as an integral member of a minority group which has specific rights and needs precisely as a group.

In my final chapter, I will attempt to suggest some ways in which the layman as an individual should answer these questions. It is necessary now, however, to spell out in greater detail the meaning and implications of the changing relationship between American pluralism and Catholics as a group.

Among the laity, perhaps no question has been raised so frequently or insistently as this: what contribution should Catholics try to make to American life? This question means not only what Catholics as individuals should try to accomplish, but also what the Church, as a community of clergy and laity, should aim for. There is still another sense in which this problem is often understood: how ought the Church seek to preserve, sustain and protect itself from harmful forces? How ought it to seek to strengthen itself internally to ensure faithful and effective service to its members? The first sense of the basic question bears on the positive, apostolic task of the Church; the second on its defensive, preservative task. At first glance, it might appear that these different senses of the question are of only academic interest. Nothing could be further from the truth. The different interpretations of the question account for very different attitudes concerning the Church and American life, and for some of the sharpest arguing among Catholics.

To grasp the significance of these differences, it is helpful to recall the early conflict among American Catholics between the established

Anglo-American Catholics and the incoming, insecure immigrants.[12] Each group, in its own way, sought to make a Catholic contribution to America. The Anglo-Americans, solidly integrated in the community, on easy terms with the Protestant majority, accepted with little complaint those liabilities which their Catholicism may have imposed on them. They sought to gain acceptance for the Church by the way of intellectual and cultural attainment, social conformity and the influence of good personal character. Sharing the language and social mores of their non-Catholic neighbor, they had little trouble adapting themselves to the life they found about them. The immigrant had few such advantages. Rejected and discriminated against by the established majority, the immigrant could not easily take a confident, positive stance toward the America he found: he had to fight and struggle for anything he got. America, if it meant some relief from the oppressions and privations of the Old Country, also meant new forms of fear, discrimination and Catholic-baiting—and some very great dangers to religion itself.

Although it is very difficult now to find many direct descendants of the Anglo-American families, it is exceedingly easy to find many children of the immigrant tradition.[13] What is important, however, are not the blood lines of descent but rather the permanent existence among American Catholics of the two different attitudes each of these traditions embodied. Thus one can find large numbers of Catholics, particularly among intellectuals, who hold that Catholics ought not to press aggressively for their rights or for public acceptance of their Church's internal needs. Instead, they should, by the quiet force of slow persuasion and good example, by dialogue with non-Catholics, attempt to make its beauty as well as its legitimate needs self-evident. Very much like the liberal bishops and clergy during the Americanist period, they assume a natural compatibility of Catholicism and American life and count on the basic good will of non-Catholics eventually to resolve any conflicts. Above all, they urge that Catholics not be tempted to band together to conduct political struggles on matters of public policy affecting religion. In particular, they deplore any manifestations of Catholic separatism and

[12] See Chapter 1 p. 16.

[13] It is worth observing that in certain Catholic schools—Portsmouth Priory, Canterbury, St. David's in New York, some of the Sacred Heart Convents—the direct heirs of Anglo-American families are heavily represented. Not surprisingly, they appear to favor Harvard, Yale and Princeton for their college work rather than a Catholic college.

would prefer to see Catholics work as individuals within pluralistic organizations rather than form specifically Catholic movements.

For many other Catholics, a more aggressive approach appears necessary. Far from believing that non-Catholics are necessarily amenable to enlightened dialogue or the quiet force of individual example and persuasion, they would hold that the forces of anti-religion and anti-Catholicism are rife in the land. If Protestantism is no longer looked upon with the old suspicion, then its place as a *bête-noire* has been taken by the powers of secularism and agnosticism. If Catholics are to make their message and their needs known, then they must be willing to enter the political thicket and use the political power potentially in their grasp. There is no suggestion, on this side, of turning America into a Catholic state; but only of making certain that Catholics have every iota of rights due them under our Constitution and every bit as much voice in the shaping of the public consensus as any other group. According to this view, the best way to gain federal aid for parochial schools is through active lay pressure groups, political lobbies, and legal efforts. The best way to combat secularism and unbelief is through public complaint, the power of the law, and an aroused citizenry ready to apply pressure where needed.

The two viewpoints sketched here are abstractions; it would be difficult to find them in a pure form in any given individual. But in their general lines they characterize the two main streams of the present Catholic response to American pluralism. Both assume that Catholics have some contribution to make; but they differ sharply on what that contribution should be or how it should be made. For the adherents of the first-mentioned viewpoint, the overriding consideration is that Catholics make some creative contributions to the problems which face all Americans. The institutional needs of the Church are of secondary importance; the first task of the Church is to bring its wisdom to all men. For the adherents of the second viewpoint, the institutional good of the Church is tantamount to the good of the nation. And the great need of the nation is not for some new, better solutions to national problems, but a return to those old, tried values which for centuries have sustained American and Western life. For the former one, the great failure of American Catholicism is that it has not sufficiently addressed itself to the common good but has remained preoccupied with its own troubles and the faults of its neighbors. For the latter, the great failure is the timidity and obsequiousness of Catholics, their refusal to stand up for their rights and their unwillingness to make their views and values forcefully evident to all.

Yet to put these broad differences in a proper light, it is essential to recognize that every emerging minority has had to face a similar choice. Significantly, the American Negro community has become divided in recent years over the issue of aggressiveness. Many of the older Negro leaders have pressed for a steady reduction in those local laws and customs which discriminate against the Negro; they have, mainly through the N.A.A.C.P., instituted court suits and carried on a program of public education on Negro problems. A younger generation, impatient with the pace of Negro emancipation, has resorted to the more direct means of the sit-in and the Freedom Ride. Similarly, the Jewish community has experienced important internal conflicts over how to get those laws and local practices changed that place the Jew in an unfavorable light or emphasize his non-Christian, minority status. For a great number of Jews, the question whether they should attempt to resort to vigorous political and legal efforts to have Sunday Blue Laws changed, crèches removed from public parks, or prayers banned in the public schools, is as tortured as the one Catholics face in seeking federal aid to parochial schools.

Each minority, of course, has to fashion its own group solution to such problems; each, especially the Negro minority, has particular difficulties not shared by the others. For the Catholic community—even if there was one voice to speak for it—no easy solution is possible; and this precisely because, unlike the Jews and the Negroes, there is very little overt discrimination against Catholics. What remains for Catholics are mainly those problems arising from successful assimilation; for a variety of reasons, the Jew and the Negro have still to overcome many of the hurdles which Catholics have now surmounted.

Yet in speaking of "successful assimilation" this cannot be taken to mean that Catholics, in general, are necessarily happy with the quality of their social acceptance. For those of a more aggressive mentality, it still leaves much to be desired. For them, an issue like that of federal aid to parochial schools shows all too well that many non-Catholics are still insensitive to the problems and difficulties felt by Catholics. For them, the measure of true pluralism would be a sympathetic hearing and a creative solution to the Catholic desire to provide a religious education for their children, to protect their children from harmful literature and movies, and to save them from being forced to pay taxes to support such things as public birth-control programs. Among others, however, genuine assimilation would mean that Catholics were making a visible contribution to the problems facing all. For them, the quality of the Catholic contribution to public education, to the rights of Negroes and Jews, and to the correction of massive social welfare ills would be a better index of assimilation.

It should be clear that the way the Catholic community eventually resolves these new dilemmas will have serious implications for the future of American pluralism. It will have no less a bearing on the kind of contribution the Catholic layman will be able to make to American life. If a broad Catholic consensus should emerge equating the good of the nation with the solution of internal Catholic problems—whether these problems are seen in such narrow contexts as the preservation of parochial schools or such broad ones as the danger of secularism for Catholic faith—then one could expect serious religious battles to erupt at regular intervals. What Catholics gained for themselves by such a course could easily be offset by the hostility it would generate among non-Catholics. Should the consensus turn in the other direction, however, there could well be some important gains for religious peace. At the same time, Catholics might also have to accept some losses in the strength of their own institutions—or find ways of solving internal problems without non-Catholic assistance.

A good example of these different implications can be seen in the 1961 decision (still in force) of the bishops to oppose any federal aid to education bill which does not make provision for aid to parochial schools. Though well aware that their stand could mean that no bill of any kind would be passed—thus hurting the public schools—they chose to wage a full-scale political campaign. Nor, in the face of Protestant opposition to such aid, could they have been unaware of the religious tensions their stand would produce. At the basis of this decision was a belief that the "rights" of Catholics would be jeopardized by a bill providing aid for public schools alone—and that they are worth whatever danger a vigorous political campaign would entail. In addition, they believed that unless Catholic rights, needs and desires were recognized at the outset of any massive federal aid program, they would possibly not be met at all; the time for pressure was before a program got under way, not after.

The result has been, of course, to exacerbate religious differences, to help stymie a federal aid to education program and, so far, to gain nothing for the parochial schools of any great importance. Yet, given their intentness on the strengthening of Catholic education and the hostility felt by many non-Catholics toward it, there was doubtless some practical wisdom in the Bishops' stand; in American politics, it has many precedents (some successful) among other minority groups.[14]

Pluralism and Catholic Solidarity

But the implications in the potential responses to pluralism are hardly confined only to the place of the Catholic Church in American life. They are just as important for the internal peace of the Church and for an effective and meaningful lay loyalty. To grasp the meaning for the Church of these new pluralistic dilemmas, one primary social fact must be kept well in mind: the Catholic layman has now almost decisively broken his old ethnic ties. In the past, for a variety of reasons already described in earlier chapters, the Catholic was forced by circumstance to look to his fellow Catholics for mutual support and protection. It was both natural and unavoidable for him to foster community solidarity; it was his best protection against a sometimes hostile and dangerous society. Now all that has changed. Not only a change in his circumstances brought about the break; but it was also brought about by his own distaste for the old state of affairs. Ghettoism, at first an asset, was soon seen to be a social liability. Catholicism itself creates enough problems; why complicate them with ethnic Catholicism? Even more, why complicate them by a species of Catholicism which is narrow, parochial and insular, ever wary of the non-Catholic world, ever ready to take offense at real or imaginary slights?

Given this changing Catholic temper, it is hardly coincidental that Catholic writing and preaching in recent years have turned on the ways in which the Church and the layman can make a positive contribution to American life. In part, of course, this emphasis has reflected a theological response to the recognition that Christianity, including Catholicism, is failing to make a vital impact on society. But it also reflects the

[14] The results of a Gallup Poll taken early in 1963, moreover, indicated a shift of non-Catholic sentiment toward federal aid for private schools. This may well reflect the success of the bishops in publicizing their case.

need of Catholics to find a spirituality which will take account of their desire to escape from a narrow, socially defensive Catholicism to a confident, positive, creative Catholicism. In sum, the great demand has been for a renewal of Catholicism which would reflect the altered social status of American Catholics. The need of the day is not for better defenses of the Church, better arguments in her favor, better justifications for Catholic belief—it is for a Catholicism which seeks the good of all, which has something to say to all (and not just to embattled Catholics), and which is a source of wisdom and unity for all.

Yet if this has been a main trend in recent Catholic thinking, it has co-existed with a more deeply-rooted belief that the American Catholic community has never received its just portion of recognition. Until the election of John F. Kennedy, however, this latter belief was all but obscured by the work of those pressing for an emphasis on Catholic responsibilities for the common good. The surge away from the ghetto was a far stronger force than that which animated many to hold firmly to their old grievances. It now appears that the election has served to strengthen both tendencies. On the one hand, it has encouraged many to seek to remove whatever lingering traces there are of an outmoded ghetto mentality. But, on the other, it has encouraged many others to press more forcefully for the recognition of Catholic needs.

It is the strengthened re-emergence of this latter tendency which is bound to be a source of friction among Catholics. For the essential condition of a reassertion of Catholic rights and needs is that the Catholic community be shaped into a cohesive, unified political body. The only way that Catholics can gain their "rights" is by political unity. But such unity can be attained only by invoking once again the spirit of communal loyalty which marked the days of immigration. For what clearly stands in the way of Catholic group solidarity is precisely their assimilation— and the power of this assimilation to dim a sense of communal solidarity can only be overcome by re-animating a sense of grievance, external threat and thwarted needs. Here is the rub: for a great number of Catholics, the one temptation they have most sought to overcome is *exactly* that of allowing these old grievances and needs to dominate their mind. The main thing they do not want, after struggling for years to overcome it, is a return to a Catholic spirit of grievance and complaint, a Catholic spirit of aggressive unity.

Now for many Americans it is taken for granted that a strong measure of aggressive Catholic unity already exists. This is hardly correct. Catholics have been for a number of years sharply divided on many major issues, ranging from domestic politics to the meaning of papal teachings. It is hard to think of a single major national issue within the past decade that did not see Catholics opposed to one another; and the same can be said of a great variety of theological issues. Moreover, since Catholics now occupy all steps on the social ladder, there are important class and educational distinctions among Catholics, differences which in practice lead to many conflicts. As far as Catholics are concerned there are good reasons to doubt the validity of Will Herberg's and Gerhard Lenski's thesis that "The successor of the ethnic subcommunity is the socio-religious community."[15] What these observers fail to recognize is that many Catholics resist strenuously any tendency to see their loyalty to the Church as equivalent to an identity with the Catholic "socio-religious community."[16] More precisely, it could be said that Catholics are now faced with a choice between trying to erase any suggestion that such a cohesive social community exists (or should exist) and trying to form such a community and making it a strong social and political reality.

Inevitably, the conflict between supporters of these two options means conflict within the Church. To those who would minimize the socio-communal aspects of American Catholicism, their more solidarity-minded Catholic brothers are like throwbacks to an era which should be buried and forgotten. In the eyes of the aggressive, the minimizers are bound to appear disloyal to the Church, or at least grossly deficient in their sensitivities to the needs of the Church. The prime instance of such conflicts —the one that overshadows all others—is, again, the one over federal aid to parochial schools.

By now it has become clear that the major tactic within the Church of the ardent supporters of such aid is the invocation of communal loyalty. Just as vigorously as various bishops, priests and lay publicists have urged the so-called "Catholic case" on federal aid to parochial schools on the nation, as vigorously have they tried to persuade Catholics

[15] Gerhard Lenski, *The Religious Factor* (New York, 1961), p. 326. Cf. Will Herberg, "Religious Group Conflict in America," *College of New Rochelle Alumnae News* (Fall, 1962), pp. 7-8, and *Catholic-Protestant-Jew* (rev. ed.; New York, 1960), p. 39.

[16] Cf. Joseph H. Fichter, S.J., *Social Relations in the Urban Parish*, Chap. IV, "Social Solidarity and Model Parishioners," pp. 40ff., for some evidence on an absence of social solidarity among Catholics.

themselves that their rights are being infringed. They have learned that they can by no means expect a unanimous Catholic acceptance of their case. The reason for this is surely that many Catholics, accepted and secure in their communities, have no sense of deprivation or grievance. More importantly, a large number of Catholics appear to resent any effort to induce such a sense; and they strongly resist being drawn back into an orbit of aggressive Catholic communal solidarity. This does not mean that they are uninterested in aid to parochial schools; but it does mean that they are not interested in jeopardizing inter-religious understanding to gain it. Nor, as citizens, are they interested in fighting for a Catholic cause if this fight will entail some potential harm to the community at large.

The fruits of assimilation are thus many. They pose dilemmas on the personal level which are sharper than those faced by earlier generations. But, above all, they raise in a direct way the question of how the layman ought to relate himself to American life. And that question in turn can only be answered by determining at the same time how the layman ought to relate himself to American Catholicism as a social community. In the end, the problem of the layman's place within the Church is inextricably related to the problem of his role as a citizen. We may now turn to this relationship.

CHAPTER 8

The Future of the Layman

NOTHING is so hard on the conventional wisdom of any given generation as rapid social change. In those societies accustomed to stability, those rooted in a rigid pattern of daily life, a sudden social or political upheaval can mean total disaster. In American society, however, change and flux have from the beginning been the rule; we have never been able to develop a fixed way of life which can be handed down intact from grandfather to father, from father to son. Every generation has been forced to shape its own conventional wisdom, and almost always with the understanding that it must be tentative and provisional, subject to overthrow or modification by those who come after.

The American Catholic has, of course, shared in the flux of our society; in fact, his very presence has been one of its causes. And like his non-Catholic neighbor, he has been forced to develop ways of coping with change and the constant transition from one style of life to another. For the Catholic, however, there have been some special problems. His religion (at its best) transcends the mores of ordinary life; it holds up to him values, ideals and goals which often set him in conflict with those about him and places before him standards which make it difficult to accept the reigning intellectual and moral fashions. In past generations, the American Catholic tendency has been to escape from such conflicts—either by a violent rejection of opposing values or by ignoring them altogether. Neither solution has proved to be workable; and neither can be called a validly Catholic one.

What the present generation is coming to see is the need for both a more vigorous and a more discriminating approach to American life. The necessity of vigor is apparent: American Catholics make at present very little special contribution to the national good. They do their part, undoubtedly, but little more. Whatever the criteria one might choose—in

171

tellectual and cultural leadership, prophetic social judgment, the leavening of a secularized humanity with the Word of salvation—American Catholicism would do badly. The necessity of discrimination is no less apparent. Neither a blind acceptance nor a fearful rejection of American life can bring any good—to the Catholic himself or to that life which swirls about him. In particular, it is no longer possible for the Catholic simply to proclaim his dedication to revered American values while, at the same time, cutting himself off from those trends and movements which attempt to give those values new relevance.

Yet if American Catholics are gradually coming to see these needs, they are still unclear about the best course to follow in the future. Almost all would agree, however, that the main burden of creating a rich, productive and mutually beneficial relationship between Catholicism and American life must be carried by the layman. It is he, and not the priest or the bishop, who is most intimately in touch with the non-Catholic; who is most exposed to the main stream of cultural and political life; who is most directly forced to wrestle with the dilemmas of giving Christian witness in a society ever ready to ignore or domesticate religion. No matter how vigorous the spiritual leadership of the bishops, no matter how brilliant the work of theologians, no matter how dedicated the ordinary priest—it will all count for nothing if the layman does not do his part.

But what is the "part" of the layman? That is the crucial question which innumerable priests and laymen have put to themselves, and to each other, in recent years. It is in answer to that question that many bishops have spoken, that many lay leaders have attempted to shape means and ends. And out of the probing and its accompanying self-criticism have come a broad consensus. The layman's task is to bring Christian values to bear in every corner of society, to speak to the needs and the agonies of our times, to show the contemporary relevance of Christianity to those great issues which trouble and divide men. Christianity, far from being opposed to the material world, is a religion of incarnation, a religion which has the obligation to accept and redeem the world. While the Christian's ultimate destiny is union with God, he must work out his salvation in this world. One cannot call oneself a Christian if one does not seek justice in this world for the oppressed, if one is not sensitive to the cares and needs of the suffering and persecuted, if one does not attempt to make one's deepest values visible and effective in society. Racial discrimination, the underdeveloped nations, the impact of automation and technology, poverty and the maldistribution of wealth, the life of reason, the arts, political institutions—all these are the proper province and concern of the Christian. And above all, they are the special concern of the layman. He lives in the world; it is up to him to redeem it.

Along with this consensus still another one has emerged: the layman must have a more significant role to play in the Church itself. It is unnecessary to describe again here those lay aspirations and desires already spoken of in previous chapters: greater freedom of speech in the Church, fuller participation in the liturgy, less clerical paternalism, a more responsible role for the trained layman. It is sufficient only to say that those laymen and priests who dissent from this common opinion are fewer every year.

Oddly enough, however, few have seen the full implications of these two consensuses, especially as they relate to each other. As a rule, the place of the layman in the Church is treated as a problem separate and distinct from that of the layman in the world. The only occasions on which the two are joined, and then only rarely, come when it is observed that a fuller and more meaningful lay role in the Church would mean a more effective layman in the world; or that the hierarchy and clergy would profit from the worldly wisdom of the laity on administrative or policy decisions. These are valid and important perceptions, but they only touch a part of the deeper issues. That few have cared to go much further is understandable: as a member of the Church the layman is under an authority very different from that of the state. There are many things about the exercise of authority in the Church which cannot be decided by democratic methods. But over and above genuine theological obstacles, there also exists a deep-rooted fear of discussing or contemplating the interaction of freedom in the Church and freedom in civil life. Trusteeism and the Americanist crisis undoubtedly had the effect of making such discussions appear a dangerous business, better avoided altogether; time has not yet healed those wounds.

Nonetheless, as I have tried to show, the attitudes of the layman toward the Church, and his conception of his place within it, are very directly shaped by his experience as a free citizen in our society. Whether one likes it or not, the fact of civic freedom and its potentiality for unlimited action and initiative provide part of the context in which the layman thinks about and responds to the Church. If he is a weak or uninformed Catholic, he may judge the Church entirely by the standards of democratic freedom—and then reject it or find himself in a permanent state of rebellion or bitterness. But even if he is a strong Catholic, able to distinguish between civil and ecclesiastical freedom, he is still likely to see areas in Church life which could profit from the stiff winds of open debate and the cooperative fashioning of goals and policies.

(What is unfortunate about the fear of facing such realities directly, about fearing to admit the influence of democratic values on the Church, is that no one asks many of the creative questions which could be asked.) Thus as part of the new consensus on the importance of the layman a basic question is constantly raised: how can the layman give an effective witness to his faith in society? Similarly, it is asked: how can the layman have a more effective voice in the Church? These two questions dominate almost every discussion of the layman. They are perfectly good questions; but they have only limited value. Neither of them so much as suggests that the values which underlie and sustain our democratic life can make a contribution to the religious life of the layman or to the Church. The first question, in particular, suggests that the relationship of Catholicism and society ought, ideally, to be a one-way relationship: what can the Church, through the layman, give society? Not, what can society give the Church? But it ought to be perfectly clear that, apart from the absence of interference with the inner life of the Church for which American Catholics have always praised our society, American values have played a substantial role in shaping those held by Catholics. If this is so, and if this is not necessarily bad (which few would assert), then it is time some different questions were posed.

Freedom and the Layman

Instead of asking only how the layman can give witness in society, let us reverse the question: how can the layman out in society give witness within the Church? This question will at once strike most Catholics as very odd. And, indeed, it would be odd and unacceptable if understood to mean that secular values could be used to judge the spiritual reality of the Church. That is not the meaning I have in mind. Instead, it is this: the layman in society can give witness within the Church by showing those who have authority in it that freedom and self-direction are not incompatible with the maintenance of legitimate authority. He can show them that one important way to form an effective Christian is by providing him with a maximum of liberty and a minimum of restraint; that just as an effective citizen must be a trained and responsible one, so too an effective layman must be no less well trained and responsible; that fear and distrust of freedom are as dangerous to the common good as a misuse of freedom; that just as political repression and the suppression of valid differences of opinion are bound to harm the political integrity and maturity of the citizen, so too an overly zealous use of ecclesiastical power will harm the spiritual integrity and maturity of the layman.

There should be no need to pose such a question or elaborate on possible answers to it. Regrettably, a lack of freedom in some non-theological and non-moral areas in the Church is recognized to be a major handicap to the development of the kind of layman the Church now needs in order to make its voice heard in the world. The layman is called upon to be vigorous, courageous and outspoken in secular society —but he is rarely encouraged (though he may be permitted) to be any of these things within the Church itself. He is told that the Church approves of the kind of give and take which prevails in American life— but he finds that it is hesitant to allow it within the Church. He is told that the Catholic school and college are as good a training ground for democracy as the public institution—yet he knows full well that the virtues often lauded within them are discipline, obedience and uniformity of opinion. He is asked, finally, to be a prophetic voice in society —but he may well be courting trouble if he tries to raise such a voice within the Church.

Now the great difficulty here is not the divinely ordained authority of the Church in matters of faith and morals. Rarely does this pose a genuine problem of conscience for the layman. The real difficulty is authoritarianism: that cluster of inclinations, concepts and attitudes which is fearful of individual freedom, reliant upon the force of law and coercion to sustain belief, and convinced that the only discipline of any value is that imposed by others. It would be false to imply that the authoritarian spirit reigns supreme in the Church, especially in America. The layman does, in fact, have open to him many options and can exercise considerable freedom. For all that, the impulse among Catholic churchmen toward freedom seems weaker than toward authoritarianism.

The layman is urged to be a free man in society; but if he observes how reliant some bishops and priests are upon docile laymen, how alarmed they become when faced with even a respectful challenge to their wisdom, then it is difficult for the layman to believe that much store is set by freedom—within the Church or outside.

Let us ask another question. How can the layman's life within the Church proclaim the relevance and value of Christianity to society? Again we have a question which, at first, may appear strange; but an answer will dispel any mystery. The layman witnesses to the relevance of Christianity in the temporal order by showing that, within the institutional bounds of the Church, Christianity enables human beings to love one another, to respect the freedom of one another and to provide a perfect basis for human cooperation and mutual enrichment. Thus if the Church within its own walls should show a tendency toward arrogance and dictatorship; if it cannot effectively unite the various social classes which make up its members; if it cannot get white Catholics to accept Negro Catholics; if its teaching authorities do not find it possible to allow legitimate differences of opinion to exist—then how is it conceivable that a skeptical world will be willing to listen to it and heed its advice? How can the world be expected to believe that Catholics can help bring to it peace and freedom if Catholics condemn and suppress each other? Who will listen?

The point of asking such seemingly odd questions is apparent. If the Church, and the laymen who are in its front ranks, are to carry the Word of Christ to the world, it is necessary to find ways of resolving those dilemmas which afflict the interior life of the Church. Insofar as the Church is a supernatural reality, the Mystical Body of Christ, there are no dilemmas. But the Church is also an institution committed into the hands of men charged with the responsibility of making its divine origin and animation apparent and efficacious. It is in the way these men, together with those who make up their pastorate, manage to incarnate the supernatural into human structures which determines the vigor and effect of the Church. Yet in our day it seems clear that on the human level the Church is beset with many of the same troubles and conflicts which beset the world at large. They are, thankfully, far less intense in character within the Church than outside of it; but they are present. If the world is searching for the ideal relationship between freedom and authority, so too it can be said that the Church is seeking, within its own institutions, the same thing. If the world is attempting to find ways to bring men of diverse temperaments, races, and aspirations together, so too the Church is, within itself, wrestling with the problem. The greatest mistake Catholics could make would be to assume that the tensions which afflict mankind in general and American life in particular do not to some degree exist within the institutional life of the Church.

Yet if there are similarities between the troubles of the world and those of the Church, then it is reasonable for the Church to appropriate where possible those insights and techniques which the world has found valuable in overcoming its problems. If, in American life, we know that a full exchange of ideas and a broad public discussion is the best way to achieve a vital consensus, then the Church can well learn from that experience. Again, if we know as citizens that the way to increase a sense of commitment and to stimulate the springs of action is by giving people responsibility, then we can only profit within the Church by attempting to find ways to tap the same spirit. The Church can learn from the world—and, by so learning, renew its own life in order to be more effective in that world.

There are, then, some good reasons why the meaning and implications of the democratic, pluralistic society we have in this country should be explored more fully. But still another reason presents itself. The laity, it seems to me, have a good basis for their complaints that clerical paternalism is a major obstacle to a more effective development of the layman. At the same time, there is considerable justice in the clerical retort that lay apathy is a reality of major proportions. How can these two viewpoints be reconciled? One can make a good beginning by asking some pointed questions about the reasons for lay apathy. One reason is surely that many laymen are responsible for their own indifference; it is their fault and no one else's. This explanation does not, however, cover those great numbers of laymen who are clearly intent upon keeping their personal religious life in good order but who show no inclination toward a vigorous social witness or fulfilling their apostolic obligations. A more plausible reason for this kind of apathy lies in the type of training the laity receives from the hands of a significant proportion of the clergy (and religious). If the layman is conditioned from his earliest days to be quiet and docile, to do what he is told, it is almost inevitable that he will be poorly prepared to act in a mature, vigorous way when he is an adult. The over-protective parent produces immature and dependent children; an over-protective clergy produces the same kind of layman.

That is not all. In our society, the Catholic as a citizen is able to exercise his constitutional freedoms to the fullest degree; the contrast between the kind of role he plays within the Church and the kind he plays within society is unmistakable. What are the implications of these contrasting roles? One is that should the layman wish to use his human talents to the utmost, he has a far better chance of doing so in the service of society than in the service of the Church. In society, imagination, initiative, and leadership are rewarded and respected; in the Church they may be the cause of suspicion and suppression.

Because of these contrasting possibilities, the compulsion to turn away from service of Church to service of society is a strong one today. Ironically, this compulsion becomes all the stronger for many laymen when they realize that there is a perfectly authentic lay vocation in the service of society. They know they can be perfectly good Catholics and even very effective ones by giving testimony to the Church and Chris- tion values in the market place. Why, then—many today seem to be asking themselves—if this kind of indirect service is possible, should they tolerate the kinds of restrictions, difficulties and tensions which go with more direct participation in the organizations and institutions of the Church?

Consider the choices open to the lay scholar. If he is well-trained and competent in his specialty, he will be able to teach in either a Catholic or a non-Catholic college. Which should he choose? In either case, he can serve the Church; each is a legitimate way of expressing his voca- tion as a layman. But should he choose to teach in the Catholic college, he knows that he will very likely have to tolerate many handicaps and restrictions: he cannot ordinarily become president of the college, he may have little say in determining administrative policies and he will have to defer to his clerical superiors in a way that he would not to lay superiors. In such circumstances, is it surprising that many lay scholars today find the non-Catholic college far more attractive? Though he will un- doubtedly encounter many vexing problems in the non-Catholic college, at least he starts out on similar footing with his colleagues: he is an equal among equals.

In the past, this kind of choice was rarely open to the layman. Often

his help was not wanted in secular institutions: he was not welcome on
the secular campus, in secular welfare work or in non-Catholic organizations in general. If he was tolerated, his opportunities were limited because of his Catholicism. Thus it was natural for him to stay closer to
Church organizations; if there were frustrations there, they were at least
more tolerable than those he met in the outside world. Today all that
has changed; the situation is reversed. It is the direct service of the
Church which entails the greater number of frustrations. The result of
this shift is apparent: a great many of the better-educated, more assimilated laymen are coming to choose the secular world as the more
congenial place to exercise their lay vocation.[1]

   There is no reason to be happy about this change. Ideally, the choice
between serving the Church in a direct way—by teaching in its schools,
by working for its parish organizations, its supra-parochial welfare, civic
and international movements—and serving it by complete integration
in secular life ought to be made on the basis of particular talents and an
individual's personal sense of vocation. It ought not, in any case, to be a
false choice—forced by the unpleasantness or frustrations of work
within Church organizations. If the Church needs the layman as a
leaven in the world, it also needs some of his energies within its own
institutions. For that matter, it could well be said that the Church most
needs those men and women whose superior talents and training make
them particularly welcome in the secular world; for its own good the
Church stands in need of some of these talents applied to its interior
problems. But it can only attract such people if its institutional atmosphere is at least as open to creativity, freedom of action and the
exercise of personal responsibility as that of the secular world. As things
now stand, the Catholic layman is almost more welcome in secular life
—to judge by the responsibilities and privileges he is given—than he is
within the organizations of the Church. Since there is every reason to
expect that the situation of the Catholic will continue to improve in

[1] In relation to this point, cf. Sally Cassidy, *Some Aspects of Lay Leadership*
(Unpublished Ph.D. dissertation, Department of Sociology, University of Chicago,
1959), p. 61: "Within the ecclesiastical institution the layman is relatively free.
As long as he does not pretend to speak for the Church he may do almost as he
pleases. . . . [But] when the laymen acts in an official capacity, as editor of a
diocesan paper, or dean of a Catholic college, or leader of a recognized Church
organization, then he comes under control and is precisely in the vulnerable
position."

American society, it is imperative that it improve within the Church. For the layman will go where he can most be himself—as a Catholic and as a person.

A Sense of Alienation

There is still another obstacle standing in the way of efforts to arouse the laity. In the previous chapter I described two important understandings of the Church's response to pluralism which have emerged in recent years: one emphasizing the necessity of serving first the common good of the nation and secondarily the needs of the Catholic socio-political community; the other aggressively prone to seek public recognition of Catholic "rights"—which are seen as tantamount to the common good. The implications of this split are enormous. If the latter succeed in shaping even part of the laity into an effective political force, they will arouse the hostility and suspicions of other laymen and drive vast numbers further into exclusive service of the secular world. This is not to suggest that the Catholic community does not have some serious problems and needs—the maintenance of the parochial school system is the most basic. Instead, it is to assert that should Church leaders appear to be interested primarily in those needs, they will only provoke the resistance of those laymen who see the Church's duty as that of service to society.

For a number of years, many laymen have publicly deplored a tendency of the American Church to reserve its major energies for those national crises which most affect its own good. These complaints reflect a growing feeling that the Church, in its own organizations, cannot always be counted upon to work effectively for society as a whole. The conclusion seems to many inescapable: if one wants to serve society as a Catholic one can better do this by rejecting or bypassing Church-sponsored societies and joining those secular groups whose motives cannot be questioned. Such a trend would be not only dangerous to the lay movement, but it could also intensify that spirit of alienation from the Catholic socio-cultural community which has gained ground among laymen in recent years. By "alienation" I mean here the inability to feel any sense of personal identification with most of one's fellow Catholics; or, more broadly, a sense of detachment, sometimes accompanied by active hostility, from all those cultural and social trappings which make up American Catholicism. In the most extreme cases, this alienation can lead to a rejection of the Church. But far more common is the emergence of a sharp division between, on the one hand, adherence to the teachings of the Church and reception of the sacraments and, on the other, to the temporal concerns and loyalties of Catholics as a group. It is thus not a rejection of Catholicism in itself, but of the way Catholicism has imbedded itself in American life. Not unexpectedly, this often seems most pronounced among those laymen whose theological literacy and cultural achievements have led them to expect better things of American Catholicism than what they observe around them.

It would, of course, be naive to think that none of this alienation springs from some baser human tendencies: snobbery, for one thing. It is all too tempting for one who is aware of recent developments in Catholic theology, at ease with his non-Catholic neighbor, and confident about his social acceptability, to reject those who are still ill-at-ease, defensive and parochial—and that means a large portion of American Catholics. Nonetheless, it would be an even larger mistake to assume that such temptations explain the existence of widespread alienation. On the contrary, since a part of American Catholicism is, in fact, still narrow, self-centered, and suspicious of the non-Catholic world, it is difficult for the educated and assimilated laymen not to find his attitudes and outlooks sharply at variance with many of his fellow Catholics. He shares with them a common faith—but he may share nothing else at all.

There is in this country, however much it may vary in intensity from region to region, an American Catholic culture. It is this culture, with its residue of outmoded fears, folkways and ghettoism which more and more laymen are coming to reject; if it is not a good reason for alienation, it is still for many a decisive one. In the past it was perhaps only a small intellectual elite who most felt a sense of strain between the popular values of American Catholicism and those different values which are the fruit of an entrance into broader streams of Catholic and secular thought. (Unfortunately for them, they often felt no happier about their relationship to the secular intellectual world; in neither direction did they find much support or understanding.) Today, one might suspect, the base of alienation has widened. As more and more laymen receive a better religious education and come to achieve an easier relationship with their non-Catholic neighbors, the contrast between what they have come to and what the more slow-moving mass of Catholics holds dear is evident. The former have found a broader, more challenging world before them: the upper reaches of Catholic thought are more dynamic and the secular world more receptive to them personally. The latter may be still firmly fixed in the ways of earlier generations. A broader group thus seems to share some of the problems once reserved for a small elite.

Any study of the American Catholic layman will be incomplete. There is much that we do not know about him and much that may never be known. Even so, there are many things which can be done to improve his situation in the Church. Already, as one fruit of the Second Vatican Council, many American bishops have instituted diocesan synods or advisory councils which include a lay representation; and a great number of bishops and theologians are attempting to find other ways of increasing the layman's sense of full participation in the life of the Church. There is every reason to expect that these attempts will grow in extent and depth; and they will undoubtedly be stimulated by the efforts now going on to fashion a fuller theology of the laity. At the same time it seems likely that new difficulties and challenges will continually arise: the very rapidity with which the Church, the world and the layman are now changing makes that almost inevitable. The need now, however, is to confront the present situation; and, in great part, this means that some goals must be established.

Four Major Goals

The history and present state of the American Catholic layman suggest to me at least four major goals. First, there is an urgent need to develop a genuine spiritual community in place of the partly artificial sense of group identity which has been the product of immigrant minority history. Second, the American Church must develop a more healthy sense of independence in our society, neither leaning upon the state for support nor being tempted to suppose that the Church alone can preserve and sustain it. Third, the Church should interpret and exercise its authority in such a way that cooperation between clergy and laity follows naturally. Fourth, the Church should set out with all dispatch to develop a mature, faithful and responsible laity—a laity capable of withstanding the harmful effects of modern life but capable also of bettering that life;

a laity fully responsive to the authority of the Church but able as well
to exercise personal judgment and to make a contribution within the
Church itself. These four requirements interpenetrate one another; none
can be neglected without seriously affecting the others.

1. *Spiritual community.* In his famous encyclical, "On the Mystical
Body of Christ,"[2] Pope Pius XII laid the firmest possible foundations
for a development of the concept of the Church as a "community."
"Our union in and with Christ," he wrote, "is first evident from the fact
that, since Christ wills His Christian community to be a Body which is
a perfect Society, its members must be united because all work together
toward a single end. . . . The cooperation of all its members must also
be externally manifest through their profession of the same faith in the
same Sacrifice, and the practical observance of the same laws." "In a
body," he said, "when one member suffers, all the other members share
its pain, and the healthy members come to the assistance of the ailing;
so in the Church the individual members do not live for themselves
alone, but also help their fellows, and all work in mutual collaboration
for the common comfort and for the more perfect building up of the
body." This same idea has been amplified by Father Yves Congar:
"The Church is built together by the intercourse of its members one
with another in a whole pattern of services, of mutual enlightenment,
of taking opportunities, by the habitual use for the benefit of the body
of the gifts each one has received: such a Church cannot be called by
any other name than 'community.' "[3]

If I am not mistaken, it is precisely this sense of community which
has been lacking in the American Church. What we have had, instead,
is a type of tribal loyalty far more conditioned by the fact of minority
status and the sharing of common immigrant problems than by considerations of the communal nature of the Church. This is not to minimize the outstanding works of charity and welfare carried on by
bishops, priests and laymen in behalf of other Catholics or the countless
instances of mutual esteem and affection among Catholics. But if one
looks at those tensions which often exist between the educated and
uneducated, liberals and conservatives, clergy and laity, the parochial
and the integrated; and if, in addition, one observes the massive urban

---

[2] *Four Great Encyclicals of Pope Pius XII* (New York, 1961), pp. 7-51.
[3] *Lay People in the Church,* trans. by Donald Attwater (Westminster, Md.,
1957), p. 234.

parish, with its hosts of Catholics unknown to, and uninterested in, each other—then one must come to different conclusions. For that matter, the very sense of community engendered by the small lay apostolate societies, by Bible and liturgy study groups, by those movements limited in membership, throws into sharp relief how little of their spirit exists among Catholics in general. Finally, if further evidence is required, one need only observe the many laymen whose sense of alienation from American Catholic culture has driven them into what seems to them the more open-ended world of secular organizations and institutions. They preserve their faith but add little to the good of that body which is the Church.

Contrary to what some important laymen and priests now advocate, the great need is not the disbanding of the specifically Catholic social, welfare or civic organizations. They still have a valuable place within the Church, enabling Catholics to share their experiences, to strengthen and animate each other. Instead, it is that Catholics should cease to view these organizations as necessarily preferable to those activities which all Americans must share together. The Catholic needs both his fellow Catholic and his fellow non-Catholic. If he chooses to unite himself only with those who share his religious beliefs, then the country as a whole will suffer; and he will suffer too from the narrowness which such exclusions carry with them. Yet if he chooses to unite himself only with those outside of the Church, he will inevitably lose that liberating sense of Christian community which should be an intimate part of his religious life. "The more we become members of one another, the closer we shall be united with God and with Christ."[4]

2. *An autonomous Church.* The need of a more pronounced sense of spiritual community among Catholics has an important bearing on the relationship of the Church to American society. In earlier periods of American history, the Church stood in a very insecure position. It was suspect to a Protestant majority, actively opposed by wave after wave of anti-Catholic bigotry, constantly forced to defend itself against the charge that Catholic principles were inimical to American freedom and pluralism. The notion that, somehow, the Church could play a very positive role in furthering freedom and pluralism crossed very few minds, Catholic or non-Catholic. By force of circumstance the Church

[4] "On the Mystical Body of Christ," *op. cit.*, p. 33.

was independent of the main streams of American life—except for the impact of their numbers, Catholics have had very little to do with the shaping of American intellectual, cultural or moral life. Now, possibly for the first time, they have a chance to do something more positive for the country. Hostility against them has been followed by indifference. Few non-Catholics think of the Church as a threat any longer; but fewer expect from it any contribution of value to all.

Can the Church make such a contribution? That depends upon many things, but the one I want to stress here is that the very possibility depends upon the ability of American Catholics to inspire confidence and respect among their non-Catholic neighbors. There can be no contribution if those who are not Catholic do not expect, or are unprepared to accept, the possibility of Catholic cooperation and assistance. But this they will never come to do unless Catholics for their part are able to demonstrate that they have the common good in mind. Nor will non-Catholics be open to Catholic cooperation unless they see very clearly that the Church is a religious community and not just another pressure group which puts its own problems before all others. As long as Catholics are quick to defend their own rights but slow to defend those of others, quick to condemn "the forces of secularism" but slow to condemn domestic injustice and discrimination, then little in the way of profitable collaboration can be expected.

There now exists a temptation among Catholics to present themselves as the guardians of true Americanism, as the true defenders of a traditional religious heritage.[5] It is a temptation which is encouraged by the breakdown of the earlier Protestant-inspired consensus on the place of religion in American life. It can be seen not only in the frequent identification of the good of the Church with the good of the nation; but it

[5] "For many reasons . . . Catholics are prone to believe that they are the prime protectors of the original ideals of this nation. This arrogant assumption argues that our political creed expresses the traditional values of the Judaeo-Christian civilization and just as the Catholic Church elaborated and sustained these in the creation of Christendom, so she defends them in present-day America." (Edward Duff, S.J., "An American Catholic Looks at Religious Freedom," in the Davenport, Iowa, *Catholic Messenger*, Nov. 29, 1962.) I cannot resist quoting in this context a witty remark by Daniel P. Moynihan: "In the era of security clearances, to be an Irish Catholic became *prima facie* evidence of loyalty. Harvard men were to be checked; Fordham men would do the checking." ("The Irish," a paper prepared for the Joint Center for Urban Studies of Harvard University and M.I.T., p. 88.)

can also be seen in the way in which many Catholics hasten forward to take up cudgels against the Supreme Court, non-Catholic minority pressure groups and political figures when they feel that religious values are being undermined. In itself, this is not necessarily objectionable; but it becomes so when Catholics presume they alone are the custodians of American religion or when they ignore the rights of other groups.

In the past the Church was independent because it had no other choice. Today, when a new choice has presented itself, it is vital that it continue to remain so. It must by all means attempt to make a creative contribution to American life. But it must not do so by attempting to gain the support of the state in creating a climate more favorable to itself. If, as seems true, the churches in this country can no longer depend upon a vague societal cushion for religion, then it would be both useless and harmful for Catholics to attempt to change the direction of American history in this respect. This country today is made up of many people who reject the old basis of American life; their number will increase. For the Church to attempt to reverse this trend by the use of its political power exercised through a militant laity would do no good and could do much harm.

As many have pointed out, the "Constantinian era" in Western history has now passed—that era from the time of Constantine up until perhaps the French Revolution which saw an intimate relationship between church and state.[6] That it has passed is all to the good; both society and the Church suffered and the Church most of all. We have had in our own country a Protestant version of the "Constantinian era" —not a formal relationship between religion and the state, but an informal, cultural one. Now, with the emergence of those who want a neutral base for our pluralism this era is coming to an end. There is no reason why a new consensus, free of Constantinian overtones, respecting both Christians and non-Christians cannot be worked out. But this new task of American pluralism will be grievously hindered if Catholics attempt to resurrect an old order, this time under Catholic auspices.

Insofar as Catholics are able to create among themselves a spiritual community capable of addressing itself to the concerns of those outside of it, they will be able to make a significant contribution to the new

[6] Cf. Archbishop Lorenz Jaeger, *The Ecumenical Council, the Church and Christendom* (New York, 1961), p. 100; and Philip Scharper, "The Second Vatican Council," *Christianity and Crisis*, XXII (Oct., 1962), pp. 161-164.

pluralistic demands. Catholics now have some of the power to play the kind of dominant role in forcing America's religious life in directions of its choosing that Protestants once possessed: they must resist to the utmost the temptation to exercise that power unilaterally or arbitrarily.

3. *Authority and lay-clergy cooperation.* I want now to shift my attention to the relationship of laity and clergy within that community which is the Church. No one is likely to deny that some improvement is necessary. What I would choose to emphasize is that the ultimate source of lay-clergy tension lies in the way authority is exercised in the Church.[7] If that problem can be clarified—and the results reflected in Church life—then many of the complicated sociological reasons for tension could at least be alleviated. "A free society like ours," Father Fichter has cogently argued, "resists authoritarian coercion to a basic, integrating and overarching value system such as the Catholic Church claims to possess. We are now at a point in history when this conflict of viewpoints has to be worked out, and the continued Americanization of Catholicism will depend upon the way in which this solution is attempted.[8]

How, within the Church, can this conflict be worked out? I have already suggested that the Church can learn from the methods of democracy in achieving cooperation and personal commitment among citizens. Yet this very possibility will be bound to arouse suspicion unless theologians are able to clarify the meaning of authority in the Church. The precise challenge, paradoxically, lies in the fact that the source of authority, entrusted to the bishops and the pope, comes from God; the Church cannot be structured the way a democracy is without destroying its very nature. Given this firm point of Catholic doctrine, how can the Church, nevertheless, avoid the danger of authoritarianism? How can it gain the human benefits of democracy while being structured in a way that is different from a democracy?

[7] Among many useful articles on authority and the layman, the following are worthy of special note: William Bertrams, S.J., "Subsidiarity in the Church," *Theology Digest*, IX (Spring, 1961), pp. 111-114; Gaston Deurinck, "Authority and the Laity," *Perspectives* (May-June, 1961), pp. 17-19 (a summary of an article entitled "Les Laics et L'Autorité dans L'Eglise, *La Revue Nouvelle*, XXXIII (April, 1961), pp. 356-364); Charles Taylor, "Clericalism," *Cross Currents*, X (Fall, 1960), pp. 327-336; Augustin Pierre Léonard, O.P., "Freedom of the Laity," *Perspectives* (July-August, 1961), pp. 8-12.

[8] "The Americanization of Catholicism," in *Catholicism and the American Way of Life*, ed. by Thomas T. McAvoy, C.S.C. (Notre Dame, 1960), p. 127.

It can at least make an important beginning by refusing to employ the imagery of secular organizations to explain its mode of authority. The Church is not an army; thus the imagery of officers and soldiers is highly misleading. The Church is not a bureaucratic government; hence the imagery of omnipotent official and loyal underling is dangerous. The Church is not a monastery or a convent; thus the imagery of religious superior (be he pastor, teacher or bishop) and zealous novice is out of place. The Church is not a totalitarian society bent on the achievement of ideological goals; thus any imagery of wise leader and unenlightened proletariat is wholly deceptive. The Church is none of these things; but it is not always clear, from popular explanations of Catholic authority (which in practice count more heavily in the shaping of attitudes than theological treatises), that this is recognized.

What of the positive requirements? Here I must defer to the theologians and be content to cite some passages which seem to offer a way out of the present ambiguous state of affairs. One in particular is worth quoting at some length: "It cannot be denied that the Church's ideal should be that of a community in which the mediatory function of hierarchical authority would remain essential, but in which, *at the same time and by the same token,* the guidance of the hierarchy would be counter-balanced by the greatest possible degree of spiritual liberty, and this because the community as a body is quickened by the Holy Spirit. This means that spiritual liberty is not the opposite pole, *but the correlative of the hierarchical idea.* It means that no obedience should be asked for which does not involve, at least to a small extent, a response dictated by love on the part of the believer under the rule of the hierarchy. It means that the ideal state of the Church is not to be found in a plethora of canonical prescriptions, but in a minimum of these."[9] Let me add to this a passage from Father Congar's writings: "Daily life goes on in conditions of community and give-and-take. It is this mutual give-and-take that I should like to see going on between priesthood and laity. The actual forms that it could take do not matter much, provided that due respect is invariably given both to fatherhood—that is, to authority—and to fellowship in community; a respect that sees in others, not simply an object, but a subject, a person, a grown-up person. What

[9] Msgr. A. Pailler, Auxiliary Bishop of Rouen, "Considerations on the Authority of the Church," in *Problems of Authority,* edited by John M. Todd (Baltimore, 1962), p. 23.

we need is a dialogue, something that takes place between adult and responsible persons, face to face."[10]

Even if the ideals so cogently stated by Bishop Pailler and Father Congar come to animate Catholic thinking on authority, much will still remain to be done on the practical level. A genuine dialogue between clergy and laity, a mutual respect for the different roles each must play, will still depend in great part on forces other than theological. Dialogue and cooperation will be impossible if the clergy are not given a training comparable to that of the laity; if the clergy are not given some of the freedom and expression and initiative which the laity now enjoy; if bishops and theologians and pastors do not have closer contact with the laity—a contact free of that stifling formality which now keeps many a layman from saying in a true and candid way what is on his mind; if the clergy do not, during their training and after, have a closer contact with the world in which the layman lives. It will also be impossible, I should add, if the educated laity seek to escape to the outside world when cooperation with the clergy seems an unbearable burden, or simply a blow to their egalitarian egos. Lastly, a considerable part of the present difficulties might be eased if it were more generally granted that the present parceling out of the layman's place as "the world" and the clergy's as "the Church" is beset with theoretical and practical weaknesses.[11] The layman has a place within the Church; the priest has a place in the world.

4. A mature laity. The final question now presents itself. What kind of layman is needed today in society and in the Church? The nature of contemporary American society suggests an answer to the first part of the question. In it, the Catholic is now accepted; he is no longer the victim of discrimination or a cultural inferior. But this very fact of acceptance also means that he cannot any longer draw on those social conditions which served in past years to fortify him: a sense of hostility against him on the part of non-Catholics, a sense of threat and danger. No religion ought to be dependent upon such forces to sustain and alert its members; yet, as with many other religions, external pressures have

[10] Yves Congar, O.P., *Laity, Church and World*, trans. by Donald Attwater (Baltimore, 1961), p. 59.

[11] Cf. James Maguire, C.S.C., "A Paradox: An Authentically Lay Vocation," *Perspectives* (May-June, 1961), pp. 3-5, and Jean Frisque, "Priest and Layman in the Church," *Perspectives* (Sept.-Oct., 1962), pp. 138-145.

been a help to American Catholicism as much as a hindrance. They are now disappearing. In the past it was not so much his religion but the Catholic himself who was rejected; today the man himself may be accepted while many of his deepest values are more rejected than ever. In itself this might pose no special problems if, as in earlier periods, the Church now enjoyed many of the natural contacts with the laity that were provided by the existence of Catholic ghettos and enclaves. There, it was at least possible for priests to know laymen, and for laymen to know each other. Social conformity was as powerful a force as preaching and exhortation.

Now Catholics are scattered, and this means one thing of great importance: what the layman comes to be as a Catholic will be almost entirely dependent upon his personal integrity and his power to sustain his values. In this respect, he is today in a situation analogous to that of those early American Catholics who chose to live on the Western frontier: all the props of social Catholicism were removed and their fate was up to them. That frontier is gone; but in its place we have the suburbs, the changing city and the fact of economic and social mobility. The layman is constantly in a new situation; there is nothing to shelter or to protect him. "Others could be taught what Freud knew for himself— that there is no longer, characteristically, in our culture, an effective community surrounding the individual, softening life often at the expense of stifling it, and organizing life often at the cost of making it rigid. . . . Where nothing else can be taken for granted, and the stupidity of social life no longer saves, every man must become something of a genius."[12]

Toward an Integral Layman

Undoubtedly, there are some who will lament the passing of the old order, who will be fearful of the layman's ability to withstand the new pressures to which he is exposed, who will doubt that he is able to muster

[12] Philip Rieff, "The Analytic Attitude," *Encounter*, XVIII (June, 1962), p. 23. Cf. also Joseph H. Fichter, S.J., *Social Relations in the Urban Parish* (Chicago, 1954), p. 177; and John L. Thomas, S.J., *Religion and the American People* (Westminster, Md., 1963), p. 246: "There is ample evidence that the traditional system of religious instruction and indoctrination, relying heavily on simple acceptance of authority, no longer adequately prepares the faithful to withstand the full impact of secular pressures in an affluent society."

the kind of genius which his new situation demands of him. But it is idle to dream of a return to the past; the old order will not return. The task now is the training and development of a layman capable of standing on his own in the society which we have and in the situation in which he finds himself. It is a task which calls for a layman who is capable of remaining true to his own values regardless of the direction in which the society moves. Such a layman would be one who remained true to the special genius of American Catholicism. That genius has been to refute the belief of the Old World which held that religion and culture were so inextricably bound together that Catholicism could not survive in a milieu which did not pay it homage.

How can such a layman be created? The primary requirement is that the freedom of the layman in society be fully recognized. For the Church this means that he is a Catholic through his free choice and in the face of competing values and ideologies. It means that he will remain faithful to Catholicism not out of mechanical conformity to rules and laws, but out of the deepest possible assent and commitment of his free personality. It means that he will be an integral Catholic, neither a conformist nor a rebel, precisely to the extent that the Church is able to show him what Catholicism in its fullness is.

In the practical order, it means that once and for all the way of conformity, docility and the attempt to condition and coerce the layman must give way to a dynamic conception of Catholic life which stresses freedom and maturity, a creative and positive assent to Church authority rather than blind, fearful obedience. Those parochial schools must change which in practice teach that not fear of the Lord but of nuns and priests is the beginning of wisdom. Those colleges must change which treat their students as incapable of regulating their intellectual and social lives. Those lay organizations must change in which the members, with fear and trepidation, await the good will of their chaplain toward their proposals. Those chancery offices must change which decide important matters behind doors closed to a lay voice. Above all, both laymen and priests must see the psychological blunder inherent in much Catholic thinking on discipline: that fear of authority is equivalent to personal integrity. Self-discipline is taught by the gift of responsible freedom, not by external coercion.

These changes are indispensable for the proper formation of laymen capable of resisting a secularized society. They are also indispensable for the development of laymen anxious and able to bring an active vision to bear in this same society. "The Church," Pope Pius XII said in an address to the cardinals in 1946, "cannot shut herself up, inactive in the privacy of her churches, and thus neglect the mission entrusted to her by divine providence, the mission to form man in his wholeness and so ceaselessly to collaborate in building the solid basis of society. This mission is of her essence." The layman will be of no help in this mission if he is not bold and daring, if he is not able to go into society armed with a free, informed and mature faith, if he has not been taught within the Church how to speak with vigor, courage and candor. More than that, the Church must hold itself up to him as a model of independence, selflessness and initiative. If the Church so much as gives the impression that it is willing to temporize for the sake of its position in the world (as it did on the Negro problem for decades), then it can hardly expect the layman to do better. If the Church will fight only when its own immediate interests are at stake, then the layman will do likewise. If the Church can bring to a secularized society only imprecations and anathemas, then the layman will bring no more.

Much has been written in our day of the "open society"—a society open to the talents of all, the contributions of all, the personalities of all, the beliefs of all. Is this an expression which holds meaning only for secular, democratic, pluralistic societies? Has it not pertinence to the Church as well? If the Church is a free community of men bound to one Lord and faithful to those who have authority in the Church; if the clergy and the laity are joined together as co-workers respectful of the rights, preogatives and sensitivities of each other; if the prophetic voice can be heard clearly amidst the voice of authority; if the Church is opened out into the world to serve and redeem the world; if the layman has both a sense of participation in the work of the Church and its reality —then the Church is truly an open society of the profoundest kind.

SELECT BIBLIOGRAPHY

INDEX

Select Bibliography

It is impossible to present here anything approximating a complete bibliography on the subject of this book. The books and articles which follow represent those I think most worthy of commending to the attention of anyone who would care to explore the various themes of this book further. In particular, it has been necessary to present only a few of the many articles written in recent years on the role of the layman in the Church and the world. Likewise, many biographies and articles on prominent laymen in the early days of the Church have been omitted, as, indeed, many articles which appeared after the 1920s on special aspects of the lay question.

For a general bibliography on the American Catholic Church, Msgr. John Tracy Ellis' *A Guide to American Catholic History* (Milwaukee, 1959) can be warmly recommended. For articles on the layman after 1930, the *Catholic Periodical Index* is the most useful source of information. For Part One of this book, the periodicals most worth consulting are the *American Catholic Historical Researches* (Philadelphia, 1884–1913); *American Catholic Quarterly Review* (Philadelphia, 1876–1924); *American Ecclesiastical Review* (Philadelphia, 1889–1944, Washington, 1944ff.); *Catholic Historical Review* (Washington, 1915–); *Catholic University Bulletin* (Washington, 1895–1928); *Catholic World* (New York, 1865–); *Historical Records and Studies* (New York, 1899–); *Homiletic and Pastoral*

Review (New York, 1899–). For Part Two, in addition to those of the above periodicals still in existence, may be added *America, The Commonweal, The Sign, Ave Maria, Perspectives, Cross Currents, The Catholic Mind.* The reader should be warned, however, that prior at least to the 1920s, relatively little was written about the layman as such; there is thus no easy route to the "mind of the Catholic layman."

PART ONE

Books

ABELL, AARON. *American Catholics and Social Action: A Search for Social Justice, 1865–1950.* New York, 1960.

BARRY, COLMAN, O.S.B. *The Catholic Church and German Americans.* Milwaukee, 1953.

BAUMGARTNER, A. W. *Catholic Journalism: A Study of Its Development in the United States, 1789–1930.* New York, 1931.

BILLINGTON, RAY ALLEN. *The Protestant Crusade, 1800–1860.* New York, 1938.

BROWNE, HENRY J. *The Catholic Church and the Knights of Labor.* Washington, D.C., 1949.

BROWNSON, HENRY F. *Orestes A. Brownson.* 3 vols. Detroit, 1898–1900.

BROWNSON, ORESTES A. *The American Republic.* New York, 1866.

———. *Works of Orestes A. Brownson.* 20 vols. Detroit, 1882–1907.

BUGG, L. H. *The People of Our Parish.* Boston, 1900.

BURNS, J. A. *The Catholic School System in the United States.* New York, 1908.

———. *The Growth and Development of the Catholic School System in the United States.* New York, 1912.

CAREY, MATTHEW. *Autobiography.* Brooklyn, 1942.

Catholicism in America. Edited by the editors of *The Commonweal.* New York, 1954.

CHRIST, FRANK L. and SHERRY, GERARD R. *American Catholicism and the Intellectual Ideal.* New York, 1959.

CROSS, ROBERT D. *The Emergence of Liberal Catholicism in America.* Cambridge, 1958.

DONOHOE, SISTER JOAN MARIE, S.N.D. *The Irish Catholic Benevolent Union.* Washington, D.C., 1953.

EGAN, MAURICE F. *Recollections of a Happy Life.* New York, 1924.

ELLIS, JOHN TRACY. *American Catholicism.* Chicago, 1956.

———. *American Catholics and the Intellectual Life.* Chicago, 1956.

———. *Catholics in Colonial America.* Reprinted from the *American Ecclesiastical Review.* Vol. CXXXVI, Jan.–May, 1957. Washington, D.C., n.d.

———. *Documents of American Catholic History.* 2nd edition. Milwaukee, 1962.

———. *John Lancaster Spalding.* Milwaukee, 1961.

———. *The Life of James Cardinal Gibbons, Archbishop of Baltimore, 1834–1921.* 2 vols. Milwaukee, 1952.

ENGLAND, JOHN. *The Works of John England.* Edited by SEBASTIAN G. MESSMER. 7 vols. Cleveland, 1903.

ERNST, ROBERT. *Immigrant Life in New York City, 1825–1863.* New York, 1949.

FOERSTER, R.F. *The Italian Emigration of Our Times.* Cambridge, 1919.

FOIK, PAUL J. *Pioneer Catholic Journalism.* New York, 1930.

FOX, MARY HARRITA. *Peter E. Dietz, Labor Priest.* Notre Dame, 1953.

FRAWLEY, SISTER MARY A. *Patrick Donahoe.* Washington, D.C., 1946.

GOLDMAN, ERIC. *Charles J. Bonaparte, Patrician Reformer. His Earlier Career.* Baltimore, 1943.

GORMAN, SISTER M. ADELE FRANCIS, O.S.F. *Federation of Catholic Societies in the United States, 1870–1920.* Unpublished Ph.D. dissertation, Department of History, University of Notre Dame, 1962.

GREELEY, ANDREW M. *The Church and the Suburbs.* New York, 1959.

GUILDAY, PETER (ed.). *The Catholic Church in Virginia, 1815–1922.* New York, 1924.

———. *A History of the Councils of Baltimore (1791–1884).* New York, 1932.

———. *The Life and Times of John Carroll, Archbishop of Baltimore, 1735–1815.* 2 vols. New York, 1922.

———. *The Life and Times of John England, 1786–1842.* 2 vols. New York, 1927.

———. *The National Pastorals of the American Hierarchy, 1792–1919.* Westminster, Md., 1954.

GWYNN, STEPHEN. *Ireland.* London, 1924.

HANDLIN, OSCAR. *The Uprooted.* Boston, 1951.

HASSARD, JOHN R.G. *Life of the Most Reverend John Hughes.* New York, 1866.

HOFSTADTER, RICHARD. *The Age of Reform from Bryan to F.D.R.* New York, 1955.

HOLDEN, VINCENT F. *The Yankee Paul: Isaac Thomas Hecker.* Milwaukee, 1958.

IRELAND, JOHN. *The Church and Modern Society.* 2 vols. St. Paul, 1905.

KWITCHEN, SISTER MARY A. *James Alphonsus McMaster.* Washington, D.C., 1949.

MARX PAUL. *Virgil Michel and the Liturgical Movement.* Collegeville, Minn., 1957.

MAYNARD, THEODORE. *Orestes Brownson. Yankee, Radical, Catholic.* New York, 1943.

———. *The Story of American Catholicism.* New York, 1941.

———. *Too Small a World. The Life of Mother Cabrini.* Milwaukee, 1945.

McAVOY, THOMAS T. *The Great Crisis in American Catholic History, 1895–1900.* Chicago, 1957.

McGURRIN, JAMES. *Burke Cochran: A Free Lance in American Politics.* New York, 1948.

MELVILLE, ANNABELLE M. *John Carroll of Baltimore.* New York, 1955.

MOYNIHAN, J.H. *The Life of Archbishop John Ireland.* New York, 1953.

NEUSSE, C. JOSEPH. *The Social Thought of American Catholics, 1634–1829.* Washington, D.C., 1945.

O'BRIEN, JOHN A. *Catholics and Scholarship.* Huntington, Ind., 1939.

O'DEA, THOMAS. *American Catholic Dilemma.* New York, 1958.

O'GRADY, JOHN. *Levi Silliman Ives, Pioneer Leader in Catholic Charities.* New York, 1933.

PAHOREZKI, SISTER M. SEVINS. The Social and Political Activities of William James Onahan. Washington, D.C., 1942.

POWDERLY, TERENCE V. Thirty Years of Labor, 1859–1889. Columbus, 1890.

POWER, EDWARD J. A History of Catholic Higher Education in the United States. Milwaukee, 1958.

Proceedings of the Catholic Congress. Detroit, 1889.

PUTZ, LOUIS J. (ed.). The Catholic Church, U.S.A. Chicago, 1956.

REYNOLDS, JAMES A. The Catholic Emancipation Crisis in Ireland, 1823–1829. New Haven, 1954.

RICE, MADELEINE HOOKE. American Catholic Opinion in the Slavery Controversy. New York, 1944.

ROTHAN, EMMET. The German Catholic Immigrant in the United States, 1830–1846. Washington, D.C., 1946.

RYAN, LEO R. Old St. Peter's: The Mother Church of Catholic New York. New York, 1935.

SCHLESINGER, ARTHUR M., JR. Orestes A. Brownson. A Pilgrim's Progress. Boston, 1939.

SHAUGHNESSY, GERALD. Has the Immigrant Kept the Faith? New York, 1925.

SHUSTER, GEORGE N. The Catholic Spirit in America. New York, 1927.

SMITH, ELLEN HART. Charles Carroll of Carrollton. Cambridge, 1942.

SMITH, JOHN. The Catholic Church in New York. 2 vols. New York, 1905.

Souvenir Volume of the Centennial Celebration and Catholic Congress. Chicago, 1893.

SPALDING, JOHN LANCASTER. Means and Ends of Education. Chicago, 1895.

———. The Religious Mission of the Irish Race and Catholic Colonization. New York, 1880.

SWISHER, CARL BRENT. Roger B. Taney. New York, 1935.

TOCQUEVILLE, ALEXIS DE. Journeys to England and Ireland. Edited by J. P. MAYER. London, 1958.

TOURSCHER, FRANCIS E. The Hogan Schism and Trustee Troubles in St. Mary's Church, Philadelphia, 1820–1829. Philadelphia, 1920.

TYLER, SAMUEL. Memoir of Roger Brooke Taney. 2nd rev. edition. Baltimore, 1876.

UNDERWOOD, KENNETH. Protestant and Catholic. Boston, 1961.

WALBURG, ANTON. The Question of Nationality. St. Louis, 1889.

WARD, LEO R. New Life in Catholic Schools. St. Louis, 1958.

WILL, ALLEN S. The Life of Cardinal Gibbons. 2 vols. New York, 1922.

WITTKE, CARL. The Irish in America. Baton Rouge, 1956.

World's Columbian Catholic Congress, with an Epitome of Church Progress. Chicago, 1893.

Articles

BARRY, WILLIAM. "The Troubles of a Catholic Democracy," Contemporary Review, LXXVI (July, 1899).

BENNETT, WILLIAM H. "Francis Cooper: New York's First Legislator," Historical Records and Studies, XII (1918).

BRADY, E.B. "Catholic Progress, Old and New," Catholic World, LI (Jan., 1890).

BROWNE, HENRY J. "Archbishop Hughes and Western Colonization," Catholic Historical Review, XXXVI (Oct., 1950).

——. "Catholicism in the United States," *The Shaping of American Religion*, Vol. 1 of *Religion in American Life*. Edited by JAMES WARD SMITH and A. LELAND JAMISON. 4 vols. Princeton, 1961.

CANEVIN, J.F. REGIS. "Loss and Gain in the Catholic Church in the United States (1810–1916)," *Catholic Historical Review*, II (Jan., 1917).

——. "The Rise and Progress of the Catholic Church in the United States," *Bulletin* of the American Federation of Catholic Societies, VI (July, 1912).

CASSIDY, FRANCIS P. "Catholic Education and the Third Plenary Council of Baltimore," *Catholic Historical Review*, XXXIV (Oct., 1948).

"Catholic Literature in the United States," *The Metropolitan* (Baltimore), II: 64–75; 133–139; 198–204 (1854).

"The Chapter 'De Fide Catholica' in the Third Plenary Council of Baltimore," *American Ecclesiastical Review*, XVI (Feb., 1897).

CROSS, ROBERT D. "The Changing Image of the City Among American Catholics," *Catholic Historical Review*, XLVIII (April, 1962).

DWYER, ROBERT J. "The American Laity," *The Commonweal*, LX (Aug. 27, 1954).

GUILDAY, PETER. "Trusteeism," *Historical Records and Studies*, XVIII (1928).

HANLEY, THOMAS O'BRIEN, S.J. "The Emergence of Pluralism in the United States," *Theological Studies*, XXIII (June, 1962).

HECKER, ISAAC P. "Shall We Have a Catholic Congress?" *Catholic World*, VIII (Nov., 1868).

HOWARD, G.H. "The English Language in Catholic Public Worship," *Catholic World*, LI (April, 1890).

HUGHES, JOHN. "The Archdioces of New York a Century Ago: A Memoir of Archbishop Hughes, 1838–1858," *Historical Records and Studies*, XXXIX-XL (1952).

KANE, JOHN J. "The Social Structure of American Catholics," *American Catholic Sociological Review*, XVI (March, 1955).

LAFARGE, JOHN. "The Survival of Catholic Faith in Southern Maryland," *Catholic Historical Review*, XXI (1935–36).

"The Laity," *Catholic World*, XLVII (April, 1888).

LYNCH, BERNARD J. "The Italians in New York," *Catholic World*, XLVII (1888).

MAES, J. "The Theological Seminary," *American Ecclesiastical Review*, XIV (May, 1896).

MARKOE, W.P. "The Catholic Truth Society," *Catholic World*, LII (Jan., 1891).

McAVOY, THOMAS T., C.S.C. "The American Catholic Minority in the Later Nineteenth Century, *Review of Politics*, XV (July, 1953).

——. "Americanism and Frontier Catholicism," *Review of Politics*, V (July, 1943).

——. "Bishop John Lancaster Spalding and the Catholic Minority (1877–1908)," *Review of Politics*, XII (July, 1950).

——. "The Catholic Church in the United States Between Two Wars," *Review of Politics*, IV (Oct., 1942).

——. "The Catholic Minority After the Americanist Controversy," *Review of Politics*, XXI (Jan., 1959).

——. "The Catholic Minority in the United States, 1789–1821," *Histor-*

ical Records and Studies, XXXIX–XL (1952).
——. "The Formation of the Catholic Minority in the United States, 1820–1860," *Review of Politics,* X (June, 1948).
——. "Orestes A. Brownson and Archbishop John Hughes in 1860," *Review of Politics,* XXIV (Jan., 1962).
McNamara, R. F. "Trusteeism in the Atlantic States, 1785–1863," *Catholic Historical Review,* XXX (July, 1944).
McSweeny, Edward. "The Priest and the Public," *Catholic World,* XLVII (Sept., 1888).
Meehan, Thomas F. "Catholic Literary New York, 1800–1840," *Catholic Historical Review,* IV (1919).
——. "A Self-Effaced Philanthropist: Cornelius Heeney, 1754–1848," *Catholic Historical Review,* IV (1918–1919).
——. "Some Pioneer Catholic Laymen in New York—Dominick Lynch and Cornelius Heeney," *Historical Records and Studies,* IV (1906).
Minahan, M. C. "James A. McMaster: A Pioneer Catholic Journalist," *Records of the American Catholic Historical Society,* XLVII (June, 1936).
Mooney, John. "Our Recent American Catholic Congress," *American Catholic Quarterly Review,* XV (Dec., 1889).

O'Malley, A. "Catholic Collegiate Education in the United States," *Catholic World,* LXVII (June, 1896).
Reilly, L. W. "The Weak Points of the Catholic Press," *American Ecclesiastical Review,* X (Feb., 1894).
Reynard, Albert. "Organize the Laymen," *Catholic World,* L (Dec., 1889).
Schrott, L. "Pioneer German Catholics in the American Colonies (1734–1784)," New York: *United States Catholic Historical Society, Monograph Series,* XIII (1933).
Shea, John Gilmary. "Converts—Their Influence and Work in This Country," *American Catholic Quarterly Review,* VIII (July, 1883).
Tracy, J. V. "Is the Catholic School System Perfect?" *Catholic World,* LI (July, 1890).
Treacy, Gerald C. "Evils of Trusteeism," *Historical Records and Studies,* VIII (1915).
"Vocations to the Priesthood and Our Seminaries," *American Ecclesiastical Review,* III (Aug., 1890).
Weigel, Gustave, S.J. "American Catholic Intellectualism: A Theologian's Reflections," *Review of Politics,* XIX (July, 1957).
Young, Alfred. "Shall the People Sing?" *Catholic World,* XL (July, 1887).

PART TWO

Books

Alonso, Arthur, O.P. *Catholic Action and the Laity.* St. Louis, 1961.
Bedoyere, Michael de la. *The Layman in the Church.* Chicago, 1955.
Cassidy, Sally Whelan. *Some Aspects of Lay Leadership.* Unpublished Ph.D. dissertation. Department of Sociology, University of Chicago, 1959.
Catholicism in American Culture. Col-

lege of New Rochelle, New Rochelle, N. Y., 1955.

CONGAR, YVES. *Laity, Church and World.* Translated by DONALD ATTWATER. Baltimore, 1961.

——. *Lay People in the Church.* Translated by DONALD ATTWATER. Westminster, Md., 1957.

DAY, DOROTHY. *The Long Loneliness.* New York, 1952.

DOTY, ROBERT L. *Trends and Counter-Trends Among American Catholics.* St. Louis, 1962.

FICHTER, JOSEPH H., S.J. *Are We Going Secular?* Milwaukee, 1960.

——. *Parochial School.* Notre Dame, 1958.

——. *Religion as an Occupation.* Notre Dame, 1961.

——. *Social Relations in the Urban Parish.* Chicago, 1954.

——. *Southern Parish. Dynamics of a City Church,* Vol. I. Chicago, 1951.

GERKEN, JOHN D. *Toward a Theology of the Layman.* New York, 1963.

GIESE, VINCENT J. *Training for Leadership.* Chicago, 1959.

GREELEY, ANDREW M. *The Influence of Religion on the Career Plans and Occupational Values of June 1961 College Graduates.* Unpublished Ph.D. dissertation, Department of Sociology, University of Chicago, 1962.

HERBERG, WILL. *Protestant-Catholic-Jew.* Rev. edition. New York, 1960.

JAEGER, LORENZ. *The Ecumenical Council, the Church and Christendom.* New York, 1961.

KANE, GEORGE L. (ed.). *Lay Workers for Christ.* Westminster, Md., 1957.

KANE, JOHN J. *Catholic-Protestant Conflicts in America.* Chicago, 1955.

LALLY, FRANCIS J. *The Catholic*

Church in a Changing America. Boston, 1962.

The Lay Apostolate: Papal Teachings. Boston, 1961.

LECLERCQ, JACQUES. *Christians in the World.* New York, 1961.

LENSKI, GERHARD. *The Religious Factor.* New York, 1962.

MASURE, EUGENE. *Parish Priest.* Chicago, 1955.

MCAVOY, THOMAS T., C.S.C. (ed.). *Roman Catholicism and the American Way of Life.* Notre Dame, 1960.

MICHONNEAU, GEORGES. *Catholic Action and the Parish.* Westminster, Md., 1955.

NEUSSE, C. J. and HARTE, T. J. *The Sociology of the Parish.* Milwaukee, 1950.

NEWMAN, JEREMIAH. *The Christian in Society.* Baltimore, 1962.

——. *What Is Catholic Action?* Westminster, Md., 1958.

NEWMAN, JOHN HENRY. *On Consulting the Faithful in Matters of Doctrine.* Edited by John Coulson. New York, 1962.

O'GARA, JAMES (ed.). *The Layman in the Church.* New York, 1962.

ONG, WALTER, S.J. *American Catholic Crossroads.* New York, 1959.

——. *Frontiers in American Catholicism.* New York, 1957.

PERRIN, J. M. *Forward the Layman.* Westminster, Md., 1956.

PHILLIPS, GERARD. *The Role of the Laity in the Church.* Chicago, 1955.

PUTZ, LOUIS J., C.S.C. (ed.). *The Catholic Church, U.S.A.* Chicago, 1956.

——. *The Modern Apostle.* Chicago, 1957.

RAHNER, HUGO. *The Parish, from*

Theology to Practice. Westminster, Md., 1958.

RAHNER, KARL, S.J. *Free Speech in the Church.* New York, 1960.

REINHOLD, H. A. *The American Parish and the Roman Liturgy.* New York, 1958.

ROBERTS, T. D. *Black Popes—Authority: Its Use and Abuse.* New York, 1954.

SCHUYLER, JOSEPH B., S.J. *Northern Parish.* Chicago, 1960.

SMEDT, EMILE JOSEPH DE. *The Priesthood of the Faithful.* New York, 1962.

TAVARD, GEORGE. *The Church, the Layman and the Modern World.* New York, 1959.

THOMAS, JOHN L., S.J. *The American*

Catholic Family. Englewood Cliffs, 1956.

———. *Religion and the American People.* Westminster, Md., 1963.

THORMAN, DONALD. *The Emerging Layman.* New York, 1962.

TODD, JOHN (ed.). *Problems of Authority.* Baltimore, 1962.

WARD, LEO (ed.). *The American Apostolate: American Catholics in the Twentieth Century.* Westminster, Md., 1952.

———. *Catholic Life, U.S.A.: Contemporary Lay Movements.* St. Louis, 1959.

WEIGEL, GUSTAVE, S.J. *Faith and Understanding in America.* New York, 1959.

WHITE, THEODORE R. *The Making of the President 1960.* New York, 1961.

Articles

ABBOTT, WALTER M., S.J. "Total Dedication in the World," *America* (May 20, 1961).

AUGUSTIN, DOMINIC. "The Catholic College Man and the Negro," *American Catholic Sociological Review,* VIII (Oct., 1947).

BAUM, GREGORY. "Conflicts and the Council," *The Commonweal,* LXXVI (September 21, 1962).

BERTRAM, WILLIAM, S.J. "Subsidiarity in the Church," *Theology Digest,* IX (Spring, 1961).

CASEY, THOMAS, S.J. "Catholics and Family Planning," *American Catholic Sociological Review,* XXI (Sum., 1960).

CONLEY, WILLIAM H. "The Lay Teacher in Catholic Education," *Proceedings of the Fifty-ninth Annual Convention of the National Catholic Educational Association,* LIX (August, 1962).

DEURINCK, GASTON. "Authority and the Laity," *Perspectives* (May–June, 1961).

DIETZ, DONALD, O.M.I. "The Bishop and the Layman," *American Ecclesiastical Review,* CXLVII (Aug., 1962).

ELLIS, JOHN TRACY. "American Catholicism in 1960: An Historical Perspective," *The American Benedictine Review,* XI (March–June, 1960).

FLEEGE, W. R. "The Coming Era of the Catholic Layman," *Homiletic and Pastoral Review,* LIV (Nov., 1953).

FRISQUE, JEAN. "Priest and Layman in the Church," *Perspectives* (Sept.–Oct., 1962).

GLEASON, ROBERT W., S.J. "American Catholic Anticlericalism," *Thought,* XXXVIII (Spring, 1963).

GRAHAM, ROBERT A., S.J. "The Laity,

the Council and the New Apostolate," *America* (May 6, 1961).

HARTE, THOMAS, C.Ss.R. "Catholic Education as a Factor in Catholic Opinion," *American Catholic Sociological Review*, X (March, 1949).

HERBERG, WILL. "Religious Group Conflicts in America," *College of New Rochelle Alumnae News* (Fall, 1962).

KANE, JOHN J. "Anti-Semitism Among Catholic College Students," *American Catholic Sociological Review*, VIII (Oct., 1947).

LÉONARD, AUGUSTIN-PIERRE. "Freedom of the Laity," *Perspectives* (July–August, 1961).

MAGUIRE, JAMES, C.S.C. "A Paradox: An Authentically Lay Vocation," *Perspectives* (May–June, 1961).

MARROU, H. I. "The Church Is Not Clerical," *Cross Currents*, VII (Spring, 1957).

NOVAK, MICHAEL. "The Priest in the Modern World," *Review for Religious*, X (1961).

O'GARA, JAMES. "Theology of the Laity," *The Critic* (Aug.–Sept., 1962).

PUTZ, LOUIS J., C.S.C. "The Apostolate," *Perspectives* (Sept.–Oct., 1962).

RAHNER, KARL, S.J. "The Lay Apostolate," *Cross Currents*, VII (Summer, 1957).

———. "Reflections on Obedience," *Cross Currents*, X (Fall, 1960).

REDLON, REGINALD, O.F.M. "The American Character and Formation in Religious Life," *Proceedings of the Second National Congress of Religious of the United States*. Notre Dame, 1962.

ROSSI, PETER H. and ALICE S. "Some Effects of Parochial School Education in America," *Daedalus* (Spring, 1961).

SCHARPER, PHILIP. "The Second Vatican Council," *Christianity and Crisis*, XXII (Oct., 1962).

TAYLOR, CHARLES. "Clericalism," *Cross Currents*, X (Fall, 1960).

WROBLEWSKI, SERGIUS, S.F.M. "Formation of Seminarians Toward a Diocesan Spirituality," *Proceedings of the Fifty-ninth Annual Convention of the National Catholic Educational Association*, LIX (August, 1962).

Index